ISLAMIC AID AND GULF STATES IN CONTEMPORARY CRISES

A mio padre

ISLAMIC AID AND GULF STATES IN CONTEMPORARY CRISES

Altea Pericoli

EDINBURGH
University Press

Edinburgh University Press is one of the leading university presses in the UK. Publishing new research in the arts and humanities, EUP connects people and ideas to inspire creative thinking, open new perspectives and shape the world we live in. For more information, visit www.edinburghuniversitypress.com.

Edinburgh University Press Ltd
13 Infirmary Street, Edinburgh EH1 1LT

Typeset in 11/15 Adobe Garamond by
IDSUK (DataConnection) Ltd
Printed and bound in the UK using 100% renewable electricity by
CPI Group (UK) Ltd

A CIP record for this book is available from the British Library

ISBN 978 1 3995 4834 2 (hardback)
ISBN 978 1 3995 4833 5 (webready PDF)
ISBN 978 1 3995 4848 9 (epub)

EU Authorised Representative:
Easy Access System Europe
Mustamäe tee 50, 10621 Tallinn, Estonia
gpsr.requests@easproject.com

MIX
Paper | Supporting responsible forestry
FSC
www.fsc.org
FSC® C013604

This book is printed using paper from well-managed forests, recycling and other controlled sources

CONTENTS

FIGURES AND TABLES

Figures

Tables

FUNDING ACKNOWLEDGEMENTS

The publication of this book has been supported by the Middle East and Contemporary World research programme and the Centre for Advanced Middle Eastern Studies (CMES) at Lund University, which made possible publication in open access (Gold Open Access).

The pre-press stage of this book project was supported by the British Society of Middle Eastern Studies through the Early Career Development Scholarship award in 2023.

ACKNOWLEDGEMENTS

This book is the product of many places, but above all, many people who have somehow crossed my path. To all of them goes my infinite gratitude. I will be forever grateful to all the people who spoke with me during both formal interviews and informal conversations. They dedicated their time to sharing their stories, experiences, dreams and hopes.

I will always be indebted to Mehmet Asutay for his intellectual generosity and deep engagement with my work. My research would not have been the same without his unwavering support and inspiration. He carefully guided me throughout my PhD, teaching me both the scientific and the human aspects of being a researcher. I am deeply grateful to him for making me feel like part of the 'Durham family' and for believing that this world can be a better place, after all.

I also want to express my gratitude to CMES director Karin Aggestam for her constant encouragement and positive energy, as well as the deupty directior, Ronny Berndtsson. To Oliver Scharbrodt and Sami Al Daghistani, for their invaluable feedback on the Islamic principles and ontological framework that form the basis of the first chapter.

To my colleagues at CMES and Lund University, where this book took its final shape – Adam Almqvist, Anna Lene Stein, Daria Davitti, Giulia Gozzini, Lina Eklund, Lisa Strömbom, Maria Småberg, Mo Hamza, Pablo Pastor Vidal, Pinar Dinc, Rafah Barhoum, Rola el Husseini Dean and Sinem Kavak – thank you for making my time in Sweden so enjoyable.

I am deeply grateful to the editorial team at Edinburgh University Press, particularly Emma House, Isobel Birks and Sarah Foyle, for their support during the publication process and to the two anonymous reviewers for their engagement with this work and their precious comments and reflections. I am also grateful to Nora Derball for her incredible and inspiring work on Saudi Arabia and charitable activities, as well as for her valuable suggestions on my book proposal.

Special thanks go to Matteo Legrenzi for his energy, enthusiasm and constant encouragement in the early, difficult stages of my career. He helped me believe in a brighter future, and for that, I will always be grateful. Thanks to Bernard Haykel and Matteo Legrenzi's support, this research will continue its journey at Princeton University and Ca' Foscari University through a Marie Skłodowska-Curie Global Fellowship.

Thanks to Antonio de Lauri and the team at the Chr. Michelsen Institute – especially Sarah Tobin, Andrea and Maria – for welcoming me into their research centre. Thank you for enriching my work. A special thanks to Mari Norbakk, who prepared me for fieldwork as a friend should do, supporting me through good and bad times.

Part of this research was conducted in Qatar, with additional remote interviews with UAE practitioners and humanitarian workers in Syria. I am deeply thankful to all those who found the time to discuss the complex humanitarian situation in the region. A huge thanks to the entire team at the Centre for Conflict and Humanitarian Studies, especially Ghassan Elkahlout, Tariq Dana and Abdulfatah Mohamed. May their work always be an inspiration.

I am incredibly grateful to Olivier Roy and Louis Blin, who supported me during the final phase of my PhD and gave me the opportunity to conduct research at the European University Institute (EUI). Thanks to Théo Blanc, for the word *courage* at the right moment. Abdullah Al Jabassini and Agnès Favier, with their project 'Wartime and Post-Conflict in Syria' at the EUI, enriched my knowledge and analysis of Syria. It was wonderful to receive their support and intellectual generosity.

I presented part of this research project at Durham University as Sir William Luce Fellow in 2024. Thanks to the critical audience and the support of Clive Jones and Anoush Ehteshami for their invaluable feedback, comments, questions and advice.

To Louise Haysey, Eva-Maria Nag, Oznur, Muchait, and the beautiful rain of Durham that soaked many wonderful days. To my colleague and friend Mehmet Artik, for reminding me of the power of hope and imagination.

To Guillaume, *merci pour tout*. You were there in many places, and I hope to find you in many others.

To Hebatallah, Pelle – and Shams, for the chaos, the love, the Asian and Middle Eastern food, and the feeling of being home in beautiful Sweden.

To my family, for patiently accompanying me on this journey, holding my hand and never leaving me alone through all the deserts and roads of the world. To my father, for being the roots, and my mother, for giving me the audacity she always dreamed of. To Evans, I am sure I am not the sister you deserve, but maybe the one you will always need. To my friends scattered around the world, it is only because of you that I can feel at home everywhere. Because wherever I go, you are with me. To Silvana and Maria Sole, I wish you both a bright future in this world.

Finally, my deepest thanks go to my old and far-away friend Giulia de Cesaris, who donated all the photos of Syria in this book. While I tried to understand the Syrian humanitarian crisis, she dedicated her life as a humanitarian worker in the country. I am glad this book can show Syria through her eyes.

NOTE ON TRANSLITERATION

The transliteration of Arabic words and titles follows a simplified pattern. Diacritics are not included; Arabic words are not capitalised; 'ayn (') and hamza (') are differentiated; Arabic words and names mentioned in the International Journal of Middle East Studies' Word List are included accordingly; accepted English spelling is used for prominent Arabic names and figures.

INTRODUCTION: HUMANITARIANISM, POLITICS AND ISLAM

Charity, Islamic Aid and Foreign Aid

A picture of a Ferris wheel in a destroyed playground in the suburbs of Deir ez-Zor, taken by my friend Giulia, a humanitarian worker in Syria, evoked in me both sadness and hope when I saw it for the first time. And imagination. The capacity to envision a future after conflicts, disasters and prolonged crises, which seem to have become part of the contemporary Middle East, at least since I began studying and observing the region as a researcher. The power to imagine that something can be done to restore 'normality', to allow people to live their lives in familiar places.

This is where my journey began: attempting to understand the humanitarian response in conflict zones, with a regional focus on the Gulf States and Islamic organisations. This book was completed during the Israeli war on Gaza after 7 October 2023, when the humanitarian response was – once again – undermined by political circumstances, leaving me to wonder whether it is truly possible to separate humanitarianism from politics, or if the answer lies in finding 'good' policies and practices for humanitarian responses.

Unfortunately, this work does not provide a solution to the humanitarian dilemma, but it offers a new narrative and insights into the Islamic understandings of aid and charity, and the under-examined Gulf donors, which represent crucial actors in regional and contemporary crises.

The central argument of this book is based on the existence of non-universal but coexisting values that inspire humanitarianism, and the confrontation between principles and practices in the implementation of humanitarian aid. The Gulf States, like any other donor states, are guided by the structural norms of the aid system and the politicisation of aid itself. However, originating from a different political and cultural background, including different Islamic understandings, they bring with them distinct practices and approaches within the system that can no longer be ignored.

When I arrived in Qatar for the first time in November 2021, Doha was an open-air construction site, preparing for the major event of the following year: the 2022 FIFA World Cup. As I observed the stadiums, buildings and roads under construction, I recalled the question posed at the beginning of Mehran Kamrava's book *Qatar: Small States, Big Politics*: 'How can a small state, with little previous history of diplomatic engagement regionally or globally, have emerged as such an influential player in shaping unfolding events across the Middle East and elsewhere?' (Kamrava, 2015: 1).

Doha's transformation before my eyes, ahead of the World Cup, was the perfect image of a country willing to invest all its efforts and resources into showcasing and projecting its power to the entire world – no matter what it took or whether it attracted positive or negative attention from the international community. However, Qatar's historical role as a mediator and its proactive diplomacy in the region were already important indicators of this intent.

At that time, I was conducting fieldwork for my PhD research on the bureaucratic transformation of Qatar's aid structure and its humanitarian response in Syria. Simultaneously, several significant events were on the agendas of regional actors, such as the 'new' Afghanistan under Taliban authority, the Yemeni crisis and the military coup in Sudan after October 2021. All these events drew the attention of and humanitarian responses from the Gulf States, including the UAE, Qatar and Saudi Arabia, each with different approaches and strategies.

In the international humanitarian landscape, these Arab actors, with their varying Islamic backgrounds and political interests, play an active role in financing and implementing aid interventions in contemporary crises, particularly in the MENA region and Muslim-majority countries. However, literature on humanitarian assistance and foreign aid has largely focused on

Western actors, often treating Islamic organisations and Gulf States as 'others' or 'emerging agents' in the international arena – despite the strong relationship between Islam and charitable practices, and the efforts of these donors dating back to the 1970s. Charitable giving and generosity have been integral aspects of Islamic tradition from the religion's origin, serving as forms of social responsibility and grassroots activities. However, the relationship between power and charity has consistently been evident in the practices of *zakat* and *waqf*, which have in some cases been either instrumentalised or secularised (Moumtaz, 2021) to supplement public welfare. Since the 1970s, the Gulf States, following the oil boom and independence, have leveraged their resources to enhance their power in various forms, including transnational support and aid.

This book challenges the existing literature on the concept of Islamic aid and foreign aid interventions by the Gulf States, bringing together an analysis of these two concepts through the study of various levels of aid implementation and policies, and examining their behaviour in a specific case study: the Syrian humanitarian response from 2015 to 2023. The analysis explores the top-down decision-making process of aid allocation by Qatar and the UAE and non-state regional actors, as well as the humanitarian negotiations and aid distribution conducted by Gulf charities and local organisations in Syria after 2015.

Due to the complexity and differences among the Gulf States, this book focuses on Qatar and the UAE as two examples from the region. This selection is based on several factors. The two countries have distinct internal structures – Qatar is a cohesive state, while the UAE is a federation – which influence their bureaucratic aid systems, including the institutions and implementing agencies involved. Moreover, following the Arab Spring, Qatar and the UAE have adopted different positions in the MENA region and the Horn of Africa, driven by their security perceptions and power projection strategies. Additionally, their stances on the Syrian crisis have diverged, making it particularly interesting to examine how aid policies may vary based on differing political positions within the same context.

The observation of these Gulf States is built by combining international relations (IR) theories and the ontological framework that draws from the Islamic perspective on aid and charity, referred to as 'behavioural norms'. The Islamic solidarity and helping the *Umma* beyond national borders inspired the Gulf States' initial steps to act as donors in crises and conflicts, albeit with differing intentions and approaches, as in the cases of Afghanistan and Bosnia (Benthall & Bellion-Jourdan, 2003: 69). Some of the instruments used by charities and governments belong to the Islamic tradition, such as *zakat*, *sadaqa* and *waqf*. However, the Islamic principles which inspire aid as a pure form of assistance have often been influenced by the pragmatism of donors – especially when the state is the main agency responsible for designing and financing aid – and have been further shaped by social and political dynamics on the ground. The different Islamic backgrounds of these donors may be irrelevant in aid strategies and implementation, where 'structural dynamics', including elite decision-making processes, bureaucratic aid systems and the geopolitical context, are the main variables influencing aid parameters and resource allocation.

Hence, this study assumes that, despite Islam providing an ethical and ontological framework (behavioural norms) within which concepts of humanitarianism can be identified, the application of these behavioural norms in the foreign aid strategies (structure) of the Gulf States results in the predominance of political needs driven by both external dynamics and the internal characteristics of these donors and recipients. However, different religious identities should still be considered in the analysis of these donors' foreign aid as a distinguishing factor in the international humanitarian order. It can offer advantages in the implementation of aid in Muslim-majority communities or countries (bottom-up analysis) and serve as a form of perceived legitimisation compared to Western organisations (Facon, 2024).

In reflecting on religious norms, it is essential to acknowledge that Islam is not a monolithic phenomenon. Drawing on Petersen's (2012) work, this analysis moves away from essentialist conceptions of Islam, instead focusing on 'making the construction and signification of Islam – and, subsequently, Islamic aid – part of the subject matter of the analysis' (Petersen, 2012: 129). Religions are not separate from historical contexts, structures and power relations; rather, they are shaped through continuous interactions with them. Therefore, when constructing Islam, actors draw upon historical cultures, traditions and practices, with varying degrees of authority and power, thus presenting their version of Islam as more valid than others (Petersen, 2012).

Analysing Gulf States' foreign aid solely as a tool of foreign policy would overlook the cultural and social components that shape their aid systems in both policy elaboration and implementation. At the same time, ignoring the significance of geopolitical interests and power projections in resource allocation would be naive and detached from the rationalist approach that the Gulf States have adopted in the region.

Three key concepts will emerge in this book that require clarification: charity, Islamic aid and foreign aid. The concept of charity in the Islamic understanding is well described by Amy Singer in her book Charity in Muslim Societies (Singer, 2008). She draws on Marcel Mauss's theory, where charitable giving in Muslim contexts is seen as part of the pervasive, ongoing gift exchanges that hold societies together. Charity is viewed through its historical dimension and its connection with Islamic economics and values, which transform charitable practices into moral and social obligations.

The term 'Islamic aid' refers to the set of behavioural norms that can be applied to the different Islamic understandings of aid and charity. This includes the financial instruments currently used to address humanitarian issues, as well as the practices of state institutions or religious-based organisations (such as charities, non-governmental organisations (NGOs) and regional institutions) involved in humanitarian responses and development interventions. As mentioned, the Islamic tradition offers instruments for charitable giving such as *zakat* and *sadaqa*. However, in this book, I focus on Islamic aid and Islamic humanitarianism as a set of behavioural norms inspired by modern political thought and built on the ontological framework of Islamic economics.

The third concept is foreign aid, intended as official development assistance (ODA) according to the OECD definition, 'government aid that promotes and specifically targets the economic development and welfare of developing countries'; this includes humanitarian responses as part of foreign aid analysis. Humanitarian aid, in fact, is a sector of ODA, aiming specifically to 'save lives, alleviate suffering, and maintain and protect human dignity during and in the aftermath of emergencies', as defined by the Development Initiative. It includes disaster prevention and preparedness; reconstruction relief; relief coordination, protection and support services; emergency food aid; and other emergency or distress relief.

This work examines both humanitarian and development interventions by the Gulf States, with a particular focus on humanitarian responses during conflicts, which excludes (or should exclude) any form of conditionality.

How, then, is foreign aid related to Islamic aid? This relationship between foreign aid and Islamic aid, in the context of regional actors and Gulf donors' strategies, reflects a combination of identities and religious motivations, alongside political interests, in the allocation and implementation of aid on the ground. Understanding Islamic charity and the Islamic concept of development and assistance can help deconstruct Western development narratives around aid strategies, promoting a new paradigm where aid models are not static schemes imposed by donors but are instead built on the beneficiaries' systems of understanding and values.

As Benthall and Bellion-Jourdan highlight in their book on the politics of aid in the Muslim world, 'the topic of Islamic philanthropy is pivotal, bringing together the richness of Islamic studies with an almost virgin field for academic research – the traditions of aid that fall outside the normal category of presumed Western largesse' (Benthall & Bellion-Jourdan, 2003: 1). These words became particularly challenging in 2003 when Islamic charities and the broader aid sector of Islamic organisations were accused of supporting and financing terrorism in some Muslim countries. After 9/11, many Islamic organisations scaled back their activities, and major donors, including the Gulf States, initiated efforts to improve accountability and transparency. Following 9/11, several NGOs were accused by the United States of funding militant camps, providing logistical support for fighters from Saudi Arabia and otherwise aiding the mujahedeen, particularly in the contexts of Afghanistan and Bosnia. Although the funds were linked to individuals from the Gulf States rather than the states themselves (Petersen, 2012), Saudi Arabia, Qatar, the UAE and Kuwait chose to institutionalise their charities in line with the Western model of accountability and transparency, aiming to reframe their aid interventions. Despite these efforts, the relevance of this issue persists, albeit for different reasons.

The importance of Islamic organisations and Arab donors emerges overwhelmingly in light of the protracted crises occurring in Muslim-majority countries (MMCs) and the high poverty rates among Muslim communities. According to the International Rescue Committee, in 2024, the worst crises in the world, in terms of the number of people in need and the humanitarian consequences, were in Sudan, Gaza, South Sudan, Burkina Faso, Myanmar, Mali and Somalia (International Rescue Committee, 2023).

These countries are predominantly MMCs, where access to aid can be influenced by various factors. These include the capacity of actors to negotiate with local stakeholders and the level of trust that communities have in humanitarian workers and organisations. De Cordier (2009) examined the existing and potential added value generated by Muslim aid actors in predominantly Muslim environments, highlighting how it is cultural proximity that influences the ability of Islamic organisations to build effective networks and implement aid interventions in each context. Although it is still challenging to assess the extent to which cultural proximity enhances the quality of aid distribution and the interaction between donors and recipients, understanding the aid schemes of donors with Islamic backgrounds – despite their heterogeneity – and the organisations operating in Muslim-majority contexts remains essential.

It is important to note that the concept of cultural proximity remains a tentative argument rather than a fully developed theory. According to this concept, the symbolic sense of community within the *Umma* extends to Muslim actors involved in the aid process – specifically, between Muslim organisations, national and local governments, local communities, and beneficiaries. As emphasised by Palmer, cultural proximity could provide added value, as solidarity in faith might enhance aid provision in different ways, such as (a) ensuring easier and safer access to Muslim countries and areas, offering logistical advantages through religious solidarity with national and local governments, as well as local communities; (b) ensuring that aid is delivered effectively and that the services provided are sensitive to religious needs; and (c) fostering positive relations between local and expatriate staff and beneficiaries, based on shared beliefs and respect for religious values and practices.

According to this line of thought, a common religion creates solidarity among beneficiaries, NGOs and other actors in the aid process, which in turn generates added value through ease of access and the provision of more culturally appropriate services (Palmer, 2011: 97). This assumption has arisen from contexts where Western NGOs encountered hostility, insecurity and logistical challenges when attempting to work in complex emergencies in Muslim countries. Palmer's conclusion regarding the cultural proximity hypothesis was not confirmed in the case of Islamic Relief

Worldwide's response to the Rohingya refugee crisis. She argues, 'It is therefore naive to presume that being Muslim will facilitate easy and effective relations between an organisation and beneficiaries, between an organisation and a host country, or between organisations' (Palmer, 2011: 107). However, in each context, cultural and religious values carry their weight and significance.

Evidence from the field and empirical studies have linked aid access and successful humanitarian negotiations more closely to the 'political' capacity of humanitarian actors or donors, particularly in their vertical and horizontal relationships with formal and informal authorities on the ground, than to a shared cultural or value-based background between donors (or implementing agencies) and recipients (Bartlotti, 2002). However, it remains a concept worth considering and assessing on a case-by-case basis.

In the pages to come, I explore answers to key questions: What principles constitute the behavioural norms of aid and humanitarianism in the Islamic understandings? What elements shape the identities of Qatar and the UAE as donors in the region? Furthermore, when observing the Syrian humanitarian response and considering the intrinsic political dimensions of aid, do the sectarian approaches to the conflict and the fragmentation of the opposition – put in place by these two external supporters – reflect how these two Gulf states implement their aid policies?

The book begins by exploring the principles that inspire aid and charity in Islamic theology and the Islamic moral economy, establishing the general framework within which the Islamic concept of aid is constructed. However, while Islam offers principles inspiring humanitarianism, aid practices must be contextualised and analysed in relation to historical and political needs. Thus, the book reconstructs the historical trajectory of aid and charity from the origin of Islam to the present, offering a new perspective on the elements that guide the foreign aid policies of Gulf donors. The politicisation and institutionalisation of aid can be traced back to the Ottoman Empire and the approach of the Muslim Brotherhood (also referred to as *Ikhwan*, the Arabic word for 'brothers'), continuing with the role of the Gulf States as mediators and donors in the region. The institutionalisation of aid from Islamic organisations and Gulf donors has been identifiable since the 1990s, becoming more pronounced after 9/11 when aid from

Figure I.1 Lusail skyline from the terrace of the Doha Institute, Qatar, November 2021. Photo by the author.

Muslim organisations and regional donors faced scrutiny and accusations of supporting terrorism.

Despite these challenges, the current transformation of aid bureaucracy in the Gulf States, along with the use of Islamic social welfare instruments by both Muslim and non-Muslim organisations (as explored in the case of UNHCR in Chapter 1), indicates that the institutionalisation process at both local and transnational levels is still ongoing.

The first part of the book, '**Principles**', explores the principles and historical dimensions of aid and charity, illustrating how the dynamics of politicisation and institutionalisation have evolved together over time. The second part, '**Practices**', examines Qatar and the UAE as state donors within the international framework, highlighting their distinct aid systems, with a specific focus on Syria's humanitarian response.

The Syrian Case and the Role of the Gulf States

The common ground for observing the aid policies and implementation of Qatar and the UAE, encompassing both state and non-state actors, is the Syrian humanitarian response from 2015 to 2023. But why is the response of the Gulf States to the Syrian crisis relevant in this analysis?

The Syrian humanitarian response has been one of the most discussed and criticised issues within the humanitarian community, primarily due to the lack of neutrality, as well as the polarisation and instrumentalisation of aid practices throughout the conflict. In the book *Everybody's War: Politics of Aid in the Syrian Crisis*, the authors examine how humanitarian aid, advocacy and service delivery have sometimes been 'complicit in a war that placed the provision, diversion, and restriction of services at the centre of the battle of the Syrian State' (Bseiso, Hofman & Whittall, 2021: 2).

As diverse actors provided aid in various parts of Syria – whether controlled by the Assad government or opposition armed groups – this provision quickly became a political issue rather than a straightforward response to the needs of the conflict-affected population. Aid distribution often reflected the interests of the donors and their positions regarding the Assad government. Consequently, this study distinguishes between two different mechanisms and dynamics of aid distribution: one within Assad-controlled areas and the other in opposition-controlled areas.

In 2011, unarmed anti-governmental protests across the country began, followed by severe crackdowns by the military and the police force. This repression quickly escalated into an all-out war and protracted crisis. Initially, large portions of Syrian territory were captured by armed opposition groups, aided by the support of international and regional actors who fragmented al-Assad's opposition. The United States provided training and arms to what were termed moderate opposition fighters, while the Gulf States supported different factions within the opposition, opting to avoid direct military engagement – unlike Russia and Iran – by using their proxies to extend their influence.

The military involvement of Russia in 2015 shifted the balance in favour of the Syrian government, leading to the retaking of various areas through 'reconciliation deals' (Adleh & Favier, 2017). By the end of 2024, however, Idlib and northern Aleppo remained under opposition control.

While this book was still in the making, at the end of November 2024, various groups of rebels and opposition forces advanced towards Damascus, and on 8 December, al-Assad's government collapsed. This 'historic moment' (Al Jazeera, 2024b), marking the end of fifty-three years of rule by the al-Assad family, ushered in a new era characterised by uncertainty and hope for the Syrian population, alongside emerging political dynamics and the prospects for future reconstruction.

Figure I.2 Destroyed buildings in Deir ez-Zor, eastern Syria, 2021. Photo by Giulia de Cesaris.

Regarding the Gulf States, there was no unified stance on the Syrian conflict. Saudi Arabia, Bahrain and Qatar were strong supporters of the rebellion and backed various rebel groups. Qatar viewed the situation in Syria as an opportunity to bolster its longstanding regional allies in the Muslim Brotherhood (MB) movement, a significant player in the Syrian political opposition (Ibish, 2016). Saudi Arabia vehemently opposed al-Assad, largely to contrast with Iranian support for the regime, instrumentalising the sectarian nature of the conflict. Riyadh assisted Sunni rebels, which contributed to the fragmentation of the opposition, differing from Qatar's alignment with Islamist groups.

The UAE also supported elements of the anti-Assad insurgency, but its role was less prominent than that of Saudi Arabia and Qatar. The UAE's focus was primarily on ensuring that Islamist forces did not gain the upper hand in the conflict. However, its position began to shift in 2018 when the country initiated a rapprochement with the Syrian regime and advocated Syria's readmission to the Arab League after its suspension in 2011. This normalisation process was also embraced by Saudi Arabia, reflecting a strategic recalibration of the kingdom's approach in the region.

In examining Qatar and the UAE's aid interventions, the Qatar Fund for Development (QFFD), the UAE Ministry of Foreign Affairs and the Abu Dhabi Fund for Development (ADFD) represent the main state institutions responsible for allocating funds and monitoring programmes in third countries. Their distinct operational methods, their partnerships and the types of projects implemented in the field reflect how Qatar and the UAE choose to allocate funds and solidify their roles in fragile contexts, including Syria.

To conduct a comparative analysis, this study considers the Syrian case as a common ground for observing how these governmental institutions and their main charities operate in Syria and neighbouring countries – namely Lebanon, Jordan and Türkiye – to address humanitarian needs and the refugee crisis. The elements outlined in the conceptual framework – (a) transnational: Islamic backgrounds; (b) internal: elite decision-making processes and institutional dimensions; and (c) external: projection of power and geopolitical dynamics – are employed to explain the identities of these two donors and their foreign aid interventions in Syria, moving beyond a simplistic understanding based solely on political agendas.

Depoliticising Humanitarian Action?

As mentioned in the opening lines, this work engages with the ongoing debate surrounding the humanitarian dilemma and the politicisation of aid interventions during emergencies and conflicts. Analysing humanitarian aid financed by state actors, including the Gulf States, necessitates an exploration of the unresolved discussion about humanitarianism and the politicisation of aid.

Humanitarianism is a contested concept (Barnett & Weiss, 2013). Although charity and philanthropy have existed throughout human history, many argue that modern humanitarianism began with the establishment of the International Committee of the Red Cross in 1864. Following this, the term 'humanitarian aid' emerged in international law and relations to describe a legitimate form of 'organised assistance and protection for people who are suffering or who are likely to suffer from armed conflict or disaster' (Gordon & Donini, 2015: 81).

Humanitarianism is often perceived as distinct from politics. However, if we examine humanitarianism for what it is and does – rather than what it should be and should do – we can observe the strong interconnection between politics and humanitarian interventions (Bradley, 2023). Humanitarianism and humanitarian aid have always been influenced by political factors and have political effects, often debated as unintended consequences of aid during conflicts (Wood & Sullivan, 2015; Narang, 2015). This dynamic contributes to the concept of the 'politicisation' of aid. According to Dany, politicisation can be defined as 'political changes that divert humanitarian aid away from its principled character' (Dany, 2015: 424).

In this book, the term 'politicisation' is used to describe the allocation of resources and the response to specific needs of targeted groups or communities that align more closely with the political agendas of the donors than with the necessities of the recipients. This does not imply that responses to conflicts or disasters should be entirely depoliticised, as it is essential to address the political solutions required by local and international actors in contexts of asymmetrical power (Facon, 2024). Instead, depoliticisation indicates that humanitarian efforts should not serve to support certain political rationales or be seen as long-term solutions to political problems. Dany further distinguishes politicisation from instrumentalisation, which occurs when 'humanitarian aid is used to advance political, economic, or security interests', thus compromising the principle of impartiality (Dany, 2015: 426).

In other words, instrumentalisation refers to donors' preference for allocating resources to certain countries based on strategic priorities and it can involve the use of humanitarian aid to either empower or disempower state or non-state actors in fragmented contexts. The literature on the impact of aid delivery to non-state actors emphasises how aid can help these entities 'win the hearts and minds' of the civilian population, thereby supporting their political objectives (Meininghaus, 2016; Loewental, Miaari & Hoeffler, 2023). A study conducted by Carnegie and colleagues, which provides an empirical analysis of aid in contested areas of Syria, demonstrates that foreign aid can enhance the credibility and support of non-state actors and rebel groups, particularly in environments lacking contestation (Carnegie, Howe, Lichtenheld & Mukhopadhyay, 2022).

In their book *Depoliticising Humanitarian Action*, Desportes and colleagues have tried to find an alternative model to the current schemes of humanitarian interventions, to eliminate political obstacles and influences in everyday practice:

> The reality of our times is that it is no longer possible to carry on with the status quo. The model of orthodox humanitarianism that emerged in the West and has been subsequently exported through colonial and neocolonial initiatives to the vast majority of the world is cracking under the weight of rising tides of change. The history of the humanitarian movement is shaped by geopolitical issues and reigning ideologies. Thus, simply relying on 'reason' or 'pragmatism' does not appear to be a satisfactory resolution to the complex problems being raised today. Rather, orthodox humanitarianism has to evolve. (Desportes, Corbet & Siddiqi, 2024: 257)

But how can humanitarianism evolve? Do the Gulf States' aid initiatives follow the hegemonic approach to humanitarian interventions, or do they present an alternative model?

To address the first question, the authors identify 'localisation' as an initial paradigm shift aimed at mitigating North–South disparities and asymmetrical power relations. However, the study of humanitarian practices must consider two analytical levels: the intentions and policies of donors in financing aid, and the implementation of aid, which involves the daily operations of aid agencies and their interactions with recipient communities. The predominant debate on the depoliticisation of humanitarian aid pertains to the second level – everyday practices of aid implementation – which significantly impacts recipients' lives and interacts with political actors and dynamics on the ground. Regarding the first level – aid policy formulation – it remains unclear how state actors in their roles as donors can genuinely depoliticise aid strategies and resource allocation, as these processes are inevitably intertwined with political considerations. Depoliticising humanitarian aid implies that the costs of humanitarian relief should be borne exclusively by donors, based on technical evaluations and needs assessments, without regard for their political agendas or positionalities. This would necessitate incorporating a pure sense of assistance into their budgets, a goal that seems distant from current realities. Moreover, as the Syrian case illustrates, the allocation of resources in a fragmented context among various state and non-state actors can inadvertently alter power dynamics.

Approach and Sources

The data presented in this book were gathered from 2021 to 2024 during my fieldwork in Qatar, complemented by remote interviews with humanitarian practitioners in Syria and key informants within aid institutions in the UAE. To ensure data triangulation regarding the Syrian case, I conducted interviews with representatives from the United Nations Office for the Coordination of Humanitarian Affairs (OCHA) in Gaziantep and Damascus, as well as Ihsan Relief and Development, a Syrian NGO based in Doha that operates as a local partner with Qatari and international organisations. Table I.1 below illustrates the actors analysed and/or interviewed in the period considered. For Chapter 1, which examines the use of Islamic social welfare instruments, I conducted interviews with the UNHCR's Refugee Zakat Fund and the Islamic Development Bank (IsDB) to gather data on the Refugee Zakat Fund and the Global Islamic Fund for Refugees (GIFR).

In Chapters 3 and 4, the research employs a qualitative approach through both primary and secondary sources. This includes official documents from the two ministries of foreign affairs, the QFFD and the ADFD, such as annual reports, bilateral agreements, official statements and press releases. While the efforts towards accountability made by the QFFD and the UAE Ministry of Foreign Affairs have resulted in the availability of more data and reports, neither institution provides comprehensive details on financed projects, sectors or beneficiaries. Consequently, a part of this research is constrained by the limited data available and the political sensitivity of the Syrian case.

Despite intentions to enhance transparency by these donors, gaps remain in both quantitative and qualitative information. However, data from international organisations, such as OCHA's Financial Tracking Service, allow for triangulation of information on multilateral interventions through UN channels. The analysis and comparison of aid are based on four main parameters: aid flow per year, geographical allocation, sectoral distribution and channel allocation of resources.

For the case of Syria, interviews were conducted with donor organisations, charities and representatives from OCHA in Damascus and Gaziantep, which oversaw operations in the opposition-controlled areas of Idlib and northern Aleppo (before December 2024).

Table I.1 Overview of the actors analysed and/or interviewed from 2021 to 2024.

Actor	**Reference – subject**	**Period of interviews/analysis**
UNHCR Refugee Zakat Fund	Chapter 1 – management of *zakat* for refugees	2022–2024
Islamic Research and Training Institute (IRTI), Islamic Development Bank	Chapter 1 – IsDB policies and Syrian refugee interventions	2021–2024
Islamic Solidarity Fund for Development	Chapter 1 – collaboration with the UNHCR for GIFR	2022–2024
Qatar Fund for Development	Chapter 3 – Aid policies	2021–2022
Regulatory Authority for Charitable Activities (Qatar)	Chapter 3 – Aid bureaucracy and management	2021
Qatar Red Crescent Society	Chapter 3 – Aid implementation	2021–2022

(Continued)

Actor	Reference – subject	Period of interviews/analysis
Qatar Charity	Chapter 3 – Aid implementation	2021–2022
Abu Dhabi Fund for Development	Chapter 3 – Aid policies	2021–2022
OCHA Gaziantep	Chapter 4 – Triangulation and Operations in Syria	2023
OCHA Damascus	Chapter 4 – Triangulation and Operations in Syria	2023
Syrian local organisations – Ihsan Relief and Development	Chapter 4 – Aid implementation	2023

The Chapters

The book is divided into six chapters, including the introduction and conclusion.

Chapter 1 explores the values and principles of the Islamic moral economy, which inspire charitable and philanthropic acts within society. This chapter provides the ontological framework and investigates the structure and instruments of the moral economy designed for redistributing wealth and enhancing social justice.

Islamic sources and principles contain tools such as *zakat*, *waqf* (endowment), *sadaqa* (charity) and *qard al-hasan* (interest-free loan), which are now managed differently by various actors and organisations. This ontological background aims to give the reader an understanding of the Islamic alternative, which, however, faces obstacles and challenges in its implementation. Moreover, it examines the implementation of financing instruments by the UNHCR Refugee Zakat Fund and IsDB in addressing the humanitarian financing gap related to the global refugee crisis, using *zakat* and *waqf*.

In the second chapter, the book traces the evolution of charitable practices from the beginning of Islam to the present day, considering crucial events that have influenced these practices and, consequently, the institutionalisation of aid within the international framework. It analyses aid in all its components to understand how contemporary practices draw on historical notions and values, resulting in specific responses to crises that differ from Western-based approaches. Key events, such as the 9/11 terrorist attacks, the 2011 Arab uprisings and the growing diversification of foreign aid efforts in the Gulf States, have contributed to an increasingly politicised aid landscape. The impact of these factors is compounded by the emergence of new young ruling elites in the Gulf States, who espouse realist, power-based thinking in international relations. Furthermore, the chapter constructs a conceptual framework to analyse the foreign aid strategies of the Gulf States, combining international relations theories to evaluate the internal, external and transnational variables that affect aid parameters.

To integrate theoretical analysis with empirical evidence, the third chapter explores the evolution of foreign aid from Qatar and the UAE, the institutional background of the two countries and charitable organisations in them. By analysing data on funded projects and the geographical, sectoral and channel allocation of aid, the chapter highlights crucial aspects of these two Gulf donors' behaviours.

Chapter 4 focuses on the modus operandi of these two Gulf States in the context of Syrian humanitarian response and early recovery, and examines their involvement. Data from 2015 to 2023 reveal that differing interests in the Syrian context are reflected in how aid policies are implemented. This top-down evaluation of aid strategies demonstrates the predominance of political choices in aid allocation, leading Qatar and the UAE to finance interventions along two parallel lines – supporting respectively the opposition- and government-controlled areas.

Since the Arab uprisings, Qatar and the UAE have found themselves on opposing sides in terms of foreign policy, which has consequently affected their foreign aid strategies. They have intervened in the geopolitical landscape of the MENA region, supporting different groups to pursue their political agendas, the Syrian case being no exception. Against this backdrop, the first stage of the research examines the evolution of their foreign aid policies, while the second stage explores whether and how the sectarian approach to the Syrian conflict, coupled with the fragmentation of the opposition, is reflected in the implementation of aid policies by these Gulf States. Moreover, the chapter considers a bottom-up perspective on aid interventions, describing the everyday practices of humanitarian negotiations and operations conducted by implementing agencies involved in current protracted crises.

In the conclusion, the book reflects on the relevance of the Gulf States in contemporary crises in the Middle East and beyond, and how the increasing number of actors in the humanitarian sector may create a new paradigm for change.

PART I

PRINCIPLES

1

ISLAMIC AID: PRINCIPLES, IDENTITIES AND RELIGION

Islamic understandings of humanitarianism and charity are grounded in the Islamic tradition and modern Islamic political thought and have evolved across diverse geographical contexts, historical periods and schools of thought. Analysing foreign aid interventions by Gulf States, particularly Qatar and the United Arab Emirates, and their implementation in a Muslim-majority country, such as Syria, does not necessarily imply that Islam directly determines aid dynamics or donor–recipient relationships. Nonetheless, Islamic principles and interpretations may influence certain dimensions of these engagements and create Islamic instruments of wealth redistribution for humanitarian purposes. This chapter traces the intellectual foundations of Islamic humanitarianism, exploring the link with Islamic economics and examining how poverty and social justice are conceptualised within the ideological frameworks developed by key figures in the field, including the founding theorists of Islamic economics and ideologues of the Muslim Brotherhood such as Yusuf al-Qaradawi and Sayyid Qutb.

The Islamic Culture of Aid and Islamic Moral Economy

Humanitarian aid and politics are part of the same story, while the Islamic understanding of charity and humanitarianism has been shaped by the political agendas of both state and non-state actors in modern-day aid. This is particularly evident when donors are state actors but also when non-state organisations operate in highly politicised contexts where humanitarian aid becomes part of the conflict or crisis. Islam, indeed, offers a set of norms that could form the framework for the behaviour of donors and implementing agencies. Whether these behavioural norms can truly resist the politicisation and institutionalisation of aid practices in the contemporary aid landscape is probably a 'matter of faith', and depends on how political and humanitarian actors define, use and instrumentalise these norms. However, Islam, as a shared value between donors and recipients, can still play a role in the dynamics of aid and power. Therefore, a critical exploration of its norms is necessary before observing how these norms have been transformed, used or adapted by different actors operating in the modern humanitarian field.

This work traces the connection between Islamic charity and Islamic economics as charity 'is of central importance to Islamic economics' (Atia, 2013: 1). The term 'Islamic economics' refers to a field of study and discipline based on the assumption that Islamic axioms exist within the social, political and legal environment – a system of values and ethics that guides the economic behaviour of human beings in Islamic society (Kahf, 2003). The central idea that defines Islamic economics and distinguishes it from positive (neoclassical) economics is its insistence on the explicit inclusion of ethics, grounded in religion, within a unified analytical framework (Naqvi, 1994).

The founding figures of Islamic economics attributed the failure of economic development in the 1960s and 1970s – particularly in the Middle East and other Muslim-majority countries – to capitalist economic development strategies that overlooked the importance of human beings and their well-being. Among various theories of development, the Islamic economic system emerged as an alternative, aiming to establish a parallel system based on Islamic norms, rules and institutions. In describing Islamic economics, Chapra argues that it emerged in Muslim countries aiming to regain independence from colonialism, as a response to the dominance of Western powers. Tracing the framework of Islamic economic paradigms, he notes that it is based on a paradigm with socio-economic justice as its primary objective (Chapra, 2001).

In an effort to localise the Islamic economic system within temporal, geographical and political contexts, Al-Daghistani traces the genealogy of modern Islamic economics beginning with the backdrop of nineteenth-century Europe. This prominent dimension of the discourse on Islamic economics is closely tied to the colonial period and the conception of the modern state, which, in many respects, represents both a response to and a continuation of the writings of Muslim reformists during *al-Nahda*, also known as the Arab Renaissance, which took place from the late nineteenth century to the mid-twentieth century. The Islamisation process, as envisioned by Ismail al-Faruqi, for instance, found its most tangible application in economic models. Despite offering theoretical critiques of the neoliberal economic paradigm, Islamic economics and banking have largely adopted mainstream political-economic ideologies, rather than fully embracing principles considered inherent to Islamic economic thought, such as socio-economic justice and the pursuit of higher moral objectives.

During the nineteenth century, at least three distinct movements emerged in the Middle East and South Asia, each responding differently to the intellectual and sociopolitical challenges facing Muslim societies. One movement sought to preserve traditional Islamic knowledge by advocating a return to scriptural teachings. A second embraced secularisation, aiming to reform Muslim societies and institutions along modernist lines. The third movement attempted to reconcile these divergent paths by integrating Islamic sources with non-Islamic philosophical traditions. In the context of the Islamisation of knowledge and Islamic economics, this third, synthetic approach is particularly relevant.

Efforts to formulate an authentic Islamic vision of socio-economic life can be traced to the early twentieth-century reformist movements. However, the development of Islamic economic literature – which eventually gave rise to the formal discipline – emerged in the subsequent decades through the contributions of figures such as Hifzur Rahman Seoharwi, Manazir Ahsan Gilani, Sheikh Mahmud Ahmad, Muhammad Hamidullah, Khurshid Ahmad, and notably, Abul A'la Maududi, whose seminal work *The Economic Problem of Man and Its Islamic Solution* played a foundational role. Some of these thinkers were influenced by the *Nahda* scholars and their reformist legacy.

Nonetheless, it was only with the broader systemic efforts to Islamise national economies and the concurrent Islamisation of knowledge movement, initiated in the late 1970s through the philosophical work of Isma'il al-Faruqi and Muhammad Naquib al-Attas, that Islamic economics began to mature into a structured field and academic discipline. Although initially conceived as a spiritual and intellectual endeavour, the Islamisation of knowledge also functioned as a strategy to decolonise and 'de-Westernise' epistemological frameworks, offering distinct and authentic contributions to global knowledge production in response to the political and economic challenges faced by Muslim-majority countries in the Middle East, South Asia and Southeast Asia (Al-Daghistani, 2021: 47–8).

Ontological framework and axioms of Islamic economics

In contrast to the secular market paradigm, human well-being is not solely dependent on maximising wealth and consumption. It requires a balanced satisfaction of both the material and the spiritual needs of the human personality. Islamic economics considers the economic behaviour of humans within the broader context of their overall existence, and it does not limit itself to market variables. It adopts a multidisciplinary and normative approach, based on ethical patterns and values. In this regard, Islamic economics must fulfil the Quranic duty of enjoining the good and forbidding the evil, suggesting ways and means to achieve *falah* (salvation) (Khan, 1984). Therefore, Islamic political economy seeks to establish a political order based on ontological and epistemological sources, namely the Quran and *hadith*, and to define a framework for the economic value system, the operational dimensions and the economic behaviour of individual Muslims. The axioms underpinning this framework shape economic activities, in terms of both intra- and intergenerational social justice. These foundations generate the behaviour of economic agents as well as the institutions in the system and hence effectively determine the micro-foundations of that economy (Arif, 1989).

One key axiom is *tawhid* (God's unity and sovereignty). The Islamic worldview is grounded in *tawhid*, which represents the vertical dimension of Islam, manifested by the inherent equality of each individual, reflected in their equal proximity to God.

The second axiom is that of *al-'adl wa'l-ihsan* (equilibrium and beneficence, or socio-economic justice), according to which individuals are expected to establish justice *('adl)* and promote beneficence (*ihsan*), which consequently 'denote a state of social equilibrium'. This axiom provides for the horizontal dimension of equality across all the virtues of the basic set of social institutions – legal, political and economic (Naqvi, 1994).

Third, the axiom of *ikhtiyar* (free will): in the Islamic economic system, humans are believed to be endowed with free will. However, this freedom must be understood within specific social contexts and adapted to changing times. This axiom forms the functional norms of economic activity within the Islamic economic system (Asutay, 2007).

The fourth axiom is *fard* (responsibility). While 'responsibility' is voluntary, individuals and society must recognise their mutual obligations to the public good, which stem from the principle of *tawhid* and, consequently, humanity's role as vicegerent on earth.

Fifth, the axiom of *rububiyyah* refers to divine arrangements that direct things towards their perfection. This axiom underscores the necessity of sustainable economic growth and development, ensuring harmony between the various components of economic and social life (Asutay, 2007).

The sixth axiom is *tazkiyah*, which refers to the achievement of perfection through purification and harmonious relationships. This is the result of *tawhid, 'adl, fard* and *rububiyyah*, guiding the individual towards self-development in alignment with economic and social progress. The result of *tazkiyah* is *falah*, prosperity in this world and the hereafter (Ahmad, 1994).

The seventh axiom is *khilafah*, human accountability before God. Allah created human beings as His vicegerents on earth. This role, known as *istikhlaf*, entails fulfilling God's will on earth – promoting what is good, forbidding what is wrong, establishing justice (*'adl*) and promoting beneficence (*ihsan*), all of which lead to attaining a high standard of living (*hayat al-tayybah*), both individually and collectively. This axiom implies universal solidarity and sustainable consumption of resources (Ahmad, 2003).

The final axiom is represented by *maqasid al-shari'a* (the objectives of *shari'a*), which defines the legal-rational framework within which Islamic economic activities should be conducted. The objectives of Islamic economics must align with the principles of *shariʿa* and ultimately lead to human well-being.

Maqasid al-shariʿa embodies a framework for development that integrates relevant 'theological' values into both the knowledge and the practice of development. For this reason, the early scholars of Islamic economics sought to adopt a new methodology that challenges centrism and universal truth claims on assumptions of rationality (Asutay & Yilmaz, 2018).

Studies in this field have sought to develop a conceptual framework for a *maqasid al-shariʿa*-based index of socio-economic development. *Maqasid al-shariʿa* refers to the objectives of Islamic law, which are categorised into three descending levels of importance: *daruriyat* (the essential), *hajiyat* (the complementary) and *tahsinayat* (the desirable or embellishments).

Al-Ghazali identified five essentials that are fundamental from the *shariʿa* perspective. These essentials are the human self, faith, intellect, progeny and wealth or property. These five necessities, according to *shariʿa* principles, must be protected and enhanced by society as a whole (Bedoui & Mansour, 2015). From this perspective, development should be realised by fostering an environment that enables individuals to achieve spiritual, moral and socio-economic well-being in this world, as well as salvation in the hereafter (*falah*). Consequently, *maqasid al-shariʿa* serves as the Islamic framework for development. In light of the importance of socio-economic development guided by *maqasid al-shariʿa* and the creation of development policies aligned with these objectives, there is a need to establish a measurement method based on them (Ali, 2019).

Building on al-Ghazali's theory, some scholars, such as Chapra and Siddiqi, have expanded this theoretical framework by introducing corollaries to the five main necessities. Placing individual *falah* at the centre of his theorisation, Chapra adopts al-Ghazali's *maqasid* framework, acknowledging that the five necessities outlined by al-Ghazali are not the only *maqasid* aimed at ensuring human well-being (Chapra, 2008b). He argues that many other principles from the Quran and Sunnah can be seen as corollaries to the first five objectives, and the realisation of these corollaries is essential for achieving the primary objectives. Chapra's reworking of *maqasid* emphasises the enhancement of the five universal necessities through the fulfilment of the set of corollary objectives (Asutay & Yilmaz, 2018).

Moreover, Chapra underscores the importance of policy goals aimed at achieving security of life and property, the removal of poverty, employment and self-employment, equitable distribution of income and wealth, education, good governance, and the development and expansion of wealth. These objectives should culminate in the revitalisation of the human self, which is one of the five primary objectives of *shari'a* (Chapra, 2008b). This evolution in the *maqasid* framework carries two significant implications. First, the concept of 'enrichment' or 'invigoration' replaces the classical scholars' notion of 'preservation' or 'safeguarding' in defining the five essentials. Second, it incorporates the social dimensions of *maqasid* through corollaries into its economic framework (Asutay & Yilmaz, 2018).

Islamic economics and social redistribution

Against this backdrop, regarding the principles that inspire the relationship between Islamic economics and Islamic charity, the ethical framework contains three main concepts: *amanah* (trusteeship) and *'adalah ijtimaiyyah* (social justice), coupled with *ihsan* (beneficence) for socio-economic equilibrium. The concept of *amanah* is strongly linked with charitable obligations and establishes the vertical relation with God and the horizontal relation with all human beings. *Amanah* refers to trusteeship, where all things that belong to God are entrusted to human beings for their collective well-being. Humans are not the owners of wealth and property; rather, they are stewards of resources. What they have is not a right but a privilege. This privilege of possessing resources comes with the moral and spiritual responsibility to use them for expanding *ihsan* (Atia, 2013).

In this ontological system and approach to development, individuals must recognise that all resources ultimately belong to God. For this reason, they are not solely for individual benefit but should be shared equitably and justly among all of humanity. These principles, therefore, provide a framework for economic activity within the social sphere that adheres to Islamic norms. They also imply vertical justice in the sense that all individuals are equal in their proximity to God and, thus, in their access to the resources He has created. The redistribution of resources in Islamic economics aims at human *falah*, achieved by organising the resources of the earth based on cooperation and participation (Khan, 1984).

These concepts of trusteeship and resource redistribution are related to practices and institutions that establish the duties of Muslim believers in society. To the extent that people observe Islamic norms, social justice will be achieved. However, if people refuse their *amanah* obligations, the state must ensure distributional equity and the redistribution of resources (Hasan, 1988). *Amanah* is linked to charitable practice, but it does not preclude income inequality – which, according to some Islamic economists, is inevitable. Nevertheless, it may be possible to avoid extreme wealth disparities, eliminate exploitative practices, and strike a balance between supporting the accumulation of wealth and promoting economic growth on the one hand and addressing concerns for justice and protecting the poor on the other (Atia, 2013). *Amanah* leads to charitable practices as a form of redistribution, making resources available to the poor. The type of charitable practice depends on the concept of social justice and the idea of which method is most effective in addressing the basic needs of the poor.

Regarding the concept of social justice and social solidarity (*'adala* and *takaful*), in his work *Al-'adala al-ijtimaiyya fi al-Islam* ('Social Justice in Islam'), Said Qutb – as one of the major ideologues of political Islam in the twentieth century – begins by examining the Islamic theory of the universe, life and mankind to understand and explain the concept of social justice (Musallam, 1993). According to his view, Islam itself contains the concept of social justice: the Quran and the *hadith* describe creation as deliberately produced by a single, absolute and comprehensive will, forming an all-encompassing unity in which each part is in harmony with the others. In this universal scheme, Islamic social justice is essentially an all-embracing justice that accounts for both man's body and his soul, not merely material and economic factors. The doctrine of *tawhid* (unity and complementarity) suggests that none can dominate over the others and indicates equality in the sight of the Creator. Therefore, it provides a rationale for a particular social contract based on the centrality of social justice and social welfare. Individuals are expected to establish justice (*'adl*) and promote beneficence (*ihsan*), ultimately attaining high levels of the good life (*hayat al-tayyibah*), both individually and collectively. According to Qutb, social justice is one of the main principles of the Islamic moral economy and refers to the equality of individuals and their equal access to resources created by Allah. In other words, *'adl* is the framework within which *falah*, as the ultimate objective, can be achieved through *ihsan*. *Ihsan* and *'adala* are complementary parts of an ontological system that ensures 'balance and reciprocity in human relations' in terms of expanding beneficence. From this perspective of social justice, it is not enough for the poor and weak to receive equal shares with others in society (equality). Instead, it is necessary that 'the poor and the weak take more than their share in social cooperation to achieve an overall social equality of the human condition' (Naqvi, 1994).

The Islamic Economic Development Paradigm

The issue of aid and charity is closely tied to the problem of poverty and underdevelopment in many Muslim countries. This aspect has been analysed for years from various perspectives to identify causes, risks and solutions from an economic standpoint. The effort is to understand what development means according to the Islamic worldview and how it might be realised. Regarding the Islamic concept of development, the primary function of Islam is to transform individual morality and build a social environment that aligns with human development and implements justice. As already mentioned, the foundation of the Islamic approach to development is based on four core principles: *tawhid*, *rububiyyah*, *khilafah* and *tazkiyah*, which together form the framework for achieving development. 'Development is concerned with growth towards perfection through the purification of attitudes and relationships. The result of *tazkiyah* is, indeed, *falah*: prosperity in this world and the hereafter' (Ahmad, 1994). Therefore, the Islamic approach to development is comprehensive, encompassing moral, spiritual and material dimensions. Islamic development is a value-oriented activity aimed at empowering the role of the human being in all dimensions of life, with the ultimate goal of achieving *falah*. The focus of Islamic development is human development. The effort is to shift attention from the physical environment to the human being, who is considered the vicegerent (*khalifah*) of God and has various duties to perform from an economic development perspective. The development of human beings is a strategy that ultimately conforms to the rules of *shari'a*. To realise these objectives and achieve economic development, human beings may use the concept of *siyasah shar'iyyah* (Islamic governance), as state *shari'a* politics, to implement reforms that protect moral values and the public interest.

Development in Islamic economics also emphasises how economic activities can reduce or eliminate unfair income distribution and poverty and promote public interest (*maslaha*). Economic development should aim to foster growth in all aspects of human well-being. For this reason, the measurement of economic growth alone is insufficient to capture the full scope of development (Kusuma, 2010).

Some scholars have conceptualised development as a multidimensional phenomenon, with economic development being just one aspect of overall human development. According to this perspective, human development is not solely indicated by increases in real per capita income, literacy rates and life expectancy at birth, as reflected in the UNDP Human Development Index. Rather, it involves considering the socio-economic and political variables that impact human well-being and influence the rise and fall of societies (Chapra, 2008b). Ibn Khaldun, for instance, attempted to address key questions regarding the approach to development, and the strength of his analysis lies in its multidisciplinary and dynamic character. He links essential socio-economic and political variables – including sovereignty and political authority, the belief systems and behavioural rules of *shari'a*, the population, wealth or resource stock, development and justice – in a circular and interdependent manner, where each variable influences the others while also being influenced in turn. In his work, Chapra (2008a) applies Ibn Khaldun's model to the contemporary Muslim world to identify which of the variables in the model have contributed to the decline of Muslim societies and continue to perpetuate the underdevelopment of these countries.

Regarding the role of Islam, numerous studies argue that Islam played a positive role in the development of Muslim societies in the past but that it has now become a victim rather than a trigger mechanism (Chapra, 2008a). The trigger mechanism identified by Ibn Khaldun is political illegitimacy, which began when Mu'awiyah, the fifth caliph, established hereditary succession by appointing his son Yazid to the caliphate in 679. In this context, Kuran highlights that the underdevelopment in Muslim countries may be attributed to certain Islamic institutions that were designed to serve laudable economic objectives but had the unintended effect of acting as obstacles to economic development (Kuran, 2004). According to him, three specific institutions have hindered growth in these countries: (a) Islam's egalitarian inheritance system from the point of view of the absence of the right of primogeniture, which prevented the establishment of primogeniture in Muslim societies; (b) the absence of the concepts of limited liability and juridical or legal personality in Islam; and (c) the Islamic institution of *waqf* (philanthropic trust). The first two factors are said to have impeded capital accumulation and the formation of corporations, both of which were essential for accelerated development in the second millennium. The third institution, *waqf*, is argued to have directed vast resources into projects that became dysfunctional over time. Furthermore, the failure to transform *waqf* into self-governing organisations stunted the development of civil society, a vital segment of the social system that exists outside direct state control (Kuran, 2004).

When integrating Kuran's theory with Ibn Khaldun's work, a fourth factor emerges that affects growth in Muslim countries: the absence of democracy (Chapra, 2008a). According to the Economist Intelligence Unit's Democracy Index, many countries in the MENA region are classified as authoritarian or hybrid regimes (Economist Intelligence Unit, 2023). This understanding of development and democracy has two important implications. First, the lack of democracy has led to corruption, scarce public resources and political and social tensions, suggesting the need for political reforms. The second implication is the importance of institutions and democratic empowerment in the context of foreign aid implementation, and it is related to the impact that aid can have on a context in the long term. This view reflects a Eurocentric perspective that regards democracy as the primary driver of prosperity and development. However, this assumption can be contested with numerous examples, such as Gulf states that have achieved prosperity without democratic systems, or democratic countries that continue to struggle with poor economic performance and high levels of corruption.

Poverty Alleviation in the Islamic Understanding

By defining development, Muslim scholars have elaborated a contemporary vision of poverty and poverty alleviation based on Islamic understanding. Among the major scholars and movements that discussed the issue of poverty in Islam, the MB emerged as the largest mass movement in Egypt, entering the political arena to address pressing issues such as poverty, property rights, the nature of the state and the distribution of power. The organisation used political engagement as a means to re-establish an Islamic order and to foster a broader spiritual revival. Sayyid Qutb was a vocal critic of the influence of Western cultural and political values on Egyptian society. He contended that the Islamic tradition inherently upholds the principles of social justice. Although he engaged with certain socialist ideas, Qutb maintained that Islam itself provides the foundational principles and institutional mechanisms necessary to ensure an egalitarian balance between the wealthy and the poor (Al-Daghistani, 2021).

The Quran addresses poverty extensively, primarily from a moral standpoint. Islam advocates a proactive approach to prevent situations that hinder human development. As the Quran states: 'Indeed, Allah will not change the condition of a people until they change what is in themselves' (Quran 13:11). It offers guidance on fulfilling the basic needs of the poor and needy, urging the wealthy to give a portion of their surplus wealth (Hasan, 2015). The concept of justice, as discussed earlier, requires that human actions in economic and social relationships be directed towards 'public benefit'. *Maslaha*, derived from the word *salih*, meaning 'social benefit/common good', refers to welfare and signifies the 'public good or benefit'. According to al-Ghazali, *maslaha* requires Muslims to engage in economic activities that create benefit, prevent harm and align with the *maqasid al-shari'a* (objectives of the law). All economic activities – whether production, distribution or consumption of goods and services – must prioritise human well-being and expand people's choices in a way that pleases God. The notion of God's ownership asserts that humans do not have dominion over resources but are entrusted with the responsibility to align their actions with nature, safeguarding the community's interests. Therefore, the community's interests are protected when individuals act responsibly, adhering to the framework of social equilibrium outlined in Islam (Hasan, 2015).

Regarding poverty alleviation through an Islamic approach, Iqbal (2002) begins with the belief that strategies for poverty reduction involve two trade-offs: the first between the interests of the 'haves' and the 'have-nots' and the second between the role of the public sector and the market. For the first trade-off, he refers to the Islamic worldview, where life in this world – including the context of poverty and disparities in income and wealth – is considered a test. Regarding the second trade-off, Iqbal proposes an 'institutional approach' to achieve redistributive goals. The market, as an institution, is permitted to play its role, while other institutions, such as *zakat*, *awqaf*, *takaful* and *irfaq* (the non-profit sector), serve as supplements to correct the inherent tendencies in market-based solutions. The idea of alleviating poverty through this 'institutional approach', as Iqbal (2002: 13) terms it, has become a key framework advocated by many Muslim scholars. Al-Qaradawi (2002: 569), an influential Islamist scholar close to the MB, views the *zakat* system as a permanent mechanism within the economy, continuously transferring income from the rich to the poor to lift the latter entirely out of poverty. This can be achieved by providing the poor and needy – two of the eight designated recipients of *zakat* – with education, training and the necessary capital and resources. However, in the mainstream approach to poverty and poverty alleviation by Muslim scholars, there are some critical points missing, including a redefinition of poverty itself and, consequently, what poverty alleviation means (Salleh, 2017).

In Sadeq's analysis, poverty is categorised into two distinct levels: the hard-core poverty line and the general poverty line. The hard-core poverty line refers to the concepts of *miskin* and *faqir*, both terms that denote poverty, although Islamic jurisprudence scholars often distinguish between them. The term *faqir* describes a person who lacks property or a lawful and adequate income to meet essential needs such as food, clothing, shelter and other necessities for themselves and their dependants in a manner that is neither extravagant nor miserly. On the other hand, *miskin* refers to a similar condition, but one that is slightly less severe. The distinction suggests that both *faqir* and *miskin* refer to economic situations where basic needs cannot be met, though the degree of severity may vary.[1]

So, what constitutes basic needs in Islam? Scholars hold varying views on this matter. Commonly included in the list of basic needs are food, clothing, shelter, medical care, education, and even a spouse. These views are based on individual interpretations of Islamic sources, which do not provide a definitive list of goods and services considered basic needs. Therefore, there is no absolute standard defining the scope of basic needs, and it largely depends on *urf* (custom) in society. This *urf* is shaped by the prevailing economic conditions and society's perception of human needs. Importantly, *urf* in Islam allows for customs that align with the spirit of Islam or, at the very least, do not exceed the boundaries of Islamic permissibility. Consequently, hard-core poverty can be understood as a condition in which an individual's Islamically *urf*-defined basic needs cannot be fulfilled (Sadeq, 1997).

In contrast, general poverty refers to a situation where all basic needs are met, but the individual has a surplus that is below the *zakat nisab*. The *zakat nisab* is the minimum wealth threshold that makes the payment of *zakat* obligatory. If a person's wealth falls below the *nisab*, they are not required to pay *zakat*. Anyone whose wealth is below the *nisab* is considered eligible to receive *zakat*, thus categorising them as poor. Therefore, general poverty can be defined as a situation where all essential expenses are covered, yet the surplus that remains is still below the *nisab* threshold (Sadeq, 1997).

Regarding how poverty has been assessed in Organisation of Islamic Cooperation (OIC) countries, the Oxford Poverty and Human Development Initiative (OPHI), in collaboration with the United Nations Economic and Social Commission for Western Asia (ESCWA), UNICEF and the Arab League, published the first *Arab Multidimensional Poverty Report* in 2017 (ESCWA, 2017). This report is based on the *Global Multidimensional Poverty Report* and covers 75 per cent of the Arab population, categorising countries into three clusters. Cluster 3 includes countries with high levels of acute poverty, such as Mauritania, Yemen, Sudan and Comoros; Cluster 2 includes Morocco and Iraq, which exhibit low levels of acute poverty but medium levels of overall poverty; and Cluster 1 comprises countries with very low levels of both acute poverty and overall poverty, such as Jordan, Tunisia, Algeria and Egypt.

The global Multidimensional Poverty Index (MPI) for 2015, which covers 5.2 billion people across 101 countries (representing 75 per cent of the world's population), includes forty-three OIC countries. These countries are home to 1.3 billion people, and in 2015, 504 million people in these forty-three IsDB countries lived in multidimensional poverty, accounting for nearly one-third of the 1.56 billion multidimensionally poor people globally (IsDB & OPHI, 2016). The largest concentrations of multidimensional poverty were found in Sub-Saharan Africa and South Asia.

A comparison of this database with the most recent MPIs from 2020 and 2024 shows some variations in different regions. In 2020, the percentage of multidimensional poverty decreased in Sub-Saharan Africa from 61.9 per cent to 57.5 per cent, but the most significant reduction occurred in South Asia, where the MPI dropped from 49 per cent to 31 per cent. In 2024, the incidence of poverty in the Arab states was over 50 per cent in 19 of the 144 sub-national regions. Yemen was home to six of these nineteen regions, with the highest poverty rate in Reimah (82.7 per cent) and al-Jawf. However, the MPI is based on three dimensions, education, health and living standards, excluding the Islamic understanding of poverty and development – and related indicators – from the measurement.

Islamic Social Welfare Instruments: *Zakat* and *Waqf*

The previously outlined axioms provide the framework within which the Islamic moral economy operates, influencing the economic structure concerning the operational and institutional nature of this system (Asutay, 2007). This value-based approach creates institutions and mechanisms, such as *zakat* and *waqf*, to address societal needs. It is considered *fard* (a religious duty commanded by God) for those who are financially capable of contributing.

Zakat *as a form of social redistribution*

Zakat, one of the five pillars of Islam, is a religious obligation designed to prevent wealth accumulation and mitigate social conflicts. It should be distinguished from *sadaqa*, which refers to voluntary charity. The term *zakat* is derived from the root *zaka*, meaning both 'increase' and 'purification.' The Quran frames this act of wealth distribution as a means of 'self-purification' (Quran 92:18). *Zakat* is categorised into two forms: *zakat al-mal* (on wealth) and *zakat al-fitr* (a charitable donation given during Eid al-Fitr, marking the end of Ramadan). *Zakat al-fitr* is a required charitable contribution for every eligible individual during Eid. The rationale behind this redistribution is rooted in equity, ensuring that even the poor can partake in the celebratory meal, marking the conclusion of the month of fasting in Ramadan. *Zakat al-mal*, as mentioned in the Quran, encompasses 'all things that people are to acquire and own'. Based on this, Muslims are categorised into two economic groups: those who pay *zakat al-mal* and those who receive it. An individual possessing moveable and immoveable assets is required to pay 2.5 per cent (for Sunni Muslims) or 5 per cent (for Shi'a Muslims) of their annual savings above the necessities of life, in charity, provided they meet the *nisab* (the threshold). *Zakat* became a formal and compulsory transfer system in 624 CE, during the second year of the Prophet Muhammad and his Companions' migration to Medina.

Two critical factors should be considered when examining *zakat* today: first, the *nisab*, which is presumed to cover basic living expenses, and second, the taxation of the most common forms of income, along with a tax on gross wealth that is not actively invested. While investment principal is exempt from *zakat al-mal*, income derived from investments is subject to *zakat* payments (Hasan, 2015).

In contrast to *zakat*, *sadaqa* is a voluntary form of giving. The term *sadaqa* is derived from the root *sidq*, which signifies the sincerity of the giver's religious intentions and spontaneous voluntary almsgiving. Unlike *zakat*, which is obligatory and directed towards specific groups, *sadaqa* is an act of charity aimed at drawing the donor closer to God. Furthermore, there are no restrictions on the recipients of *sadaqa*, distinguishing it from *zakat*, which has defined beneficiaries, which definitions need to be adapted to contemporary contexts and meanings.

Regarding the jurisprudential criteria of *zakat*, the primary sources are the Quran and Sunnah, both of which contain numerous references to *zakat* and the related concept of *sadaqa*. The Quran features thirty-two references to *zakat*, the majority of which are attributed to the Medinan period, marking the Prophet Muhammad's ministry after the *hijrah* and his efforts to address community administration. While *zakat* is associated with prayer and piety throughout the Quran, there is a shift from voluntary to compulsory participation during the Medinan period. This transition aligns with the needs of the growing spiritual, political and economic community of Medina. The revelations from Mecca established broad principles of stewardship and charity, while the Medinan verses formalised these principles into actionable rules for the Muslim polity. The Quran states:

> The alms are only for the poor and the needy, and those who collect them, and those whose hearts are to be reconciled, and to free the captives and the debtors, and for the cause of Allah, and [for] the wayfarer; a duty imposed by Allah. (Quran 9:60)

This passage is crucial in Islamic jurisprudence as it specifies the eight groups who are eligible to receive *zakat*, though the term *sadaqa* is used for offerings and alms. In more detail, the eight categories of *zakat* recipients are:

1. The poor (*fuqara'*): Those who are in material need.
2. The needy (*masakin*): Similar to the poor but with some nuance in Islamic jurisprudence. While some scholars treat these two categories as synonymous, a more traditional interpretation places the poor above the needy in terms of priority, although some jurists argue that the needy takes precedence.
3. Those who collect *zakat*: This group refers to those tasked with the collection and distribution of *zakat*. Historically, the costs associated with collecting *zakat* were justified as state administrative expenses when it was collected as a state tax.
4. Those whose hearts are to be reconciled: This category refers to individuals whose hearts are either fully reconciled or in the process of reconciliation with Islam. One interpretation includes recent converts, while another broader interpretation extends to those sympathetic to Islam but not yet Muslim. This latter interpretation has been used to justify financial support for missionary activities and potential converts.
5. Captives (*al-riqab*): This refers to the freeing of captives, typically through ransoming prisoners of war or purchasing the freedom of slaves.
6. Debtors (*al-gharimin*): This category includes individuals burdened by debt. While this could encompass enslaved persons, it also applies to others suffering from financial obligations.
7. The cause of Allah: Historically, this category referred to warriors defending Islam. However, due to the absence of a limiting interpretation in *fiqh* (jurisprudence) literature, it can also encompass a wide range of activities that support the broader cause of Islam.
8. Wayfarers (*ibn al-sabil*): This category supports travellers, which could include both the needy and, in some interpretations, wealthy travellers who lack access to their funds (Powell, 2010).

The concept of *zakat* as a tool for redistribution has been revitalised in recent decades within the discourse of scholars such as Yusuf al-Qaradawi, who addressed issues of cooperation and social responsibility in the contemporary

Muslim world while articulating a well-defined ideological stance within Islamist thought. Indeed, al-Qaradawi is associated with the ideology of the Muslim Brotherhood, described in Chapter 2. His interpretation of *zakat* harks back to the earliest conception of mutual social responsibility in Islam, extending beyond its religious function. Moreover, *zakat* plays a significant role in social security and solidarity, both of which are deeply intertwined with the Islamic economic system. In his book *Fiqh al-Zakat*, al-Qaradawi identifies three primary functions of *zakat*. The first is its role as an act of worship. *Zakat* embodies a fundamental religious value, often mentioned alongside prayer (*salah*) in the Quran, highlighting the intrinsic connection between the two obligations. According to al-Qaradawi, while prayer is the pillar of religion, *zakat* serves as the bridge. If a Muslim successfully crosses this bridge, they will be ensured safety (al-Qaradawi, 2011).

The second function of *zakat* is its contribution to the state's financial and economic system. This role emphasises economic values, as the payment of *zakat* helps reintroduce wealth into circulation. The third function pertains to *zakat*'s establishment of the first institution of mutual social responsibility in Islam, aimed at alleviating poverty within the community. This concept of mutual social responsibility encompasses both smaller units – the individual, family and neighbourhood – and larger units such as the state and the *Umma*. Its universality remains pertinent across time and space, and *zakat* should be extended to all Muslim societies worldwide, ensuring its distribution reaches all corners of the globe. The principles of mutual social responsibility and the use of *zakat* as a financial resource for the *Umma* form the foundation for the flow of financial assistance and aid within the Muslim world (Nurlaelawati, 2010).

Al-Qaradawi's theory on *zakat* not only asserts that it is a religious obligation but also reveals its multifaceted functions within Muslim society, religious, economic and social. The integration of these three functions highlights the fact that the obligation of *zakat* is inherently tied to the concept of ownership. As a religious function, *zakat* embodies the belief that God is the sole owner of everything and that what individuals possess is a trust and deposit bestowed upon them by Him. Economically, *zakat* provides strong support for the investment of wealth for the benefit of society and encourages individuals to refrain from hoarding wealth (Nurlaelawati, 2010).

This relationship between *zakat* and the concept of ownership is crucial in understanding the ongoing debate regarding the use of *zakat* in activities, its beneficiaries and the management of this instrument by different actors. In the case of using *zakat* for microfinance, for instance, some studies have contributed to creating a framework for *zakat*-based Islamic microfinance institutions (MFIs). Charity-based Islamic MFIs can achieve both financial and social sustainability by embracing the concepts of brotherhood, local philanthropy and volunteerism. *Zakat*-based Islamic MFIs would focus on providing resources for both consumption and productive purposes, enabling them to address the economic and social needs of the most impoverished members of society. These institutions might help reduce indebtedness, lessen the unequal distribution of wealth and enhance the capacity of the poor to become more productive, thus fostering greater independence from wealthier individuals (Ismail and Possumah, 2013). However, despite its potential, *zakat* has missed, over time, the opportunity to serve social needs and address poverty. Starting from the 1930s and the emergence of modern Islamism, *zakat* returned to the Middle Eastern political discourse, but 'Islamism missed an opportunity to make this Islamic institution relevant to solve major contemporary problems in complex society' (Kuran, 2023: 275) due to the lack of a strong civil society and political priorities related to non-Islamic taxation. On the other hand, Islamic movements in certain contexts have tried to create a sort of civil society in politically repressive contexts, especially through their charitable work.

Waqf *in the contemporary understanding*

Within the Islamic system, *waqf* refers to a form of perpetual charity wherein certain property is held and preserved for specific philanthropic purposes. Under classical Islamic law, a *waqf* is a foundation that an individual establishes by turning privately held real estate into an endowment (Kuran, 2023: 50). The Quran does not mention *waqf*, which suggests that it emerged after Muhammad's death in 632. *Awqaf* can be classified into several types based on their intended purposes or uses:

- Religious *awqaf* focus on the maintenance of religious institutions, such as mosques and schools, along with their associated properties.

- Philanthropic *awqaf* aim to support the poor, particularly through services like healthcare and education.
- Finally, family *awqaf* are a distinct form of *waqf* in which the proceeds are primarily allocated to the family and descendants of the founder, with any surplus directed towards aiding the poor.

The establishment of a *waqf* entails certain legal requirements, including the following: (a) the property must be a tangible asset that retains an enduring value, such as land, buildings, livestock (e.g. camels, cows, sheep), books or jewellery; (b) the property must be given permanently; (c) the founder must be legally competent, meaning that individuals such as children, those deemed insane or those without ownership of the property are not permitted to create a *waqf*; (d) the *waqf* must serve a charitable purpose, in terms of both *shariʿa* law and the founder's intentions; and (e) the beneficiaries – whether individuals or causes – must be living and legitimate. Additionally, *awqaf* can take the form of cash. In the first century of the *hijrah*, two primary forms of cash *waqf* were practised: cash for interest-free lending to beneficiaries and cash invested with the net returns designated for the beneficiaries (Hassan & Ashraf, 2010).

As for *zakat*, there were missed opportunities within the *waqf* institution for it to fulfil its intended goals and contribute meaningfully to society. The potential decentralised structure of *waqf*, which involves numerous NGOs and diverse social objectives, could have influenced state policies by aligning with individual preferences based on the actual needs of society. This is particularly significant because it is the founder of the *waqf* who determines its purposes rather than the state. According to this view, a *waqf* could serve as a sort of bottom-up approach to serving society in line with its needs and a possible starting point for autonomous non-state organisations in delivering social services in perpetuity. However, the Islamic *waqf* did not produce a vigorous civil society due to some limitations in its internal structure, including the lack of formal participation of beneficiaries in *waqf* activities (Kuran, 2023).

Zakat and *Waqf* in Poverty Alleviation

Historically, *zakat* was never fully institutionalised in Islamic societies, as it was primarily regarded as a religious obligation rather than a formal financial mechanism. This effort appears to be characteristic of modern Islamic economics and finance.

Assessing the impact of *zakat* and *waqf* on society and poverty reduction is a complex task. If we assume that the extent of poverty in an economy is quantified by the number of poor individuals and the funds required to lift them out of poverty, the next step would be to calculate the potential amount of *zakat* that could be collected within the economy. A comparative estimation of the required funds for poverty alleviation and the potential *zakat* collection demonstrates the potential of *zakat* in addressing poverty (Ahmed, 2004). In Ahmed's study, *zakat* collection is compared with the amount needed to move the poor above the poverty line by transferring USD 1 per person per day. In countries with low per capita income and high poverty concentration, *zakat* collection alone may not be sufficient to provide income for poverty alleviation. However, the transnational nature of *zakat* can mobilise funds beyond national borders. According to Ahmed, the focus should be on using *zakat* funds to increase the productive capacity of the poor. This approach would positively influence poverty alleviation efforts in the long term. By becoming productive and able to generate income, households would not only escape poverty but would also eventually be able to contribute *zakat* themselves, supporting wealth redistribution to a larger portion of the poor. This strategy should be considered in both national and transnational contexts, with governments and civil society organisations using *zakat* as a financing tool.

For this reason, *zakat* distribution needs to incorporate a long-term perspective, taking into account the specific characteristics of the destination context. In this long-term view, further consideration may be necessary. Most studies in this field measure poverty and development using conventional methods, such as GDP or the Human Development Index. It may be beneficial to consider alternative approaches for measuring gaps or goals aimed at enhancing the impact of *zakat* and identifying sectors of implementation.

A study conducted by the Islamic Development Bank and the World Bank estimated in 2015 that the worldwide value of *zakat* is potentially USD 200 million to USD 1 trillion annually (World Bank & Islamic Development Bank Group, 2016). What is evident is that there is a significant gap between the actual global collection of *zakat* and its potential reach. The challenges facing the *zakat* administration are due to various factors, including jurisprudential interpretations and management issues. Traditionally, *zakat* was managed by the government and individuals; however, current practices reveal that it is now administered through three key channels: the government, non-profit organisations and individuals. Unlike in the past, governments in most contemporary Muslim countries do not play an active role in *zakat* administration, or if they do, the amounts collected are generally small with limited impact on the beneficiaries.

One of the reasons for the low *zakat* collection is mismanagement, which discourages individuals from paying *zakat* to state institutions. In the absence of credible public *zakat* institutions, people often give their *zakat* directly to individuals they know or to non-profit welfare organisations they trust. Since this *zakat* is typically distributed in small amounts without long-term planning, it fails to address the broader needs of the recipients and has negligible effects (Lessy, 2013).

The potential *zakat* that could be used for socio-economic development depends on the wealth and income levels within a society. However, the total amount of *zakat* collected also depends on jurisprudential interpretations of what constitutes 'zakatable' assets or property. For example, traditional views, as captured in historical texts, define zakatable assets narrowly, thereby excluding most contemporary sources of income and assets (Kahf, 1989). Scholars counter this by arguing that the nature of wealth has evolved, and *zakat* should encompass modern forms of assets and income. While the traditional perspective includes assets such as agricultural output, livestock, trade inventory and cash holdings, some contemporary scholars advocate including returns on fixed assets, salaries, wages and the capital value of fixed assets in the *zakat* base (Kahf, 1989; Kahf, 1999). Furthermore, given that much of modern-day wealth is invested in the financial sector, financial assets such as investment accounts, stocks and *sukuk* (Islamic securities or bonds) should also be considered zakatable wealth. Including these assets could significantly increase *zakat* collections, providing additional resources to mitigate poverty and enhance social welfare (Ahmed, 2020).

Defining the role of *waqf* in poverty alleviation and measuring its impact is a more challenging task. Two primary issues complicate this: first, the lack of relevant aggregate data on *waqf* institutions, and second, the difficulty in identifying which *waqf* institutions can be leveraged for poverty mitigation.

The social welfare role of *awqaf* depends on the type and size of the institutions. While many Muslim countries possess a large number of *waqf* assets, the majority are tied to religious institutions like mosques and cemeteries. However, there are also substantial *waqf* assets that could be used for socio-economic development. For example, the Islamic Research and Training Institute (IRTI) and Thomson Reuters report that Indonesia holds 1,400 square kilometres of *waqf* land valued at USD 60 billion (IRTI & Thomson Reuters, 2015). With an annual return of 5 per cent, this *waqf* could generate USD 3 billion annually for various socio-economic purposes. Furthermore, the potential for using other *waqf* assets, such as cash, for social development is vast but largely untapped.

Despite this potential, much of the *waqf* pool in many Muslim countries remains unused for socio-economic development. Several factors contribute to this stagnation, including the loss of *waqf* deeds, mismanagement, corruption among *mutawallis* (managers or custodians of *awqaf*), and the sale or liquidation of *waqf* assets. A significant issue, however, is the role of governments in the *waqf* sector, in particular with the creation of modern nation-states. While a *waqf* is intended to be a non-governmental entity, historically, various states have attempted to control *waqf* assets. Muslim rulers sought to confiscate *waqf* and convert it into state assets as early as the Fatimid period in the tenth century CE. This trend reached its peak during the Ottoman rule under Sultan Mehmed II in the 1470s, when all arable land, including *waqf*, was brought under the ownership of the sultanate (for more details see Chapter 2, 'The role of the *waqf* in the Ottoman Empire'). These trends continued throughout the twentieth century, with *waqf* being controlled by governments through ministries or public administrators in most jurisdictions (Mandaville, 1979).

Although *waqf* remains underdeveloped in most countries, making minimal contributions to socio-economic development, some nations have taken initiatives to revitalise the sector. For example, Sudan established the autonomous Awqaf Corporation in 1986, which included an investment and construction department to develop existing *waqf* properties and initiate new *waqf* projects through soliciting donations (Kahf, 2004). Similarly, the General Secretariat of Awqaf was established in Kuwait in 1993 to create specialised investment funds for various objectives and to solicit donations. While the responsibility for managing the funds lies with a specialised investment department, an autonomous board for each fund decides how to allocate the revenue. This secretariat also oversees an investment and construction department responsible for renovating and developing existing *waqf* properties (Kahf, 2004). A few other countries, such as Qatar and Bahrain, have reorganised their *waqf* sectors following Kuwait's model.

There are also developments in regenerating the *waqf* sector in countries with Muslim minorities. For instance, in the UK, Islamic Relief Worldwide established a *waqf* where supporters can donate *waqf* shares, which are then invested, with the returns directed towards various social and developmental projects. In 2018, the Islamic Relief *waqf* disbursed a total of GBP 407,814 to fund six projects globally (Islamic Relief Worldwide, 2019).

Managing *Zakat* and *Waqf*: Theories and Practices

As has emerged from the literature and been observed in practical cases, *zakat* and *waqf* are today managed in various ways and for different purposes. Among Muslim communities, many believe that *zakat* is a powerful tool for poverty alleviation, as it fulfils socio-economic functions similar to those of a formal social security system (Shirazi, 2006). However, who is in charge of administering these resources, including collection and distribution, is not clearly defined, especially when it comes to *zakat*.

For some scholars, the administration of *zakat* (its collection and distribution) should be carried out by the state as an institution. The people responsible for these tasks should be knowledgeable about their calculation and collection, and they must be employed or designated as collectors and distributors of *zakat* (De Zayas, 2003; al-Qaradawi, 2011). Al-Qaradawi (2011: 13) states: 'Zakat is an institution of social welfare supervised by the state, and a form of organised taxation administered by an autonomous public organisation on behalf of the community as a whole and the state as its legitimate leadership.' From this perspective, the state is responsible for enforcing and supervising the collection and distribution of *zakat*.

However, in the absence of an Islamic state, any Islamic organisation can perform this obligation on behalf of the Muslim community. Despite this, the enforcement aspect of *zakat* may not necessarily align with the state, and the government's role in collection and distribution should be supervisory only. In other cases, the state can supervise, but it should not fully control the *zakat* institution, unlike the control it exerts over government taxes (De Zayas, 2003). The government and/or its designated agencies should only oversee *zakat* collection and distribution, without the power to modify, increase, decrease or suspend it, as they would with regular taxes. The role of the state, therefore, is limited to enforcing the Quranic injunctions regarding *zakat* (Owoyemi, 2020).

Recent developments in *zakat* management have seen a proliferation of modern Islamic philanthropic institutions and faith-based organisations. This trend of institutionalisation in Islamic charity and philanthropy has led to the rise of numerous actors who use *zakat* funds to assist the poor. One key issue that may emerge in such a context is coordination between different stakeholders – governmental and non-governmental – operating in the same space. A second issue concerns the policies and strategies that governmental organisations and NGOs implement in the allocation of funds, as well as the significant impacts this allocation has at both the micro and macro levels.

UNHCR Refugee Zakat Fund: A Non-Muslim Organisation Managing Religious Funds

A relevant case in the context of current *zakat* management practices is represented by the UNHCR, which established a fund aimed at collecting and distributing *zakat* to address the needs of Muslim refugees. The Refugee Zakat Fund (RZF), a component of the Islamic Philanthropy programme, began as a two-year pilot project in 2015, focusing on Syrian refugees in Jordan, and was formally launched in 2019. Before the establishment of the fund, UNHCR sought guidance from numerous Islamic scholars and organisations across the Muslim world to ensure legal validation and receive clear guidelines for its initiatives. To date, seventeen *fatwas* have confirmed that the UNHCR's distribution of *zakat* is *shariʿa*-compliant. In alignment with *shariʿa* principles, the organisation developed a 100 per cent *zakat* distribution policy, which sets rules for the allocation of *zakat* and defines eligibility criteria for both the organisation and its beneficiaries. This policy stipulates that all donations deposited into a dedicated non-interest-bearing bank account are distributed directly and in full to the most vulnerable refugees and internally displaced persons (IDPs). Operational and administrative expenses are covered through alternative funding sources, such as *sadaqa* (UNHCR, 2019).

In contrast to *waqf* and *sadaqa*, *zakat* distribution is governed by jurisprudence, which, as we have seen, outlines eight categories of eligible beneficiaries and activities that must be adhered to when redistributing these funds. Among these categories, the wayfarers (*ibn al-sabil*) are considered a relevant reference group within which refugees and IDPs may be included, along with the poor (*fuqara'*) and the needy (*masakin*). *Ibn al-sabil* refers to a traveller who lacks sufficient funds during their journey. This individual is eligible to receive *zakat* to complete their journey, even if they are financially well off in their home country. If they are unable to access their wealth during the journey, *zakat* may be provided to them. Based on this definition and the absence of specific guidelines regarding who may act as an intermediary between *zakat* donors and beneficiaries, UNHCR, as a secular organisation, is thus authorised to distribute *zakat* to the most vulnerable Muslim refugees globally.

The various *fatwas* have further clarified key issues concerning the use and distribution methods of *zakat* funds. For example, in 2021, the Al-Azhar Islamic Research Academy issued a *fatwa* confirming that refugees fall within the eight categories of eligible beneficiaries (UNHCR, 2021). It also affirmed that *zakat al-fitr* may be distributed either in cash or in kind, depending on what is most convenient for *zakat* payers and most suitable for the beneficiaries. In terms of goods distribution, the Tabah Foundation had already approved the use of goods in place of cash in 2020, provided that these goods are purchased at fair market prices (UNHCR, 2020). Furthermore, *zakat* funds may be used to cover associated costs, such as storage and transportation, when cash distribution is not feasible.

In 2021, another significant *fatwa* was issued by the Fiqh Majlis of Canada, permitting UNHCR to use *zakat* funds to pay tuition fees directly to educational institutions on behalf of eligible refugees (UNHCR, 2022). The *fatwa* stipulates that *zakat* funds should be distributed directly to deserving recipients. However, the payment of tuition fees to educational institutions on behalf of a beneficiary is permissible under the following conditions: (a) a thorough selection process is undertaken to identify qualified, deserving and committed refugee students; (b) a dedicated agent (*wakeel*) is appointed to act on behalf of UNHCR's Islamic Philanthropy programme, who will also monitor the progress of refugee students until their graduation; and (c) tuition fees should only cover essential subjects, such as engineering, trade, teaching or medical studies.

In 2023, the North American Imams Federation issued a *fatwa* endorsing UNHCR as a suitable organisation for the collection and distribution of *zakat* funds from North American Muslims to refugees worldwide. This *fatwa* outlined three key conditions, including the 100 per cent *zakat* distribution policy. First, full compliance with *shariʿa* law regarding *zakat* collection and distribution, ensuring that 100 per cent of the funds reach eligible recipients within the designated refugee populations of the global Muslim community. Second, the implementation of transparent financial management and accountability practices, including the deposit of funds into a dedicated non-interest-bearing bank account and ensuring fully traceable fund disbursements. This commitment to transparency is further reflected in the regular provision of customised *zakat* fund reports to partners, contributors and other interested parties within the wider Muslim community. Finally, the establishment of consistent review and oversight mechanisms to ensure that UNHCR's RZF remains in full adherence to Islamic principles governing *zakat* collection and distribution.

Thus, several of these *fatwas* have established guidelines to ensure that this international organisation remains in compliance with Islamic principles and *shariʿa*, particularly as evolving circumstances and emerging crises necessitate the adoption of both traditional and innovative approaches to addressing such challenges.

The evolution of the Refugee Zakat Fund

Initially focused on supporting eligible refugees in Jordan and Lebanon, in 2022 the RZF distributed *zakat* contributions to twenty countries, including Bangladesh, Egypt, Iraq, Malaysia, Mauritania and Yemen. The fund also possesses the capacity to expand its geographical reach in response to crises, as demonstrated in the case of Ukraine in 2022. The RZF adopts a bottom-up approach, with activity planning rooted in compliance with the implementation requirements and eligibility criteria for *zakat*. Additionally, it collaborates with partners on the ground who are responsible for executing activities and distributing funds, particularly in cases where cash assistance is provided directly to individuals. According to UNHCR data, global *zakat* contributions in 2018 amounted to USD 76 billion, far below the potential USD 356 billion. Saudi Arabia, Indonesia and Türkiye were identified as the primary contributing countries. The humanitarian funding need was estimated at USD 21.9 billion, with a requested budget of USD 7.9 billion. These figures underscore the potential of *zakat* to address humanitarian needs and help bridge the funding shortfall for refugee crises, provided the funds are collected and managed effectively.

Prior to its formal launch, from 2016 to 2018 the RZF raised USD 14.4 million, which was directed towards cash assistance programmes in Jordan, Lebanon and Yemen. The project drew inspiration from the work of BAZNAS, the semi-governmental institution in Indonesia that collects and distributes *zakat* funds domestically, with 40 per cent allocated to humanitarian assistance (Pericoli, 2023b).

In 2019, the total amount collected by the fund was USD 43.2 million in *zakat*, including USD 3.5 million raised through the digital platform, alongside USD 222,907 in *sadaqa* donations and purification funds. This total accounted for 12 per cent of UNHCR's overall budget.[2] The fund assisted 1 million beneficiaries across eight countries during its first year. These included Syrian refugees in Jordan, Lebanon and Egypt; Rohingya refugees in Bangladesh and Malaysia; Malian refugees in Mauritania; and IDPs in Yemen and Iraq. All assistance was meticulously provided through *zakat*-compliant cash and in-kind distribution activities, including in remote areas (Refugee Zakat Fund, 2020: 6).

In 2020, the number of *zakat* beneficiaries rose by 59 per cent, increasing to more than 1.6 million across ten countries, with new projects launched in Niger and Pakistan. *Zakat* was distributed in both cash and goods. The total amount collected grew to USD 48.6 million in 2020, surpassing the USD 43.1 million raised in the fund's inaugural year. The majority of *zakat* donations, 97 per cent, originated from the Middle East and North Africa, with institutional partners and philanthropists contributing 87 per cent of the donations and the remaining 13 per cent coming from digital platforms. *Zakat* received in 2020 accounted for approximately 20 per cent of UNHCR's expenditure on activities deemed *zakat*-compliant, compared to 12 per cent in 2019. These activities included cash and goods distribution. Furthermore, *sadaqa* donations experienced a significant increase in 2020, reaching a total of USD 12.9 million, largely due to new philanthropic partners, including the Sheikh Thani Bin Abdullah Bin Thani al-Thani Humanitarian Fund.

In 2021, the total number of beneficiaries decreased from 1.6 million to 1.2 million and remained stable in 2022. Yemen, Bangladesh, Lebanon and Jordan were the top four countries that received the highest percentage of *zakat* and *sadaqa* in terms of amount and where the greatest number of people benefited from those funds. The total amount collected in 2021 was USD 35.4 million, including USD 23.6 million in *zakat* and USD 11.8 million in *sadaqa* funds. A key development in 2022 was the geographical expansion of the fund, which grew from twelve to twenty countries, including Ukraine. In 2023, Lebanon was the first recipient country of *zakat*, followed by Bangladesh, Yemen and Afghanistan, while Syria, Kenya and Pakistan were the top three recipients of *sadaqa*. A total amount of USD 21 million *zakat* and USD 25 million *sadaqa* was collected in that year.

In 2022, the RZF had forty-two Islamic Philanthropy partners, including the Kuwait Zakat House, the Sheikh Thani Bin Abdullah Bin Thani al-Thani Humanitarian Fund, the World Assembly of Muslim Youth and Mohammed bin Rashid Al Maktoum Global Initiatives. In April 2019, HE Sheikh Thani Bin Abdullah Bin Thani al-Thani made a historic *zakat* contribution in support of Rohingya refugees in Bangladesh and displaced Yemenis through the fund. This was the largest contribution UNHCR had ever received from an individual donor and the first major *zakat* donation of its kind in the organisation's history. In 2022, the Sheikh Thani Bin Abdullah Bin Thani al-Thani Humanitarian Fund supported over 84,000 IDPs and host community members in Yemen with a *zakat* contribution, providing cash assistance to meet their urgent food needs.

The prominent role of Gulf States' donations within the RZF influences the allocation of resources, as well as fluctuations in *zakat* and *sadaqa* funds, which explains the decrease in *zakat* and *sadaqa* from 2019 to 2022 and a new increase in 2023. The political dimensions of the refugee issue also impact donor decisions. Since the RZF depends heavily on large donors rather than individual contributors, the allocation of *zakat* and *sadaqa* remains linked to the donors' political interests and willingness rather than to the actual needs on the ground (Pericoli, 2025c). As a result, the RZF is being pushed to diversify its sources of funding and income.

A waqf *for refugees: the Global Islamic Fund for Refugees*

In March 2022, together with UNHCR and the Islamic Solidarity Fund for Development (ISFD), the IsDB launched the Global Islamic Fund for Refugees (GIFR), intending to provide effective, efficient and predictable support for programmes and projects aimed at refugees, IDPs and host communities in Organisation of Islamic Cooperation (OIC) member countries. The focus areas include health, education, WASH (water, sanitation and hygiene) and economic empowerment through microfinance.

The establishment of the GIFR marks an important step towards diversifying humanitarian funding sources and bolstering relief efforts. The fund aims to mobilise immediate and multi-year funding to support humanitarian programmes and operations in situations of forced displacement across various sectors. The partnership between the IsDB and UNHCR is grounded in their common interests and experience regarding refugee issues and their capacity to advocate for resource mobilisation.

The GIFR platform is structured around two components: a cash *waqf* part (both permanent and temporary) and a 'cash non-*waqf*' component that provides grants in different sectors. The initial phase relies on a temporary cash *waqf* for ten years, along with a cash non-*waqf*. It is funded equally by the ISFD (USD 50 million for the cash *waqf* part) and UNHCR (USD 50 million for the cash non-*waqf* part), totalling USD 100 million in seed capital. This amount has been supplemented by contributions from other sources, such as the governments of Saudi Arabia and Bahrain, bringing the total to USD 114 million at the beginning of 2024. In its starting phase, the GIFR counted seventeen potential donors, including the King Salman Humanitarian Aid and Relief Centre and the Qatar Fund for Development, and aims to reach its target of USD 500 million to address the refugee issue within the OIC.

The GIFR's steering committee, composed of UNHCR, ISFD and any other donor contributing over USD 10 million, is responsible for the decision-making process regarding the geographical and sectoral allocation of the fund's resources. The key distinction between the cash *waqf* and cash non-*waqf* components lies in the legal framework, which allows UNHCR to withdraw funds from the latter in case of emergencies, such as bankruptcy.

Due to the highly sensitive and political nature of the refugee issue, despite the positive outcomes demonstrated by Islamic social welfare instruments, the reliance on the decisions of more influential donors – rather than on the technical evaluations of the organisations themselves – risks exposing these mechanisms to the same financial gaps that already exist in conventional humanitarian financing. As a result, the GIFR grants greater decision-making power to the IsDB and UNHCR, untying it from donors' political considerations (Pericoli, 2025a).

Conclusion

Islamic understandings of humanitarianism, poverty and development form a set of behavioural norms that underpin the operations of various actors, including state, non-state and faith-based transnational organisations. The deconstruction and decolonisation of humanitarian values – traditionally viewed through a Western-centric lens – challenge prevailing understandings of humanity, poverty and the actions associated with development. Humanity, as a universalist category, is no longer (or has never been) the exclusive domain of Western humanitarian discourse. Moreover, aid policies are usually linked to a Western development conceptualisation, aligning with the current trend often described as the 'globalisation of aid' (Swiss, 2021). Despite the diversity of donor interests and motivations, there is frequently a convergence in their approaches to development policy and programming priorities, even amid divergent national interests, cultural contexts, development conditions and organisational structures (Swiss, 2021). Shedding light on Islamic perspectives on humanitarianism, charity and poverty provides a foundation in the following chapters for examining how these norms and values have been applied across different historical periods and by various actors.

Notes

1. These two interpretations reflect the view of Malik ibn Anas, Abu Abdullah Muhammad bin Idris Al-Shafiʿi and Ahmad ibn Hanbal.
2. USD 222,907 in non-*zakat* funds, including USD 117,812 in *sadaqah*, in addition to USD 105,095 in purification funds. The donation for purification funds is the first of its kind ever received by UNHCR and reflects the donation of funds earned by Islamic banks from transactions that are not *shariʿa* compliant, for instance late payment fees.

2

INSTITUTIONALISATION AND POLITICISATION OF AID

The evolution of foreign aid by the Gulf States requires contextualisation within broader historical dynamics. The history of aid and charitable practices, from the Ottoman Empire to the present day, provides a crucial backdrop for understanding the conceptual framework in which these dynamics should be situated. Both external and internal factors – such as the internal transformations within these countries and shifting geopolitical dynamics – help explain how foreign aid and charitable practices have evolved in the region. Additionally, the transnational variable, represented by varying Islamic understandings and Gulf States' perception of political Islam and Islamist movements (with a particular focus on the Muslim Brotherhood organisations), connects the internal and external dimensions of the analysis, shedding light on the inter-state relationships between donors and recipients. This chapter analyses the historical evolution and establishes a conceptual framework through which the foreign aid of Qatar and the UAE can be examined in the region and the specific case of Syria.

The Roots of Charity in Islam: From the Prophet to the Empire

Any analysis of the role of charity and poverty in Islamic societies must trace its roots back to the origins of Islam and the pre-Islamic period. In early Arabic narratives about the first Muslim community and its conquests and conflicts, *zakat* and *sadaqa* were prominently featured during several critical moments. These include the beginning of Muhammad's prophetic path in Mecca when some of the earliest scriptures emphasise almsgiving above all other human activities. Moments of crisis also encompass the *ridda* or apostasy wars of 632–4 CE, shortly after Muhammad's death. During this period, many Arabs across the peninsula refused to continue paying *zakat* to the central authority in Medina. In response, Abu Bakr, upon assuming leadership, swore to compel them to pay. He deployed armies that subdued these rebels or 'apostates' in large-scale battles, which were soon followed by the expansive Islamic conquests beyond the Arabian Peninsula itself (Bonner, 2003).

In recent years, some of the most influential historical accounts of the rise of Islam have highlighted the significant role of charitable practices and the structures that evolved from them. However, charity in Islam is complex and intertwined with other ideas. In pre-Islamic Arabic writings, generosity and hospitality were highly regarded traits.

During the Ottoman Empire, a 'mixed economy of charity' emerged, as Singer defines in her book *Charity in Islamic Society*. She characterises the Ottoman Empire as a 'welfare society' rather than a welfare state, comprising extensive welfare networks. People belonged to and sought support from overlapping networks formed by families, neighbourhoods, villages, professional groups, households and communities of similar geographic origins or religious affiliations. Within each network, assistance was provided in ways that were either formalised or loosely structured.

The welfare ethos and the responsibility for providing relief were embedded within society as a whole, and the entire society – including the sultan – participated in delivering social services, not solely or even primarily through the state. The large imperial *awqaf* perhaps came closest to functioning as state welfare agencies during much of the Ottoman period. Ottoman public kitchens, or *imarets*, further illustrate why the Ottoman Empire could be viewed as a welfare society rather than a welfare state. Over approximately 550 years, more than 200 *imarets* were established throughout the empire. Almost all of them shared standard features: soup and bread were served twice a day, with richer dishes prepared on holidays. There is no evidence that these activities were coordinated by any central authority or even among the *imarets* themselves. Charity and philanthropy in the Ottoman Empire remained a decentralised experience, often influenced by the characteristics or geographic location of the recipients (Singer, 2008).

The role of the waqf *in the Ottoman Empire*

The *waqf* played a significant role in providing educational, religious and infrastructure services in Ottoman society. Starting in the mid-nineteenth century, a dedicated ministry for *awqaf* was established in the Ottoman Empire, and various laws regarding *awqaf* were enacted. The most notable among these was the Law of Awqaf of 29 November 1863 (19/6/1280 AH). This law remained in effect in several countries (Türkiye, Syria, Iraq, Lebanon, Palestine and Saudi Arabia) for many years after the dismemberment of the Ottoman Empire in 1918 (Akgündüz, 2011).

The Ottomans integrated the *waqf* system to support the social, economic, cultural and religious fabric of society. Proof of the success of this system was the presence of *waqf* institutions even in the most remote villages. The Ottomans institutionalised the *waqf* despite the dominance of Hanafi jurisprudence, which initially opposed it. While Abu Hanifa, the founder of the Hanafi school, did not support property *waqf* or cash *waqf*, his students eventually allowed their establishment.

Therefore, the Ottoman *ulema* also considered the tendencies, traditions and views of Abu Hanifa's students regarding cash *waqf*. A philanthropist wishing to establish a cash *waqf* first prepared a settlement deed (*waqfiyah*) and registered it at the *qadi*'s office. The founder of the cash *waqf* specified in the *waqfiyah* the names of both the founder and the trustee, the amount of the donation, the conditions governing the donated money, how the funds would be managed, and the purpose of the *waqf*. The establishment process was as follows: the founder presented the document to the qadi; the founder recited the conditions outlined in the *waqfiyah* in the presence of the *qadi*; the trustee confirmed the founder's statement; finally, the *waqf* was formally established (Bulut & Korkut, 2022).

In administrative terms, cash *waqf* underwent several stages of regulation throughout its history in the Ottoman Empire (Mandaville, 1979). One of the attempts to reform *waqf* administration occurred during the reign of Mustafa III (1757–74), involving the transfer of responsibility for collecting revenues from large imperial *awqaf* to the head of the Imperial Treasury. This change was intended to prevent abuses in *waqf* administration and ensure that *waqf* properties were used for charitable purposes.

However, this period was also marked by a series of fiscal crises. As a result, these regulatory efforts were probably tied to broader fiscal centralisation reforms and aimed at utilising previously untapped *waqf* revenues to support state finances. These early reforms were eventually reversed by Sultan Abdulhamid I (1774–89) due to their political costs. Nevertheless, the Imperial Evkaf Ministry was established and reached its fullest development under Sultan Mahmud II (1808–39).

The most significant transformation of the *waqf* system took place after 1839 as part of the broader bureaucratic reform movement known as the Tanzimat. Mahmud II's efforts focused primarily on centralising and unifying the administration of various religious foundations under a dedicated ministry. This was an ambitious undertaking, as, by the early nineteenth century, at least half of the landed property in the Ottoman Empire held *waqf* status. The centralisation policies aimed to redirect the revenues from these lands to the central administration (Mandaville, 1979).

Before the establishment of the ministry, the state's control over *awqaf* was inconsistent. In certain cases, such as the *awqaf* of sultans or those managed by the Imperial Treasury, the state held direct control and acted as the trustee. In other cases, it only supervised the actions of trustees. There were also unique cases, such as *awqaf* established by founders of dervish orders or *gazis*, where the state's role was minimal. For notable local families, who often used the *waqf* system to protect their property from central authority, these centralisation efforts meant that they had to allocate their incomes to causes dictated by the government in Istanbul.

Consequently, centralising religious foundations became a laborious process, further hindered by resistance within the Ottoman bureaucracy, which benefited from the semi-autonomous nature of the old system (Çizakça, 2000; Kuran, 2004). The Imperial Evkaf Ministry was established as a fully independent ministry only after the successful abolition of the janissaries in 1826, an event that strengthened the sultan's position against political opposition. Nonetheless, the state still had to collaborate with local notables to manage *waqf* properties, which limited the revenue that could be raised from *awqaf*.

In 1863, a new regulation reorganised the *waqf* administration in the provinces. From 1876 onwards, the independent administration of provincial *waqf* by the Imperial Evkaf Ministry was discontinued, and *waqf* oversight was placed in the Ministry of Finance. These regulatory changes brought notable administrative implications for cash *awqaf* and, most importantly, stricter accounting rules. Since cash *waqf* revenues were primarily used for local public services, maintenance of key local buildings and support for local producers, centralisation efforts likely posed a threat to these activities by imposing closer supervision.

During the initial reform period, the establishment of an independent Imperial Evkaf Ministry also meant that anyone wishing to establish a cash *waqf* had to apply to the ministry. Despite the increased oversight, the ministry lacked the local knowledge and expertise needed to manage these funds effectively and provide local public services. Consequently, previous practices were restored, allowing trustees to regain their rights to manage *waqf* funds.

Additionally, the 1863 regulation mandated that unused cash *waqf* funds be sent directly to the Treasury instead of remaining with trustees, to prevent misuse and enhance central government revenues. From 1863 to 1912, cash *awqaf* operated within these constraints while maintaining a degree of local autonomy. In 1912, however, a Directorate for Endowed Money was established in Istanbul to improve cash *waqf* management and credit operations. Shortly after, in 1914, the Bank of Religious Foundations (Evkaf Bankasi) was founded. This bank was authorised to accept deposits, with its main objective being to manage *waqf* funds according to modern banking principles.

The nineteenth century saw extensive centralisation efforts across the entire *waqf* system through a series of reforms. However, regarding cash *waqf*, it can be concluded that these reforms had a limited impact, allowing cash *waqf* to retain its semi-autonomous status at least until 1912 (Karagedikli & Tunçer, 2018).

Power and Welfare: the Muslim Brotherhood's Experience

The collapse of the Ottoman Empire left a void in social welfare systems. This gap was sometimes filled by civil society and grassroots organisations, the most prominent of which was the Muslim Brotherhood (MB). Established by Egyptian schoolteacher Hassan al-Banna in 1928, just a few years after Egypt's independence and the Ottoman Empire's fall, the Brotherhood aimed to merge Islam with modernity (Mitchell, 1969; Munson, 2001; Soage, 2008). Under al-Banna's leadership, the Brotherhood embraced the benefits of modern innovations in technology, science and industry (Mandaville, 2007) while rejecting Western, colonial models of modernity. Instead, it sought to interpret modernity within an Islamic framework, asserting that 'Islam is the solution'.

The Brotherhood quickly expanded to other Middle Eastern countries, establishing branches in Syria in the early 1930s, Palestine in 1935 (followed by Hamas in 1987) and Jordan in 1942. Later, MB organisations emerged in several African countries, including Sudan and Libya in the late 1940s and Somalia in the 1960s. Meanwhile, branches began to appear in North America and Europe, established by Muslim immigrants.

As a teacher, Hassan al-Banna held a strong sense of social responsibility and saw providing aid to the poor as a key duty for both the Brotherhood and all Muslims. In his pamphlet *The Message of the Teachings*, he stated:

> Be active, energetic, and skilled in public services. You should feel happy when you offer a service to other people. You should feel compelled to visit the sick, assist the needy, support the weak, and give relief to the ill-fated, even if it is with a good and affectionate word. Always rush to do good deeds. (Banna, 1993)

In its early years, the MB focused more on social welfare activities – such as relief work and building schools and hospitals – rather than formal politics (Yaylaci, 2007: 12). This approach provided an alternative to the largely ineffective state. Brotherhood movements in other countries adopted similar methods. In Jordan, for example, the Brotherhood established the Islamic Center Charity Society, an organisation dedicated to aiding the poor. It is still one of the largest NGOs in Jordan, operating nearly 100 community centres, forty health clinics, several schools and universities and two hospitals (Clark, 2004; Sparre & Petersen, 2007).

Education became a core activity for the Brotherhood, not only for teaching and sharing knowledge but also as a means to shape individual conduct, deepen faith, stimulate activism and contribute to the Islamisation of society. Through education, the Brotherhood aimed to instil an Islamic identity in new generations, thereby strengthening and reforming the Muslim community. The focus was on guiding Muslims back to righteous Islam, with the conversion of non-Muslims being secondary (Hatina, 2006).

As Mandaville (2007) notes, for al-Banna and the Brotherhood, education was closely linked to the concept of *tarbiya*, which refers to a holistic approach to personal growth and development through religious knowledge. However, it was not merely about cultivating individual spirituality in isolation; education was also seen as a tool to purify faith and nurture activism (Hatina, 2006). Islamist voluntary associations have often demonstrated their capacity to deliver effective welfare and relief services, particularly in contexts where the state has been unable or unwilling to provide such support. However, it is equally clear that these organisations have frequently sought political benefits from their activities (Benthall, 2018a). In line with this vision, Islamist mobilisation comes from the grassroots and is 'an attempt to create a seemingly seamless web between religion, politics, charity, and all forms of activism' (Clark, 2012b: 70).

In Egypt, for instance, the MB played a prominent role in providing aid after a major earthquake struck Cairo in 1992 (Degg, 1993) and again following severe flooding in the south of the country in 1994. In February 2002, after a tragic railway accident in al-Ayatt, 70 kilometres south of Cairo, the Mubarak government reportedly banned the Brotherhood from raising funds or organising assistance for the victims. This incident foreshadowed a broader conflict between government priorities – focused on political and security concerns – and humanitarian imperatives. This clash became especially pronounced in subsequent humanitarian crises, with adverse effects on disaster and conflict victims, as the United States government intensified measures against material support for terrorism as part of the 'global war on terror'. These measures claimed a worldwide jurisdiction and bore especially hard on Islamic charities deemed, justly or not, to have links with terrorism. The War on Terror after 2001 consistently impacted the work of charities, Islamic NGOs and states with regard to aid financing and implementation (Benthall, 2018a).

The Emerging Role of the Gulf States

Apart from the Brotherhood, the Gulf countries played an important role in shaping the culture of Islamic aid during the 1960s and 1970s. While the

MB's aid was primarily shaped by national needs and carried out by local and grassroots associations, the movement from the Gulf countries had a transnational and missionary outlook, evident in organisations such as the Muslim World League, the International Islamic Council for Da'wa and Relief and the Organisation of the Islamic Conference (OIC), which would become the Organisation of Islamic Cooperation in 2011. Many of these transnational initiatives originated in Saudi Arabia, reflecting the country's growing importance in the Islamic resurgence. Underlying many of these new Saudi initiatives was a pan-Islamic ideology, largely articulated as a counterbalance to Nasser's secular Arab nationalism (Hegghammer, 2010). The sharp rise in oil prices following the Yom Kippur War in 1973 led to a significant increase in the disposable revenue of oil-producing countries, including Saudi Arabia and Kuwait. This increase seemingly shifted the economic power balance between the oil-producing countries of the Muslim world and the industrialised states in the West (Petersen, 2015).

Modern Gulf state donorship began during and after the 1967 Arab–Israeli War. Countries bordering Israel and Palestine, known as the 'front-line states' for absorbing large numbers of Palestinian refugees, became primary targets of Gulf state aid, receiving more than half of all assistance from the Gulf region from the late 1960s to the late 1970s (Porter, 1986). This aid primarily went to Egypt, Jordan, Lebanon and Syria between 1967 and 1978. Egypt was removed from this list following its peace agreement with Israel in 1979 (Barakat & Zyck, 2010).

In a report from the World Bank, Momani and Ennis (2012) estimated the average donation by Kuwait, Saudi Arabia and the UAE at 1.5 per cent of their gross national income (GNI) between 1973 and 2008. The combined net official development assistance (ODA) from these three countries nearly doubled on a yearly average during the global financial crisis (2008–10) and doubled again following the Arab unrest in 2011. It reached a record of USD 19 billion in 2014, almost 0.8 per cent of their GNI (Rouis & Shomakhmadova, 2018). This rate is higher than the Development Assistance Committee (DAC) average of 0.3 per cent for the same period and exceeds the United Nations target of 0.7 per cent, a goal set over the last five decades (Riddell, 2007). Despite a common perception of Gulf state donorship as a recent trend, the region has a longstanding history of international cooperation and development assistance. In 1980, during a period of high oil prices, Saudi Arabia's ODA was more than three times that provided globally by the United Kingdom (Porter, 1986). Even earlier, from 1974 to 1979, aid contributions from Qatar, Kuwait, Saudi Arabia and the UAE amounted to between 6 per cent and 8 per cent of their respective GNIs, while DAC countries' contributions represented only about one-third of 1 per cent (Neumayer, 2004). These contributions took the form both of projects, such as Saudi Arabia's USD 36 million loan to Morocco in 1974 for the construction of the al-Massira dam, and of budget support, with over USD 100 million provided to Morocco's National Development Bank by Kuwait, the UAE and Saudi Arabia during this period. In 1978, the combined funds from Saudi Arabia, Kuwait and the UAE equalled 40.3 per cent of the aid provided by OECD-DAC member states (Barakat & Zyck, 2010).

The Organisation of Islamic Cooperation: a regional effort towards Islamic solidarity

Along with the creation of institutions responsible for managing development and humanitarian aid in third countries, a regional attempt was made in the name of solidarity across the Muslim world. The OIC is today the second-largest international organisation after the United Nations, composed of fifty-seven member states representing 1.8 billion Muslims worldwide. Established in 1969, its twenty-five founding states aimed to foster solidarity among Muslims and promote the interests of the global Muslim community or *Umma*.

The OIC's Charter and the OIC-2025 Programme of Action represent the strategy and values of the organisation. The Charter includes the strengthening of Islamic solidarity, cooperation in the political, social, cultural, economic and scientific fields, and the safeguarding of human dignity, independence and the national rights of all Muslims residing anywhere in the world. Peace and conflict resolution remains one of the main issues, and the Charter also enumerates the principles governing OIC activities: full equality among member states; support for the right to self-determination and non-interference in the internal affairs of member states; support for the sovereignty, independence and territorial integrity of each member state; the settlement of disputes by peaceful means such as negotiations, mediation, conciliation and arbitration; and a pledge to refrain, in relations among member states, from resorting or threatening to resort to the use of force against the unity, territorial integrity or political independence of any one of them.

Since its establishment, the OIC has witnessed numerous conflicts among its member states. Historically, the OIC's conflict resolution efforts have primarily focused on mediation and the provision of humanitarian aid, often in collaboration with other international organisations. In 2008, it took a significant step by establishing the Islamic Cooperation Humanitarian Affairs Department (ICHAD) to coordinate the activities of various humanitarian organisations – both non-governmental and bilateral – and to facilitate access to aid during crises. For example, in response to the devastating famine in Somalia in 2011, the OIC coordinated efforts by more than forty Islamic aid organisations and other civil society groups to provide relief supplies across the country (Svoboda, Zyck, Osman & Hashi, 2015). Beyond its political efforts to protect Muslim communities worldwide, the OIC's concrete initiatives to finance aid are carried out through its financial institution, the Islamic Development Bank (IsDB). ICHAD and the OIC's Ten-Year Programme of Action (TYPOA) both illustrate the organisation's commitment to strengthening its involvement in humanitarian action. While humanitarianism emerged as a key focus for the OIC, sovereignty concerns and the differing positions of member states in crisis-affected scenarios led it to limit the scope of action in the TYPOA to natural disasters, rather than conflicts (Pericoli, 2021). ICHAD established a code of conduct for humanitarian interventions by NGOs and member states, but its mandate remains unclear (Tok & D'Alessandro, 2019). Additionally, the relationship between ICHAD and the IsDB in financing and implementing programmes in conflict-affected or fragile countries is still not fully defined.

The role of the OIC in dealing with regional crises has demonstrated structural weaknesses, including the vague and non-disciplinary nature of its membership regime, as well as the lack of a rule-enforcing body (Bacik, 2011). The elusive efforts of the organisation in Yemen (Qadir & Rehman, 2015) and its dialogue-oriented approach to the Syrian crisis have highlighted inter-state rivalries and the OIC's incapacity to act as a supranational entity (Pericoli, 2024).

Islamic solidarity and Afghan conflict – 1979

In the name of Islamic solidarity, several organisations began to emerge in 1979, following the Soviet invasion of Afghanistan, to provide aid to Muslim communities in need. Notable examples include the International Islamic Relief Organization (IIROSA, based in Saudi Arabia), the Islamic African Relief Agency (IARA, founded in Sudan in 1981) and Islamic Relief (established in Britain in 1984). In her study *For Humanity or the Umma*, Petersen describes how the Afghan conflict, along with the famine in the Horn of Africa, marked a pivotal moment in the development of Muslim transnational NGOs. Many viewed the 1979 Soviet occupation as an attempt by an atheist regime to intimidate a devout Muslim population, sparking a surge of solidarity among Muslims worldwide. In response, Muslim groups and organisations began collecting funds and in-kind donations to send to Afghanistan (Petersen, 2015).

Some well-established transnational Muslim organisations, including IIROSA, the International Islamic Charitable Organization and Muslim Aid, provided aid to Afghanistan. However, the war also acted as a catalyst for the creation of new Muslim NGOs. Many of these new aid organisations were based in Saudi Arabia, Kuwait and other Gulf countries; they included the Royal Saudi Committee for Support of Afghanistan, led by Prince Salman; the Islamic Call Committee, established in 1986 by Kuwait's Society for Social Reform (al-Islah), the social welfare branch of the MB; and the Benevolence International Foundation and Al Haramain Islamic Foundation, both founded by Saudis in Karachi in 1988 (Ahmed, 2009).

Muslim NGOs from other Middle Eastern countries also played a significant role in Afghanistan. In 1985, the Egypt-based Arab Doctors Union established the Human Relief Agency to channel aid to Afghanistan. Similarly, the International Islamic Council for Da'wa and Relief, an umbrella organisation established in Egypt during the Soviet withdrawal from Afghanistan in 1988, was actively involved in delivering aid to the country.

Muslim migrants in Europe and North America also established several Muslim NGOs, including Canada's Human Concern International (founded in 1980) and the US-based Mercy Relief International (1986). These organisations opened offices in Pakistan, where they ran hospitals and clinics along the Afghan–Pakistani border and provided various forms of relief to refugees.

In Afghanistan, relations between Muslim NGOs and Western NGOs were often tense. Although many Muslim NGOs appreciated US government support for the mujahedeen, they viewed Western NGOs as representatives of atheism and culturally inappropriate norms and practices, which they believed could negatively impact Afghan society. Some Western NGOs were even suspected of supporting certain political parties. As a result, many Muslim NGOs chose to collaborate exclusively with other Muslim NGOs rather than partnering with Western organisations. In 1986, the Saudi and Kuwaiti Red Crescent Societies, IARA and the Muslim World League created an Islamic Coordination Council (Benthall & Bellion-Jourdan, 2003).

Two years later, the Agency Coordinating Body for Afghan Relief (ACBAR) was established to improve coordination among all NGOs working in Afghanistan. However, most Muslim NGOs chose not to join, perceiving ACBAR as dominated by Western organisations (Bennett, 2013). Only a few Muslim organisations, such as IARA and the Aga Khan Foundation, became ACBAR members, although many other Muslim NGOs did not regard the Aga Khan Foundation as a 'true' Muslim NGO.

For some Muslim NGOs, providing aid was not merely about offering relief to suffering Muslims; it was also about supporting them more directly in their struggle against the enemy. In other words, while aid in Africa was sometimes seen as a combination of relief and *da'wa* (the practice of inviting people to embrace Islam), in Afghanistan, it was often regarded as both relief and jihad (Benthall & Bellion-Jourdan, 2003).

The Iraq–Kuwait conflict and the war in Bosnia – the 1990s

From the 1980s through the 1990s, Gulf Arab foreign aid declined as oil revenues decreased. In the early 1990s, the broader Gulf region underwent economic restructuring in response to falling state incomes and rising security expenses, including the costs associated with the 1991 Iraq–Kuwait war. This conflict encouraged many Gulf countries to adopt a more isolationist stance, focusing on internal security concerns. As a result, Gulf foreign aid commitments remained low throughout the 1990s, even lower than in the 1980s.

Even when oil prices began to rise again in the late 1990s and early 2000s, Gulf states were hesitant to increase their aid levels, especially in the wake of 9/11. During this time, Gulf Arab aid to countries like Pakistan and Taliban-controlled Afghanistan faced increased scrutiny, particularly from Western nations (Momani & Ennis, 2012).

In the early 1990s, the focus of many transnational Muslim NGOs shifted from Afghanistan, where conflict was devolving into civil war, to Bosnia, as the Bosnian War (1992–5) erupted. The beginning of the 1990s saw a new wave of Muslim NGOs focusing their efforts on the victims of the Bosnian conflict. Many of these organisations were established by immigrant communities in the West, such as the British NGO Muslim Hands (founded in 1993) and the North American Global Relief Foundation (1992) (Benthall & Bellion-Jourdan, 2003).

Established organisations such as Muslim Aid, Mercy Relief International and Islamic Relief saw significant increases in donations during these years, which supported their expansion. In 1993, Islamic Relief opened offices in Tuzla and Zenica, followed by Mercy Relief International in 1994. The Bosnian War also spurred the emergence of the first transnational Turkish NGOs, including the Foundation for Human Rights and Freedoms and Humanitarian Relief (commonly known as IHH), which was founded in 1995 by representatives of Millî Görüş, the Turkish Islamic political movement created in the 1970s (Solberg, 2007).

Similarly, Iranian organisations like the Foundation for the Oppressed and the Iranian Islamic Centre for Help to the People of Bosnia-Herzegovina played key roles in providing aid to the Bosnian people. As in Afghanistan, much of the aid came from Gulf-based organisations. Saudi Arabia's King Fahd donated USD 103 million to Bosnia between 1992 and 1996. While some of this aid was distributed through governmental committees, a significant portion was channelled through Muslim NGOs such as IIROSA and al-Haramain. Under the local name IGASA, IIROSA implemented substantial aid programmes targeting Bosnian Muslims who had sought refuge in Croatia and Slovenia (Benthall & Bellion-Jourdan, 2003).

Similar to Afghanistan, the war in Bosnia saw the more or less direct involvement of certain Muslim NGOs in the armed struggle. As Hegghammer (2010) notes, the 'Bosnian jihad' became the first major pan-Islamic battleground after the Afghan jihad, attracting large numbers of Arab volunteer fighters. According to a 1996 CIA report, as many as thirteen Muslim organisations operating in Bosnia were somehow involved in the conflict, including the Human Relief Agency and al-Haramain. Other sources mention the Islamic Benevolence Foundation and the Office for Services to the Mujahedeen, both allegedly involved in sponsoring volunteer fighters and shipping weapons and military equipment to Bosnia. Additionally, IIROSA was reportedly involved in providing services like visas and fake ID cards to Arab combatants (Benthall & Bellion-Jourdan, 2003; Hegghammer, 2010). However, Bosnia represented a different experience from Afghanistan for several reasons. Firstly, there was greater international control over the area, Bosnian Muslims were more secular and less connected to the Arab world, and national and international authorities were not as welcoming of Islamic fighters as they had been in Afghanistan. Moreover, the 1990–1 Gulf War had strained relationships between the United States, Saudi Arabia and Islamic movements, as the latter condemned the participation of Muslim countries in the US-led coalition against Saddam Hussein (Benthall & Bellion-Jourdan, 2003).

Secondly, the atrocities in Algeria and Egypt, as well as the February 1993 attack on the World Trade Center in New York, illustrated with great clarity the threat posed to authorities by the so-called Arab Afghans (Hegghammer, 2010). A few years later, the bombings in Riyadh in 1995 and Khobar in 1996 prompted the Saudi government to crack down on veterans of the Afghan and Bosnian jihad. Mass arrests and interrogations marked the beginning of a more confrontational phase between the Saudi state and the Islamic movement and more generally, between Arab regimes and the Islamic movement (Hegghammer, 2010). The involvement of some transnational Muslim NGOs in the 1993 and 1998 attacks on American territories – first the World Trade Center and then the bombings of the US embassies in Kenya and Tanzania – only led to increased control of these organisations, manifested in a decrease in public funding, the arrest of individuals and bans on some of the organisations. Most famously, five transnational Muslim NGOs suspected of involvement in the embassy attacks were banned by the Kenyan government in 1998: Mercy International, Help African People, al-Haramain, IIROSA and the Ibrahim bin Abdul Aziz Ibrahim Foundation, the first two having headquarters in the US and the last three based in Saudi Arabia (Salih, 2002).

The turning point of Islamic aid after September 11th

Regarding historical events that have influenced Islamic aid and its actors, September 11th marked the evolution of Islamic NGOs and donors' trajectories towards professionalisation of aid in terms of transparency and accountability. Since the 1980s, several transnational Muslim NGOs have (rightly or wrongly) been accused of financing or otherwise supporting so-called terrorist networks (Alterman & von Hippel, 2007). Suspicions of involvement in militant activism have surged from time to time, particularly concerning the work of transnational Muslim NGOs in Afghanistan and Bosnia. In these contexts, several NGOs were suspected of funding militant camps, facilitating logistical support for fighters coming from Saudi Arabia and otherwise supporting the mujahedeen. While the US and other governments initially turned a blind eye to such relations, seeing the mujahedeen as their allies in the fight against the communists, this changed with the end of the Cold War and shifting political dynamics. The understanding of transnational Muslim NGOs as *de facto* accomplices in militant Islamic activism was further solidified by the September 11th attacks on the Twin Towers and the Pentagon in 2001. Within a year of the attacks, several transnational Muslim NGOs, including al-Haramain, the Revival of the Islamic Heritage Society, the Global Relief Foundation and Benevolence International Foundation, were accused by the US government of supporting or being otherwise related to al-Qaeda. Several other governments followed suit, banning many transnational Muslim NGOs from operating within their territories (Petersen, 2012).

On 23 September 2001, President George W. Bush issued Executive Order 13224 under the International Emergency Economic Powers Act, marking the start of heightened counterterrorism measures targeting the financial networks of foreign terrorists (Glaberson, 2001). This order allowed the US Department of the Treasury to cooperate with other nations to suppress terrorism and share intelligence. The increased scrutiny that followed has caused significant anxiety among Islamic charity staff. Advocacy organisations, through best practice programmes, have worked to instill a 'legal consciousness' (Silbey, 1992: 42) focused on risk avoidance in everyday actions. Programs like online *zakat* calculators have been developed to help Muslims comply with both religious and legal requirements, mitigating the risk of violating US laws. These auditing practices have created a climate of fear, with many American Muslims concerned about governmental reprisals. As a result, there has been a pervasive stigma surrounding charitable giving, leading to a decline in donations within Muslim communities and between Muslim and non-Muslim recipients, both domestically and internationally. This fear has even resulted in the return or suspension of charitable contributions (James, 2019).

Regarding transnational effects of these US policies, in 2003 the Saudi government, after pressure from the US, closed al-Haramain's office in Somalia because the organisation was accused of supporting al-Qaeda. In the following years, governments and intergovernmental organisations introduced a wide range of new policies, instruments and regulations aimed at preventing and obstructing NGO involvement in terrorist activities. In July 2003, for instance, the Saudi Arabian Monetary Agency announced a set of new regulations governing Saudi aid organisations, including requirements for the consolidation of funds into a single bank account licensed by the government. Later that year, Saudi charities were banned from transferring funds abroad. This was followed in 2004 by the announcement of the National Commission for Relief and Charity Work Abroad, which would oversee all NGO activities and public donations, facilitating greater governmental control over the use of charitable funds (Harmer & Cotterrell, 2005). In March 2007, the Kuwaiti government introduced similar initiatives while also forbidding cash collections in streets or mosques (Benthall, 2007).

The War on Terror not only led to a focus on supposedly 'extremist' Muslim NGOs involved in financing terrorist activities, but it also encouraged a growing interest in cooperation with so-called moderate Muslim NGOs, viewed as potential bridge builders between Islam and the West (Howell & Lind, 2009). Through so-called soft measures, governmental aid agencies, particularly in Europe, began encouraging cooperation with (certain) Muslim NGOs. One example is the Montreux Initiative, initiated by the Swiss Federal Department of Foreign Affairs in 2005 under the title 'Towards Cooperation with Islamic Charities in Removing Unjustified Obstacles'.

These soft measures coincided with a growing interest in religious NGOs among governmental and intergovernmental development agencies. Failures in hegemonic aid provision, coupled with disappointment in 'regular' NGOs, among other factors, forced development agencies to seek alternative ways of delivering aid. In this context, many turned to religious NGOs, or faith-based organisations, as they are often called, viewing them as a potential panacea. With large constituencies and established trust and credibility in local communities, religious NGOs were expected by development agencies to provide added value to development aid. They were seen as having great potential as promoters of development aid, capable of galvanising moral commitment, translating principles of aid into the idioms of faith and mobilising popular support for donor initiatives (Clarke, 2007).

As part of this trend towards increased cooperation, several aid agencies opened funding opportunities for Muslim NGOs. The British Department for International Development (DfID), which in 2020 merged with the Foreign and Commonwealth Office to become the Foreign, Commonwealth and Development Office (FCDO), is one of the donor agencies that was most active in this regard. Despite initial scepticism, after 9/11, the agency was involved in several initiatives to strengthen cooperation with Muslim NGOs. Islamic Relief had a framework agreement with the DfID, and several other Muslim NGOs received grants from the department. The DfID's civil society team conducted workshops, including one in cooperation with the Muslim Council of Britain, specifically targeting Muslim organisations to encourage them to apply for funding and to support them in the process. Other initiatives for cooperation with Muslim NGOs include the DfID-sponsored research programme Religions and Development at Birmingham University, with Islamic Relief as the only non-academic partner. Similarly, the DfID was involved in the Tony Blair Foundation's seminar series Faith and Development, hosted in collaboration with Islamic Relief, World Vision and Oxfam (Petersen, 2015).

However, this trend towards increased cooperation with Muslim NGOs includes only certain organisations. Emerging from strongly secularist aid traditions, the DfID and other aid agencies have come to prefer NGOs whose religiosity is largely relegated to the private sphere, serving as personal motivation and underlying values, but who can utilise their claim to religious identity as a tool in the implementation of development activities. As noted by James (2009: 5), '[donors] want to engage with the institutional forms of faith (the religious institution) but remain suspicious about the spiritual dimensions of faith'.

As such, the secular distinction between 'religion' and 'aid' as fundamentally separate categories was maintained: religion can be a tool in the provision of aid, but it cannot be part of the aid itself. Paraphrasing Zaman (2004), those religious organisations are acceptable in the aid field only when they unequivocally recognise the functional differentiation of social spheres; that is, when they agree to operate within the framework of secularisation. By combining discourses on faith-based organisations as tools for the effective implementation of secular development with War on Terror discourses regarding politically 'moderate' and 'extremist' Muslim NGOs, the development culture, led by governmental aid agencies such as the FCDO, has come to perceive a quasi-secular, invisible religiosity as a sign of 'good aid' and 'moderation', while a visible, orthodox religiosity is seen as a sign of 'bad aid', 'fundamentalism' and perhaps even 'extremism'. This new focus on faith-based organisations, along with the War on Terror, has brought transnational Muslim NGOs into the hegemonic aid field (Petersen, 2012).

Aid and Arab uprisings: the geopolitical dimension of aid

The 2011 Arab uprisings have increasingly politicised the Gulf States' foreign aid in terms of both political survival and competition. These new trends in the Gulf States' foreign aid emerged at a time when these countries witnessed the rise of new realist leaders who believed that economics and the balance of power should be the main tenets of their foreign policy. The uprisings' deafening cry, '*Al-sha'b yurid isqat al-nizam*' (the people want to overthrow the regime), resonated across the Arab world as authoritarian regimes braced themselves for a wave of popular protests. At the same time, the Gulf monarchies adopted different positions and instrumentalised aid to support their geopolitical interests in the region.

Saudi Arabia's stance vis-à-vis the popular uprisings was shaped by its realist geopolitical objectives: to insulate the kingdom from the winds of the Arab Spring, protect the survival of monarchical regimes and undermine Iran's power in the region, given the well-known Iranian efforts to export the Islamic revolution by supporting Shi'a Islamist groups in Gulf Arab countries since the 1980s, as occurred in Bahrain. It thus used its military forces, financial largesse and political clout to contain the effects of the uprisings on the Arabian Peninsula, especially in Bahrain, Yemen and Oman. Riyadh also extended financial assistance to bolster the monarchies of Morocco and Jordan against mounting domestic calls for reform. While Qatar supported the regime change in Libya and the Muslim Brotherhood in Egypt, Saudi Arabia drove the Arab League and rallied the Gulf Cooperation Council (GCC) and the OIC in its battle to overthrow the Syrian regime. Riyadh's use of sectarianism as an instrument of regional policy became even more pronounced than in the pre-uprising period. It instrumentalised Sunni–Shi'a divisions and sentiments to shore up support for its regional allies and isolate Iran and its Arab allies. Riyadh justified its intervention in Bahrain's uprising by characterising it as the work of Iran's Shi'a agents in the Gulf. It clamped down harshly on the opposition in the kingdom's Eastern Province, labelling the demonstrators as Iranian agents. Riyadh supported sectarian opposition against Iraq's pro-Iranian Maliki government and the Hezbollah-allied government of Najib Mikati in Lebanon, accusing Tehran of meddling in the kingdom's security backyard by supporting and arming Shi'a Houthi rebels in northern Yemen (Salloukh, 2013).

In the case of the UAE, despite not facing an immediate, direct threat to its regime, it adopted a policy of hyper-securitisation from the outset (Bianco 2024). Following the Arab Spring, there were various perceptions of security threats emerging from different directions. First, the UAE perceived Iran as a significant threat, due to its potential influence through Shi'a proxies. More importantly, however, the primary concern was Iran's regional policy, which was viewed as an external threat to the regional equilibrium. The second major security concern was the rise of Islamist movements, which will be explored further later, and the UAE's evolving relationship with the MB both domestically and regionally.

This factor may help explain the UAE's behaviour towards countries where the status quo was challenged by uprisings. In the case of Egypt, the UAE leadership was relieved by the overthrow of President Mohamed Morsi in 2013, which led to a shift in policy towards reinvesting in the country through development and humanitarian assistance. In Libya, Abu Dhabi developed ties with a coalition of anti-Islamist factions, including the Zintan Brigades, under the command of General Khalifa Haftar. Similar dynamics were observed in the Horn of Africa, particularly in Sudan and Somalia, where the rise of MB movements aligned with the central government influenced UAE engagement

(Roberts, 2017). Islamist movements and security concerns are intertwined in the UAE's strategic perception, driving the alignment of its foreign policy and foreign aid to preserve a 'safe space' both regionally and domestically.

The Arab uprisings also altered the systemic roles of Qatar and Türkiye. Both states abandoned their former pragmatic stances and jumped on the uprisings' bandwagon to carve out new regional roles for themselves. Qatar used its affiliations with the MB to co-opt Islamist parties that assumed power after the authoritarian regime's breakdown, aiming to bolster its geopolitical weight. The small sheikhdom played a proactive role in regime change in Egypt and Libya, shelved its former differences with Riyadh and openly endorsed regime change in Syria, offering military and material aid to Islamist rebels, particularly the MB. It led an Arab League campaign to ostracise Damascus and expel it from Arab organisations, threatened to apply the full weight of the UN Charter's Chapter VII against the regime, successfully engineered Hamas's exit from the Iranian–Syrian alliance, and emerged as a proxy for NATO and Washington in their efforts to contain Iran. Later, Doha embraced the politically beleaguered and fiscally crippled MB government in Egypt. Al Jazeera played an instrumental role in popularising and defending the MB's position in the contest between Islamist and secular groups over the drafting of a new constitution. In January 2013, in a clear show of support for President Morsi, Doha committed USD 18 billion to a joint Qatari–Egyptian economic project and raised its deposits in Egypt's central bank from USD 2.5 billion to USD 4 billion, triggering speculation in Cairo regarding Qatar's political and commercial interests in the country (Salloukh, 2013).

In this scenario, intending to pursue both internal and external interests, Gulf monarchies managed aid according to their objectives. To accentuate its leadership role among the Gulf monarchies, Saudi Arabia pioneered initial moves in response to the destabilising ramifications of the Arab uprisings. This was manifested in the immediate response of King Abdullah, who released substantial financial packages estimated at around USD 130 billion as a royal gift in social, unemployment and housing benefits. The funds aimed to appease the political demands of the Saudi people and fend off potential contagion from public revolts. This was followed by reports of likely assistance estimated at USD 10 billion for Bahrain alone, a country whose population slightly exceeds 1 million. Saudi Arabia also decided to grant asylum to Tunisia's ex-president, Ben Ali, and to support Egypt's ex-president, Mohammed Hosni Mubarak, during Egypt's uprising in 2011 (Isaac, 2014).

Therefore, in terms of aid flows, all these dynamics are reflected in three main features: (a) the increase in funds invested in development assistance, especially through bilateral aid; (b) the interruption of the correlation between oil prices and aid resources during the period of 2012–13; and (c) the geographical allocation of funds in line with geopolitical objectives. These three dimensions reflect the politicisation of aid flows during the Arab uprisings.

New Regional Diplomacy, Same Aid Trajectories?

Among the most recent events in the MENA region and the Gulf sub-region that have affected Arab Gulf States' foreign policy and foreign aid strategies, three main crucial moments can be identified: the Gulf crisis and the consequent Qatari embargo from 2017 to 2021; the normalisation process with Israel and the Abraham Accords; and the war on Gaza after October 2023, with the consequent twelve-day conflict between Iran and Israel in June 2025. In the summer of 2017, the Gulf Cooperation Council faced the gravest crisis since its formation when Bahrain, Saudi Arabia and the UAE, along with Egypt, cut political and diplomatic ties with Qatar, imposing an air, land and sea embargo. The main accusation was Qatar's support for terrorist organisations and its collusion with Iran and Iran-backed militias to undermine the stability of the GCC. The 'quartet' of Bahrain, Saudi Arabia, the UAE and Egypt included in their definition of terrorist groups jihadist militias fighting in Syria with ambiguous connections to al-Qaeda affiliates, such as Jabhat Fatah al-Sham, as well as groups affiliated with the MB, which all four countries had designated a terrorist organisation in 2013–14.

However, the roots of this dispute can be traced back to 2014, when Qatar's emir, Sheikh Hamad bin Khalifa al-Thani, decided to step down in June 2013 and hand power to his 33-year-old son, Sheikh Tamim bin Hamad al-Thani. In March 2014, Bahrain, Saudi Arabia and the UAE withdrew their ambassadors from Doha, accusing Qatar of breaching the comprehensive security agreement signed in November 2013 between Doha and Riyadh. In this 'Riyadh Agreement', the two parties committed to avoiding interference in the internal affairs of the GCC states and not granting asylum to any citizen of those states who had opposed their country's regime. Furthermore, there was an explicit reference to the Muslim Brotherhood and to opposition groups in Yemen that could threaten neighbouring countries. In November 2014, a second document was signed to reinforce some of the points of the previous one, with particular attention given to Egypt's stability and security following the military coup against the elected government of Mohammed Morsi, the leader of the MB, who had been substantially backed by Qatar (Bianco & Stansfield, 2018).

In 2017, to resolve the dispute, the quartet gave Qatar a list of thirteen demands to comply with within ten days. These demands included: curbing all ties except economic ones with Iran; severing all ties with individuals, groups or organisations that had been designated as 'terrorist' by the quartet; shutting down Al Jazeera and other news outlets that received Qatari funds; immediately terminating any military cooperation with Türkiye; disclosing and halting all contacts with political opposition figures in the quartet countries and handing any such individuals over to the country of origin; paying compensation for losses caused by Qatar's policies; consenting to audits for compliance; and aligning with the other Gulf and Arab countries militarily, politically, socially and economically (Wintour, 2017). Qatari leaders immediately rejected this list, and the crisis began to attract international attention (Bianco & Stansfield, 2018).

The 2017 Gulf crisis revealed the weakness of the dispute resolution mechanism within the GCC charter. Kuwait attempted to soften the dispute and build bridges between the conflicting parties. However, the erosion of shared strategic visions, particularly in terms of threat perceptions, and the involvement of external players narrowed the space for reconciliation.

On several occasions, common security concerns also failed to help bridge the divide. This was illustrated when talks between Qatar and Saudi Arabia in late 2019 ran into a dead end. There were three rounds of talks, one involving their foreign ministers in Riyadh, which started in October and ended abruptly in January 2020. Since Qatar's only counterpart in the talks was Saudi Arabia, this pointed to deeper tensions with the UAE. Likewise, the COVID-19 pandemic, which posed major challenges worldwide and became the main theme of the most recent GCC meetings, incentivised the parties to engage in low-level cooperation through video conferences between health ministers.

Figure 2.1 Doha skyline, November 2021. Photo by the author.

US mediation injected occasional shots of optimism, as US policymakers announced several times that the sides were close to a deal. Between April and December 2020, talks resumed with direct US support, and by the end of 2020, reports began suggesting that an agreement had been reached. After much speculation on the seriousness of the positive statements coming from Kuwait, Riyadh and Doha, the emir of Qatar attended the GCC summit in al-Ula on 5 January 2021 – his first visit to Riyadh following the lifting of Saudi restrictions on Qatari use of its airspace. The al-Ula Declaration was signed that day, effectively ending the sanctions on Qatar and announcing the resumption of diplomatic ties (Al-Ansari, Aras & Yorulmazlar, 2021).

Meanwhile, another event was shaping the Middle East, with consequent effects on security and stability. The Abraham Accords, signed between Israel, the UAE, Bahrain and the US in Washington in September 2020, marked the official rapprochement between some Arab states and

Israel. Israel also concluded agreements with Morocco and Sudan. Middle Eastern scholars have interpreted this peace agreement as a shift in threat perceptions in the region (Quamar, 2020; Madani, 2024), and, at the same time, as an illiberal peace process that facilitates authoritarian practices (El Kurd, 2023).

The proliferation of Islamist forces and the expansion of Iranian influence altered the threat perception of some of the Arab Gulf states. Moreover, the changing role of the US as a guarantor of regional security pushed them to redesign their alignments in the region to counterbalance external threats. There was no mention of a Palestinian state or concrete steps to resolve the Israeli–Palestinian conflict (Asseburg & Henkel, 2021). The only reference was the commitment to 'work together to achieve a negotiated solution to the Israeli–Palestinian conflict that meets the legitimate needs and aspirations of both peoples, and to promote peace, stability, and overall prosperity in the Middle East'.[1] This, however, was quite vague and did not provide any tools for addressing the root causes of the conflict.

Following the Abraham Accords, the latest event that has affected the region with both direct and indirect involvement of the Gulf States is Hamas's attack on Israel in October 2023 and the subsequent war in Gaza (still ongoing at the time of writing). Despite increasing international calls for a ceasefire, the Israeli government, led by prime minister Benjamin Netanyahu, has remained adamant about continuing military operations until Hamas is dismantled. This approach has resulted in significant civilian casualties, widespread destruction in Palestinian territories (Madani, 2024) and an increase in internal insecurity in Israel.

Could all these tensions lead to an increase in regional cooperation and the regionalisation of crisis management? A reflection on two concepts – regionalism and regionalisation – is necessary before examining the impact of these processes on foreign aid strategies in the region. As defined by Fawcett (2023b: 179–80), 'regionalism is a policy-driven process in which states (and other actors) pursue common goals and policies in a given region', while 'regionalisation is a broader process encompassing an increase in regionally based interaction and activities'. However, regional cooperation and regional institutions do not have a successful track record in the MENA region.

Formal institutions are underdeveloped, their charters weak and non-binding, and decision-making processes are usually led by the most powerful actors, such as Saudi Arabia in the OIC. Insecurity, lack of trust and lack of enforcement mechanisms have led to a preference for bilateral agreements or informal institutions, which seem more robust than formal institutional cooperation. Despite shared values and the influence of Arabism and Islamism, there has been considerable reluctance among MENA states to pursue deeper regional integration (Fawcett, 2023b). The creation of the GCC appears to be an exception, though it has its limitations, as the GCC crisis demonstrates.

The normalisation process with Israel and the reactions to Hamas's attack and the subsequent Israeli war on Gaza have shown Gulf States acting as separate entities in the international and regional arenas, pursuing their political agendas instead of seeking a cohesive response through regional organisations. Their approaches remain focused on national security interests and their differing perceptions of threats and alliances. However, after the escalation between Israel and Iran, a new regional equilibrium could emerge and constitute an incentive for the Gulf States to create a more cohesive response to the region's instability.

From the Gulf to the *Umma*: A Conceptual Framework for the Foreign Aid Analysis

The historical evolution of the Gulf States as donors in the MENA region and beyond needs to be contextualised within the analysis of foreign aid from an international relations perspective, which remains a contentious issue in the literature.

Starting from the question *What is foreign aid?*, this work problematises the concept of foreign aid as a Western notion where the relationships between donors and recipients are based on asymmetrical power dynamics and, often, principles of conditionality. This contextualisation is useful before applying the concept to 'non-traditional' donors such as the Gulf States. They are termed 'non-traditional' because, according to the prevailing narrative, foreign aid finds its roots – in the political-realism view – in the Cold War, where it served as a tool to influence the political judgements of recipient countries in a bipolar struggle (Liska, 1960; Morgenthau, 1962;

Hook, 1995). From the perspective of liberal internationalism, foreign aid comprises a set of programmatic measures designed to enhance the socio-economic and political development of recipient countries (Baldwin, 1966; Riddell, 1996). According to world-systems theory, it serves as a means of constraining the developmental path of recipient countries, promoting the unequal accumulation of capital globally (Wood, 1986).

These three definitions were challenged by Hattori in 2001, who seeks to reconceptualise foreign aid. His approach is grounded in critical naturalism, and he posits a critical assumption that diverges from all three aforementioned theories of foreign aid: 'the agency of states can be approached similarly to the agency of individuals, i.e., as "socially constituted": it is based neither on its subjectivity nor on its objectivity, but rather on its social relations with other states' (Hattori, 2001: 634; see also Wendt & Duvall, 1989).

Therefore, state actions, including foreign aid decisions, cannot be reduced to the instrumental assumptions of security or profit maximisation. This implies that anthropological and sociological considerations are essential in the analysis of foreign aid. If we accept this theoretical assumption as a starting point, the foreign aid strategies of every state result from a combination of ideological values and political demands, with no exception for the Gulf States.

From complex realism to complex constructivism

The starting point of this analysis is rooted in the theory of complex realism, as elaborated by Hinnebusch and Ehteshami, and in Fawcett's (2023a) effort to identify theoretical and analytical gaps when IR theories are applied to area studies, particularly in the Middle East. According to these scholars, the foreign aid policies of Middle Eastern countries cannot be analysed through the framework of realism or constructivism alone. Several realist assumptions pose challenges when applied to the MENA region for the following reasons: first, states do not necessarily act as cohesive entities; second, the environment in which foreign policymakers operate is more multilayered than that portrayed by realists; and third, foreign policy is also influenced by trans-state identities and the global hierarchy within which regional states are embedded. Within this framework, constructivism is used to understand the trans-state level, where identity plays a critical role. As Hinnebusch and Ehteshami

(2014: 3) note, 'in the Middle East, sub- and supra-state identities compete with state identity, inspire trans-state movements, and constrain purely state-centric behaviours'.

This element is particularly important due to the high level of incongruence between state boundaries and identity in the MENA region. While realism assumes a congruence between national and state identity, envisioning states as cohesive units whose policymakers pursue unified national interests, such unified interests cannot be assumed in this context (Hinnebusch & Ehteshami, 2014: 9). Furthermore, two elements of supra-state identity – pan-Arabism and pan-Islam – should be considered in analysing foreign policy and foreign aid. Consequently, different levels of identity coexist and create incongruence: sub-state, state and supra-state.

With this in mind, Hinnebusch and Ehteshami developed the complex realism framework to incorporate both domestic and international dimensions in understanding state behaviours. According to them, regime security is generally the foremost priority for foreign policymakers, with perceived threats to it being the primary drivers of foreign policy decisions. However, these threats and corresponding strategies are complicated by the multi-level structure of the regional system.

At the same time, Fawcett addresses the gap between IR and area studies, seeking to bridge it through an analysis of the 'regionalisation' process. Regionalism – the policy and practice of regional cooperation – is central to understanding the international politics of the MENA region. This is due, first, to broader global trends in regionalism that make it a significant aspect of international politics; and second, to the high levels of regional tension and the specific nature of its security dilemmas, which make regional cooperation particularly important (Fawcett, 2023b: 174).

Institutional theories fall short in explaining the Middle East context, where, despite the influence of Arabism and Islamism, there has been considerable reluctance to pursue deeper regional integration. Furthermore, Fawcett argues that constructivism is essential for understanding the norms, historical experiences and social dynamics of a region where multiple, overlapping identities compete and influence state preferences (Barnett, 1996).

How, then, can we explain and understand foreign aid by the Gulf States through the lens of IR theories? The answer may lie in balancing constructivist approaches with the view of foreign aid as a direct consequence of foreign policy priorities, embedding the perspective of critical naturalism in the understanding of foreign aid. This approach incorporates the idea that foreign aid, at its core, is a form of giving, and that Gulf States – like other states – are socially constituted, influenced by sub-state, state and supra-state dimensions. Thus, the analytical framework shifts from *complex realism* to *complex constructivism*, where norms, identities and elite perceptions of security and cooperation take precedence over material power.

Three variables affecting aid parameters

Against this backdrop, the conceptual framework to analyse foreign aid by the Gulf States combines the variables characterising the top-down formulation of aid strategies by donors, which affects aid parameters at the implementation level. This system of variables, constructed and tested through various case studies, including that of Syria, posits that while Islam provides an ontological basis (behavioural norms) in which concepts of humanitarianism can be identified, the application of these norms in the foreign aid strategies (structure) of the Gulf States primarily reflects political needs – shaped by elite decision-making processes, projection of power and geopolitical dynamics – as well as transnational elements related to the Gulf States' perception of Islamist movements and political Islam and the relationships between elites in donor and recipient countries (Pericoli, 2025b).

Nevertheless, the religious identities and ideological values of these donors should be considered in the analysis of their foreign aid, as these elements distinguish them within the international humanitarian order. Such factors can enhance the implementation of aid in Muslim-majority communities or countries (bottom-up analysis) or serve as a form of legitimisation (Facon, 2024).

- The first variable (transnational level) pertains to the role that Islam plays in the identity of both donors (Gulf States) and recipients (targeted communities, when relevant). It encompasses the framework that constitutes the behavioural norms for transnational assistance within different Islamic understandings. It can be applied to the state, in the evaluation of top-down policies, or to the implementing agencies at the implementation level in the bottom-up analysis of aid projects.

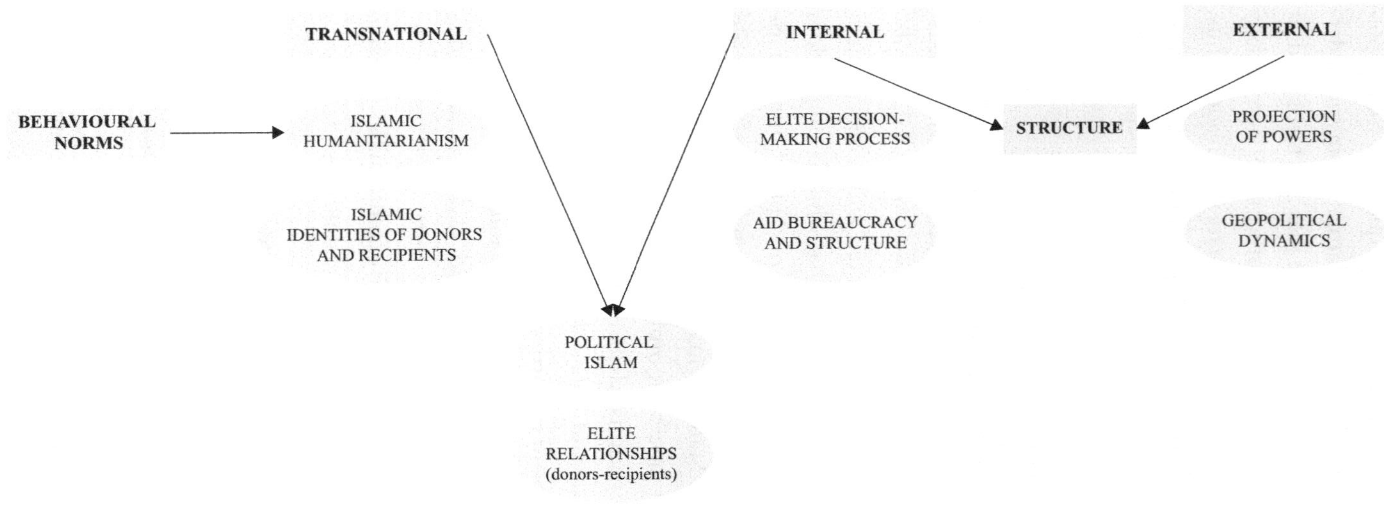

Figure 2.2 Three variables in the conceptual framework for analysing Gulf donors' foreign aid strategies.

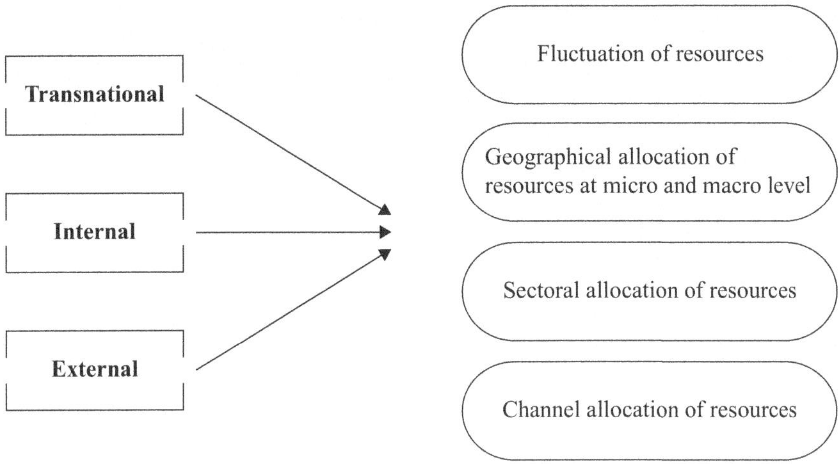

Figure 2.3 Three variables of foreign aid that affect aid parameters.

- The second variable (domestic level) addresses internal dynamics, focusing on the elite decision-making process and the structure of aid bureaucracy (institutions). This aspect involves the institutional system of aid in each country and the elite's role in resource allocation for humanitarian and development aid in third countries.

  Between the transnational and domestic levels, two additional elements must be considered: the perception of Islamist movements (both within the country and in the region) and the relationships between elites in donor and recipient contexts.
- The third variable relates to the influence of external geopolitical dynamics on foreign aid and the various strategies employed for projecting power.

All three variables represent key elements in the evaluation of foreign policy and aid implementation, affecting four main aid parameters: (a) fluctuation of resources over time; (b) geographical allocation of resources at both macro (selection of countries) and micro (selection of areas within the targeted country) levels; (c) sectoral allocation of resources; and (d) channel allocation of resources (multilateral, bilateral, through international NGOs or through Gulf state-based charities). In the multilateral allocation, the difference between earmarked and core contributions is considered in the analysis to observe the unrestricted (core) or specific (earmarked) allocation in the multilateral organisation. With earmarked contributions, indeed, the donor can maintain its preference for certain projects and sectors, potentially distorting programmes priorities by limiting the proportion of funding.[2]

Variable 1: Transnational level and political Islam

Regarding the first variable, this study incorporates multiple levels of analysis: (a) the Islamic understanding of aid and humanitarianism, discussed in Chapter 1, which constitutes the behavioural norms; (b) the role Islam plays in shaping the identities of both donors and recipients; and, finally, (c) Gulf States' perception of Islamism and political Islam. The Islamic identity of these donors influences foreign aid strategies by interacting with domestic, regional and international dynamics. However, as Mandaville (2023) notes, the substantive presence of Islam in the foreign policies of Middle Eastern nations, including the Gulf States, is difficult to discern.

A balanced approach to analysing Islam's role in international relations and foreign policy lies in avoiding an 'orientalistic' perspective that attributes all Muslim behaviour solely to Islam. On the other extreme, it should also avoid viewing Islam merely as a tool to justify policies whose true motivations lie elsewhere (Mandaville, 2023). In this regard, the goal is not to identify a direct causal relationship between Islamic norms and policy in aid strategy formulation but to understand how (if and which) Islamic values and norms are incorporated in policy development at different levels – whether in top-down policy elaboration or bottom-up aid implementation.

This book primarily observes the top-down analysis of the policymaking processes in the Gulf States, while the bottom-up analysis examines how social actors, humanitarian organisations and recipients interact with each other. It mainly explores the top-down policy formation of the Gulf States, but the study of aid must always consider it as a complex system involving diverse actors, asymmetric power dynamics and the gap between donor intentions and aid implementation.

Concerning the Gulf States' perception of political Islam and Islamist movements, it can play a role in explaining resource allocation. Islamism and political Islam are contested concepts without a settled definition and are used interchangeably in this context (despite there being no agreement in the literature on whether they can be considered the same phenomenon). This study adopts the definition of Valbjørn and Gunning (2025: 4), who cenceptualise Islamism as a 'modern political ideology associated with social, political, or armed activism concerned with the implementation of an ideological vision of Islam in the state or in the society'. Moreover, the main movement considered in this book among Islamist movements to trace the behaviours and perceptions of Saudi Arabia, Qatar and the UAE is the Muslim Brotherhood and its branches within the three countries and in aid recipient contexts.

Political Islam has often represented both a national and transnational phenomenon, significantly influencing the Gulf States' decision-making processes, including their resource and aid allocations in third countries. Following the Arab Spring, the Gulf States' relationship with the Muslim Brotherhood, in particular, impacted aid dynamics, as in the cases of Syria, Sudan, Somalia, Gaza, Egypt and Tunisia.

(a) The Muslim Brotherhood in Qatar. In the case of Qatar, the MB branch was formally formed in 1975 as a result of internal and external influences. In the mid-1950s members of the Egyptian Brotherhood arrived in the country after Nasser's crackdown and with the Assad regime's repression in Syria in 1980s, new members of the Syrian MB moved to Doha. Yusuf al-Qaradawi – a prominent figure of the MB in Egypt – for instance, left Cairo in 1961 under political pressure and relocated to Qatar, thereby increasing the MB's influence on the religious establishment and civil service (Kamrava 2015).

One of the main motivations of importing Brotherhood members was the basic need for educated employees in different roles including education and bureaucracy (Roberts, 2014). However, in 1999 the organisation decided to dissolve and they never expanded beyond the social sector (Freer, 2018). Freer identifies different causes of the dissolution, including the fact that the organisation could operate without having an organised structure, or the complicated relation with the mother organisation in Cairo and the disagreement between the two. Among other reasons, the positive stance of the Qatari government towards the organisation, due to its perceived complementary role to the government agenda, perhaps pushed the *Ikhwan* to convert from a more structured organisation to a trend inside Qatari society, away from the pressure of a regulatory framework (Freer, 2018: 90).

As Kamrava noted in 2013, the link between Doha and the MB goes beyond mere instrumental and strategic motivations. The movement has played a significant role in Qatar's nation-building process, with the MB's vision becoming a source of national identity. The Brotherhood's interpretation of Islam emerged as an ideological contrast to the Wahhabism of Saudi Arabia, despite Qatar being a Wahhabi state itself (Roberts, 2014a). Since the 1960s, Wahhabi clerics from Saudi Arabia were gradually replaced by figures from the MB as part of Qatar's effort to assert an identity distinct from that of Saudi Arabia (Kamrava, 2013). Therefore, the Qatari government has historically granted space for the MB to operate in the religious social sector, and the group in turn 'praised the government for its Islamist policies', reinforcing al-Thani's power and internal stability (Freer, 2018: 94).

(b) Islah in the UAE. In the UAE, evolving relations with the MB have shaped the country's Islamic identity and influenced its internal and external dynamics. From 1973 to 1983, the UAE's MB-linked Jamʿiat al-Islah wa-l-Tawjih al-Ijtimaʿi (Islah) enjoyed a 'golden era', playing an active role in the federation's political dynamics. However, their influence began to wane following educational reforms initiated by Nahyan al-Nahyan, which the MB opposed unsuccessfully. By the end of the 1980s, the federal government became concerned about the influence of Islamism in political spaces beyond its role in the education sector. Hence, despite the initial positive attitude of the Emirati government towards Islah, and its concession of ministerial positions to its members into the early 1980s, this decisively changed in the early 1990s, when the organisation became powerful enough to pose a political threat (Freer, 2018: 102). In 1995, the UAE disbanded Islah's administrative council, restricting its activities abroad and placing all of its branches under the supervision of the Ministry of Social Affairs.

As the MB adopted an increasingly oppositional discourse, criticising corruption and political malpractice within the UAE, its stance evolved. By the time of the Arab Spring, the Brotherhood's rhetoric had become both religious and political (Başkan, 2021), leading the Emirati government to view the MB's political ambitions as a threat to its domestic and regional agenda. Domestically, Emirati leaders, particularly in Abu Dhabi and Dubai, feared that al-Islah could mobilise economically disadvantaged segments of society, potentially undermining national unity and the legitimacy of the UAE's monarchical system. Regionally, the UAE perceived the Brotherhood not as a solution to socio-economic issues but as a transnational force challenging the concept of the nation-state (Borck, 2024). Consequently, the UAE saw the need to contain the MB both at home and abroad (Roberts, 2017) and in 2014 included it in the list of terrorist organisations, along with al-Qaeda and ISIS (Gulf News, 2018).

Apart from the relationship between the UAE and the MB, different alignments exist regarding religion and political authority. The leading emirate, Abu Dhabi, and its ruling family, the Bani Yas, differ from both Qatar and Saudi Arabia in their adherence to the less literalist Maliki legal tradition, a distinction that provides some distance from Saudi religious influence. Nevertheless, other legal traditions are present in the UAE, including the Hanbali tradition in other emirates (Diwan, 2021).

Following the Arab Spring, Crown Prince Mohammed bin Zayed sought to promote an alternative Islamic discourse, both domestically and internationally. Like Qatar, the UAE lacked an indigenous clerical establishment through which to project this authority. Therefore, leaders in Abu Dhabi began developing a transnational clerical body to convey a 'moderate' interpretation of Islam, emphasising peace, stability and religious tolerance.

In 2014, the Forum for Promoting Peace in Muslim Societies was established in Abu Dhabi. The primary clerics of the forum, Abdallah bin Bayyah and Hamza Yusuf, argue that political authority and social hierarchy are essential for ensuring stability within the Muslim community, even under conditions of injustice. In this manner, Abu Dhabi promoted a 'centric' vision of Islam intended to ensure stability within the UAE while countering Islamist movements – particularly the MB – during uprisings, as seen in Syria and Egypt. This vision aimed to provide an alternative not only to the Qatari and MB approach but also to the Saudi religious establishment, challenging its extensive role in propagating a fundamentalist interpretation of Islam (Diwan, 2021).

(c) Al-Sahwa al-Islamiyya in Saudi Arabia. The case of Saudi Arabia presents unique dynamics. With the rise of Nasser's Arab nationalism, the MB became a key asset for the Saudi kingdom, allowing it to counter nationalist ideology with an Islamic alternative. As analysed by Lacroix (2015), from the 1960s onwards, the MB – known locally as al-Sahwa al-Islamiyya – emerged as a blend of Wahhabi religious culture and Brotherhood ideology. From the 1960s to the late 1980s, Sahwi networks played a stabilising role in Saudi politics, acting as a conservative force whose mobilising potential largely served the regime (Lacroix, 2015: 174).

However, a turning point came in 1990 with the Iraqi invasion of Kuwait. Saudi Arabia's call for Western troops to protect the kingdom led to internal dissent and the rise of an Islamist reform movement. This event deepened the rift between the Brotherhood and the Saudi government, creating space for *Sururi* Salafism (al-Saif, 2014) to gain influence. *Sururi* Salafism adopted a new form of Islamic activism in harmony with Wahhabi theological precepts (Lacroix, 2011: 69). By this point, the Saudi elite increasingly perceived the MB as a destabilising force within the public and political spheres. This perception peaked in 2014 when Saudi Arabia officially designated the Brotherhood as a terrorist organisation, framing it as a subversive transnational movement with a revisionist agenda aimed at undermining regional states, including the kingdom itself (Borck, 2024: 35).

The experience of the Sahwa movement represented a distinctive form of Islamism compared to its Middle Eastern counterparts, as its ideology was not merely an importation of the Muslim Brotherhood's discourse, but rather an adaptation to the Wahhabi tradition to ensure its acceptance within the Saudi context. The governmental crackdown and consequent transformation of the movement did not completely repress the Saudi Islamism that still exists as a local and transnational phenomenon (Lacroix, 2011) and that the kingdom is now trying to transform into a 'moderate Islam' (Bunzel, 2025).

These three examples of MB organisations in the Gulf States, and their subsequent co-optation or repression, are essential for understanding the relationships with the movement's branches in the region. In contrast to the Saudi and Emirati approaches, the Qatari regime opted to co-opt rather than repress the MB organisation. This strategy created a space within the country's social fabric where the movement – de-institutionalised after 1999 – could continue to play a role in society, thereby reinforcing rather than contesting the political authority of the ruling family. Consequently, Qatar has never perceived MB movements beyond its national borders as a threat to its stability or to the legitimisation of its internal power, unlike Saudi Arabia and the UAE. This is relevant for observing the allocation of resources and foreign aid strategies that have characterised these Gulf States since the Arab Spring, as well as in the contrasting roles assumed by Doha, Riyadh and Abu Dhabi as donors in the same, fragmented context as the Syrian one.

However, internal characteristics of these three countries influence their relations with the Islamist movements and even their foreign policy choices. In Qatar, political authority is concentrated within the ruling al-Thani family, operating within a highly personalised framework. The al-Thanis' ascent to power was facilitated by the absence of competing influential families and a weak merchant class, which minimised challenges to their rule. Islam serves as the principal ideological foundation for Qatar's population; however, its influence remains largely informal and uninstitutionalised. Within Qatar's personalised political system, it is therefore unsurprising that the Muslim Brotherhood's influence lacks formal institutional representation.

In contrast, the UAE presents a more complex political environment. Despite internal divisions among its constituent emirates, government departments and authorities remain largely opaque and secretive. In this context, the federal government has at times struggled to assert full control, leading to the repression of opposition movements, particularly Islamist groups. Nevertheless, the fragmented nature of the UAE's federal system has allowed the MB to persist for several decades (Freer, 2018: 42).

Variable 2: The elite decision-making process and the institutional framework

The second variable, related to the domestic dimension, concerns two different aspects: the elite decision-making process and the aid bureaucracy in each Gulf state. The analysis of these elements is generally outlined below and applied to Qatar and the UAE in the following chapter.

(a) The elite decision-making process in aid policies. To understand the policymaking process in foreign policy analysis, Hinnebusch and Ehteshami identify three main components: foreign policy role, the balance of power between interests and the foreign policy process, and leadership.

> A state's foreign policy role implies identity and defines orientations toward neighbors (friend or enemy), toward great powers (threat or patron), and the

> state system (revisionist or status quo). Roles are constructed by elites in interaction with other states and with their publics. (Hinnebusch & Ehteshami, 2014: 28)

In regimes where power is personalised and concentrated, and especially in times of fluidity or crisis, the leader's personal style, values, perceptions – and misperceptions – can make an enormous difference (Dawisha, 1988).

In the case of foreign aid, the role of the elite in the decision-making process is intertwined with other factors that influence policy formulation and the structure of the aid bureaucracy in various ways. Rentierism, dynastic monarchism and tribalism are among the factors that shape these dynamics. Moreover, the establishment of aid institutions in the Gulf States can also play a role in influencing the process of decision-making.

In this regard, a general reflection on decision-making choices in the Gulf States is probably necessary. Coates Ulrichsen (2024a: 5) describes this process as the result of 'political outcomes of the competition among different groups of actors for influence and resources'. Rulers and ruling families sit at the apex of the power structure, but multiple spaces for influence exist through formal and informal actors, both within and outside governmental institutions and the bureaucratic framework. In the case of foreign aid, the institutional structures in each state and their social constituencies differently affect the power dynamics shaping aid decisions.

Rentierism and dynastic monarchism. Observing the Gulf States reveals structural characteristics that influence the institutional framework and decision-making processes in foreign aid: rentierism and dynastic monarchism. However, Qatar, Saudi Arabia and the UAE exhibit notable differences. Qatar is a rentier autocracy ruled by a single dynasty, the al-Thanis. The UAE, by contrast, is a decentralised state composed of seven emirates, where power remains within an intertribal structure of ruling families. Moreover, there are varying levels of rentierism among the emirates, with Abu Dhabi as an extreme rentier and Dubai as a non-rentier. Saudi Arabia is an autocracy ruled by a single dynasty, considered a rentier state with a growing attempt to internationalise its economy towards a post-rentier model (Freer, 2018).

According to the literature, rentierism illustrates how the relationship between rulers and agents (such as aid bureaucrats or para-public aid workers) in rentier states leads to the emergence of multiple principals and risk-averse attitudes among agents. Dynastic monarchism shows how family relations in the Gulf States reinforce multiple principal models, although with different outcomes in Qatar compared to the UAE (Lestra, 2017). A rentier economy has bureaucratic characteristics that affect how foreign aid is mobilised and disbursed. In principal–agent theory, rentierism highlights that Gulf polities are not composed of voters or taxpayers but of individuals co-opted by the state, primarily through the provision of public jobs. Hertog (2010) explains that as state bureaucracy expands into large public sectors that heavily resist reforms, it becomes increasingly difficult to re-engineer the state. According to Lestra (2017), in the aid landscape, this expansion allows for the coexistence of different – and often redundant – organisations.

The analysis of the Gulf sub-region has, for a long time, been observed through rentier state theory, the dominant theory to explain state–society relations in states that generate a large proportion of their income from rents or externally derived, unproductively earned payments (Gray, 2011: 1). But starting in 2011, late-rentiers theory emerged, highlighting the oversimplification of social and economic phenomena in the Gulf in light of the rentier state (Mason, 2024). According to Gray and Mason, while rents and rentierism remain crucial to understanding the nature of Gulf regimes, other non-rentier characteristics also affect the political dynamics of the region. These include the role of institutions, population change and new international imperatives, which have pushed political elites to develop a more nuanced approach to society and policymaking (Gray, 2011). Regarding foreign aid, rentierism may influence the number of organisations in the aid system (Lestra, 2017) as well as the relationship between foreign aid and the social acceptance of aid expenditure during a given crisis.

According to Bradley (2023), one of the key components of humanitarian emergencies and interventions is how events are understood and constructed. Different events, including conflicts, famine and displacement, can be seen through various lenses, and the perception of a problem often leads to corresponding solutions. The concept of 'humanitarianisation' refers to how humanitarian emergencies are perceived. It involves: (a) discursive practices through which certain privileged actors claim that the lives of a group of people are at risk and that their suffering should be alleviated, (b) the acceptance of that claim by a wider public and (c) the consequent legitimation of international humanitarian assistance. However, the perception of humanitarian intervention as legitimate does not necessarily lead to a real and appropriate mobilisation of resources (Bradley, 2023). In the case of rentier states, where expenditure for foreign aid interventions does not require the acceptance of the wider population (bottom-up), social mobilisations are typically supported, co-opted or repressed according to political necessities. However, they may not represent a significant element in the decision-making process.

Along with rentierism, dynastic monarchism is closely linked to the decision-making process and the proliferation of actors. According to Herb (1997), dynastic monarchism is a mechanism of elite accommodation: an institutionalised – yet informal – dispute settlement method used by members of a ruling autocratic family. Since it prioritises regime survival over political reform, dynastic monarchism often leads to sub-optimal policy outcomes, as it accommodates the interests of various family members within the dynasty. Conversely, the ruler can only impose reforms on aid if other principals – family members or close allies – agree to them. If they do not, dynastic monarchism reinforces the logic of the multiple-principals model. Regarding foreign aid, dynastic monarchism rewards members of the ruling family and their close allies by allowing them to participate in aid initiatives with minimal oversight, often by establishing their own organisations. This proliferation of donors strains state administration. Therefore, the success of any reform or effort to improve aid transparency depends on the cooperation of the relevant family members (Lestra, 2017).

Tribalism, aid and resources. The Western concepts of rentierism and monarchism should be integrated with a key element characteristic of the Gulf States: the tribal dimension. Scholars have yet to reach a consensus on the precise definition of a tribe. Broadly, 'tribe' may refer to a localised group organised primarily through kinship, whose members perceive themselves as culturally distinct in customs, dialect or language, and origins (Dukhan, 2014). According to Ibn Khaldoun's cyclical theory, tribes adapt to the state's economic and political environment when the state is strong; however, when the state weakens, it becomes susceptible to revolution by the tribes it previously sought to control.

Evans-Pritchard (1969) uses segmentary lineage theory to describe tribal dynamics, suggesting that solidarity shapes social groups that interact in predictable ways within a cultural system, maintaining a balance of power. Gellner expands on this approach, identifying key characteristics of tribes, especially in their interactions with the state. One such characteristic is the 'mercenary option', which allows tribes to shift external alliances to ensure group survival (Gellner, 1995). The state, in turn, relies on tribal systems for authority, sustaining a reciprocal relationship that preserves tribal authority. Thus, patronage is a fundamental social relationship, emerging when kinship alone cannot guarantee subsistence and physical security (Dukhan, 2014).

'Tribe' and 'tribalism' are distinct concepts. While 'tribe' refers to a social group defined by shared social, cultural and other values, 'tribalism' refers to the politics of identity, which, in the GCC context, includes tribal, ethnic and sectarian dimensions. Tribalism involves mobilisation around specific identity components, such as kinship, ethnicity, religion and sect, among others. This mobilisation may or may not directly involve an actual tribe, and it extends far beyond kinship in uniting or dividing people. According to al-Ghithami (2009), tribalism is essentially an exclusive, ethnic or discriminatory concept, relying on group solidarity against others.

In the GCC countries, building national identities required the state to create new forms of solidarity and cohesion within the nation-state framework, potentially replacing tribal identities. In a Khaldunian sense, the success of the national project depended on eroding tribal *'asabiya* (social solidarity) and replacing it with a national identity. This transformation was facilitated by factors such as oil wealth, which provided states with substantial resources to establish social contracts. Through these contracts, the state retained political control while citizens benefited from wealth in a rentier state system (Al-Kuwari 2019).

In the 1960s and 1970s, when most Gulf states gained independence, tribes played a crucial role in state formation. Their allegiance to ruling families, acceptance of the new state order and support for the national project enabled the formation of these states with minimal resistance – particularly in smaller entities such as Kuwait, Bahrain, Qatar and the UAE. Additionally, the fluidity of tribal connections across borders allowed the emerging states to develop political structures without substantial opposition from tribes (Eickelman, 2016).

The development of national identities in the Gulf region has often relied on the state's ability to distribute wealth to citizens, making access to wealth and resources central to the concept of citizenship. Consequently, the national identity project in the GCC has, from the outset, been somewhat weak and incomplete, heavily dependent on the state's capacity to control and distribute wealth and to provide welfare. This arrangement has formed the core of the social contract between the state and society since independence (Peterson, 2012).

While this social contract has effectively sustained national identities, it may no longer suffice today, given the mounting pressures on it. Population growth, fluctuating oil revenues, increasing demands for development and political participation, and the lack of economic diversification have all intensified the strain on the social contract. As Peterson (2012) aptly describes it, these factors contribute to the 'fraying of the social contract' in Gulf countries, challenging the state's capacity to build a unified national identity.

Beyond the challenging realities faced by Gulf states, the policies of these states may have inadvertently strengthened tribalism as a form of sociopolitical activism and mobilisation based on a modern concept of *'asabiya*. The tribe has maintained its legitimacy at a time when the state is struggling to uphold its own. As a result, tribalism offers tribes a viable alternative to the weakening state. Gulf states appear fully aware of this issue. However, rather than reinforcing the state's legitimacy, some have chosen to exploit tribalism for political advantage, particularly in relations with neighbouring countries. This tactic takes advantage of the fluid, dynamic nature of Gulf identities, which are subject to change, transformation and even manipulation.

Before the Gulf crisis of 2017, Saudi Arabia attempted to exploit tribalism to undermine neighbouring states and expand its political influence. This was pursued, for example, through financial payoffs to tribes with kinship ties to Saudi counterparts. Historically, Saudi Arabia has used this approach to instigate or exploit tribal tensions in neighbouring countries, especially in Yemen and Jordan. During the Syrian uprising, Riyadh employed a similar tactic, providing financial and military support to tribes with kinship ties in Saudi Arabia to weaken the Syrian regime (Al-Kuwari, 2019).

However, resource distribution remains a means of co-optation by ruling elites, who use it to consolidate power and authority among select social groups (Lowi, 2024). In modern states, tribalism and genealogical ties – such as those seen in Saudi Arabia (Al Fahad, 2015) – serve as tools for asserting social belonging. By distinguishing between individuals with tribal affiliations and those without, tribalism not only reinforces social hierarchies but also enables the selective distribution of resources, often to the detriment of the unaffiliated (Lowi, 2024). Observing the distribution of *zakat*, the analysis of Qatar and the UAE shows that this religious resource, collected by the state, is primarily distributed domestically to enhance social welfare. This highlights the significance of the tribal dimension and demonstrates that resource distribution is closely tied to the social contract and the *bayʿa* (allegiance) between the leader and the population.[3]

(b) Institutional aid framework. The institutional dimension of aid in each Gulf state affects the policy elaboration and aid implementation on the ground and, therefore, is essential for understanding foreign aid dynamics within and outside these donor countries.

In the case of Qatar, the institutional dimension of the aid system is highly centralised, in terms of both policy formulation and implementation. The Department of International Cooperation and the minister of state for international cooperation are part of the Ministry of Foreign Affairs, which is responsible for developing the policy directions for foreign aid strategies outlined in the Qatari National Vision 2030 and the Third National Development Strategy (2024–2030). In 2002, the Qatar Fund for Development (QFFD) was established to take over the executive responsibilities of the International Development Department and to develop a strategic framework for Qatari aid. The QFFD became the public development institution committed to allocating the government's budget for projects aligned with the country's main strategic priorities, focusing on four key sectors: education, health, economic empowerment and humanitarian response.

To better coordinate policy and implementation, the State of Qatar created the Regulatory Authority for Charitable Activities (RACA) in 2014.

The authority is tasked with developing, supporting, regulating and supervising charitable activities carried out by organisations in Qatar. Under the Law Regulating Charitable Activities, all charities are monitored and must comply with RACA's oversight.

At the implementation level, the two main charities operating in third countries are the Qatar Charity and the Qatar Red Crescent Society. These organisations operate through both governmental and private funds, but the flow of funds to third countries requires prior approval from RACA.

In the UAE, the first governmental agency created to administer foreign aid was the Abu Dhabi Fund for Development (ADFD), established in 1971. The ADFD is currently responsible for financing development interventions exclusively through bilateral channels with soft loans and grants. In 2008, the UAE Cabinet established the Office for the Coordination of Foreign Aid (OCFA), signalling the government's commitment to transforming the UAE's aid sector. OCFA was tasked with documenting and coordinating UAE foreign aid, assessing its impact and supporting capacity-building within UAE organisations.

In 2013, OCFA's mandate evolved, leading to the creation of the Ministry of International Cooperation and Development (MICAD). MICAD continued OCFA's responsibilities while also developing the UAE Foreign Assistance Policy. In 2016, MICAD merged with the Ministry of Foreign Affairs to form the Ministry of Foreign Affairs and International Cooperation. In 2017, the Foreign Assistance Policy was launched to enhance the effectiveness of UAE foreign aid. On the implementation front, the Emirates Red Crescent was established in 1983 as the UAE's primary humanitarian agency, marking an important milestone in the country's foreign assistance efforts. During the same period (1980–90), the nation's leadership further supported the creation of sponsoring aid organisations and charities in each emirate (Almezaini, 2017).

Compared to Qatar, the decision-making process in the UAE appears more fragmented, with various figures within the elite managing different aspects of foreign aid. Foreign aid strategies result from a federation-based (centralised) process, elaborated by multiple actors, particularly within the elite circles of Abu Dhabi and Dubai. This system has produced numerous players in the humanitarian and development landscape, each with distinct financial and implementation roles (e.g. the Ministry of Foreign Affairs, the

Abu Dhabi Fund for Development, the Emirates Red Crescent, the Khalifa Bin Zayed Al Nahyan Foundation and the Al Maktoum Foundation, among others). Most of these entities are linked to key personalities from different emirates, reflecting the fragmentation of policies and priorities concerning foreign aid. The institutional aid structure of Qatar and the UAE will be analysed in depth in Chapter 3.

Saudi Arabia presents some peculiarities compared to the previous countries in terms of aid institutional architecture. The right to formulate all its policies rests in the hands of the royal family with the influence of related institutions. The policymaking bodies surrounding the royal family include the Saudi Ministry of Foreign Affairs, the Ministry of Finance and the Cabinet. The Ministry of Finance also oversees the Department of International Development Cooperation. The Cabinet may also issue new decrees to manage development assistance, as stipulated in Article 7 of Royal Licence No. M/48 (Li, 2019).

In 1984, the kingdom established the Saudi Fund for Development exclusively for development interventions in third countries, providing economic support through soft loans and grants (similar to the ADFD). However, starting in 2015, with the creation of the King Salman Humanitarian Aid and Relief Centre (KSRelief), Saudi Arabia clearly distinguished between humanitarian and development interventions in terms of aid strategies and funding. Therefore, the country presents a clear institutional distinction in terms of humanitarian and development aid management compared to Qatar and the UAE. The creation of KSRelief has multiple reasons and objectives. The first one is the restructure of the Saudi aid landscape, through a unified institution and approach towards 'universality' instead of 'Islamic solidarity'. This effort was made to centralise the aid response, which was, in the absence of a ministry of international development or cooperation, administered through various channels, with royal and non-royal Saudi individuals involved in aid implementation through their charities (Derbal, 2022a).

At the operational level, the Saudi Red Crescent Society is the main implementing agency for humanitarian responses, alongside the International Organization for Relief, Welfare and Development, formally known as the International Islamic Relief Organization (Benthall, 2018b). The creation of KSRelief and the reorientation of the Saudi aid landscape in recent years have affected the implementation capacity of these two organisations, which were among the most active actors in the aid strategies of the kingdom but no longer match the new political and strategic directions of the Saudi aid landscape (Derbal, 2022b).

Variable 3: Projection of power

The correlation between foreign policy and foreign aid, which characterises any approach to foreign assistance by a state as the donor entity, affects the technical aspects of the aid itself. Therefore, this variable concerns the projection of power by the Gulf States, intended as the set of strategies and behaviours these states have adopted to interact with external actors, both regionally and internationally.

Qatar's foreign policy autonomy and diplomatic hyperactivism are rooted in two distinct yet complementary sources: massive revenues from hydrocarbon exports, particularly from liquefied natural gas, and elite institutional cohesion, which facilitates policymaking decisions and ensures diplomatic agility. This agility is further reinforced by Qatar's comparative advantages over its neighbours. It is more politically stable than Bahrain, more cohesive than the UAE, more aggressively self-assured than Oman, and more effective at branding than Saudi Arabia. These characteristics have shaped its image as a donor and enhanced its ability to exercise soft power over time. In addition to these structural dynamics, certain political goals and priorities distinguish Qatar from the other Gulf states, including the UAE, which has prioritised economic interests and security concerns over political considerations. Four main traits sum up Qatari foreign policy: (a) the relationship with Saudi Arabia, characterised by a form of independence, especially after 1995; (b) the relationship with the US, which has increased since the 1990s, aimed at securing military protection from external threats; (c) the controversial relationship with Iran, which stands in evident opposition to Saudi Arabia; and (d) its hyperactivism in diplomacy, which has allowed it to act in ways that most other states of its size cannot. Qatari leaders 'have transformed survival strategies into sources of influence and perhaps even power' (Kamrava, 2013: 72).

In the decade from the Arab uprisings to 2021, the foreign policy of the UAE became more assertive, influenced by internal factors such as its relationship with Islamism, national security concerns and human rights issues

(Mason, 2023). This phase of UAE foreign policy is characterised by a prioritisation of security and defensive alliances. Security and defence are projected through the UAE's 'model' of economic development and humanitarian diplomacy, which helps explain the geographical allocation of resources over time and the preference for bilateral and infrastructural development in foreign aid.

The UAE shifted from using soft power to deploying hard power in the region, bolstered by its economic development and investments in the military and infrastructure. Over the past two decades – and particularly after the 2008 global financial crisis, which hit Dubai hard – Abu Dhabi has come to be seen as the primary centre of gravity in Emirati foreign, defence and security decision-making. Concurrently, Mohammed bin Zayed al-Nahyan, crown prince of Abu Dhabi from 2004 to 2022 and UAE president since 2022, became the country's most important decision maker. This shift in leadership explains the centralisation process in foreign aid decisions as well (as discussed in the previous section). At the regional level, the UAE was a driving force in the effort to politically and economically isolate Qatar from 2017 to 2021, supported the USA's pressure campaign on Iran, and played a key role in the normalisation process with Israel (Borck, 2024).

Regarding Saudi Arabia, its foreign policy has been shaped by the combination of the kingdom's position as the world's leading oil exporter and its status as the host of Islam's holiest sites, which defines its Sunni identity. During the Arab Spring (2010–11), Saudi Arabia sought to prevent some revolutionary changes while attempting to capitalise on others (Borck, 2024: 9). Similar to the UAE, the rise of the Muslim Brotherhood in the region represented a significant concern for both internal stability and external alliances.

With the succession of King Salman in 2015 and the ascent of Crown Prince Mohammed bin Salman, several changes were made in both domestic and foreign policies. The new leadership worked to reduce fragmentation and centralise the decision-making process, adopting a more assertive political approach to regional issues, including the Yemeni war and the Gulf crisis (Borck, 2024).

Conclusion

The effort to integrate various International Relations theories with the behavioural norms that characterise the Islamic understanding of humanitarianism represents a critical step towards developing a more inclusive and culturally grounded analysis of regional aid dynamics. Drawing on a conceptual framework that incorporates internal, external and transnational levels of analysis, this approach reconceptualises foreign aid through a lens of *complex constructivism*. It moves beyond the assumptions of *complex realism* by recognising values and norms as fundamental components of aid practices and of the interactions between donors and recipients. Social and religious norms have been conceptualised as elements of social structure that emerge from the actions and beliefs of actors within specific communities, while simultaneously shaping those actions and beliefs by constituting the actors' identities and interests (Hoffmann, 2017). The identification of social and religious norms in the Gulf States, along with the consideration of these analytical variables, helps to trace their 'donor identities' and construct the conceptual framework through which aid parameters are examined.

Notes

1. The Abraham Accords Declaration, US Department of State, available at https://www.state.gov/the-abraham-accords/
2. Technical note on definitions, sources and coverage, https://www.un.org/en/ecosoc/qcpr/pdf/technical_note_on_funding.pdf
3. See more details on *zakat* management in the Gulf States in Chapter 3.

PART II

PRACTICES

3

QATAR AND THE UNITED ARAB EMIRATES AS DONORS IN THE REGION

The conceptual framework outlined in the previous chapter incorporates the analysis of the internal structure and institutionalisation of aid practices. This institutionalisation of aid in Qatar and the UAE is crucial for understanding how these two states have developed as donors within the MENA region, and how internal and geopolitical dynamics have shaped this transformation. This chapter examines the internal structure of the foreign aid system, focusing on the bureaucratic and ministerial management of aid, from the decision-making process to its implementation. The control over funding, efforts to ensure transparency and the relationship between higher-level ministries and lower-level implementing agencies illustrate the interaction between central authority, aid decisions and the evolution of aid practices in these two Gulf states.

Qatari Aid Structure: Institutionalisation and Control

During my fieldwork in Doha, an interesting debate was underway between the Regulatory Authority of Charitable Activities and the ministries of Social Affairs and Foreign Affairs regarding the reorganisation of the aid system and coordination of charitable operations on the ground. Understanding the aid bureaucracy and system in the country requires an effort in two main directions: the historical evolution of the country as a donor and the institutional framework that governs the aid system.

Historical evolution of Qatar as a donor

Analysing the evolution of Qatari aid through a historical lens helps understand the extent to which aid strategy and allocation have been influenced by internal and regional events, from the Arab uprisings to the Gulf crisis and beyond, as well as other key factors. From Qatar's independence in 1971 until 1995, Qatari aid reflected the common characteristics of Arab aid in the post-independence era, as well as the Muslim revival of unity and solidarity inspired by nationalist movements and Saudi Arabia's regional hegemony. During this period, Qatar's aid primarily targeted Arab and Muslim countries, and it was often channelled through multilateral organisations such as the Muslim World League, the Arab Fund for Economic and Social Development, the Arab Monetary Fund and Islamic financial institutions like the Islamic Development Bank (IsDB). The main foci of these projects were economic development, social welfare programmes and educational and cultural activities. From 1970 to 1995, Qatar's aid disbursement was estimated to total about USD 2 billion, which represented approximately 2 per cent of total Arab aid during that period. This volume of aid ranked Qatar far behind other countries such as Saudi Arabia (64 per cent), Kuwait (17 per cent) and the UAE (10 per cent). A significant shift in Qatar's aid policy occurred when Sheikh Hamad bin Khalifa al-Thani ascended to the throne in 1995. His leadership contributed to a radical change in Qatar's internal and foreign policies, which in turn influenced the country's approach to foreign aid. The volume of Qatar's aid significantly increased and expanded to cover a wider range of development and humanitarian programmes across several regions worldwide. This shift was likely linked not only to a new political strategy but also to the growing financial resources accumulated primarily from the gas industry. This dynamic has continued to shape Qatar's aid policy to this day (Bashir & Abdelsalam, 2021).

Before the Arab Spring, Emir Hamad bin Khalifa al-Thani (1995–2013) and his prime minister, Sheikh Hamad bin Jassim, developed an 'aggressive' strategy to transform Qatar into a dynamic regional actor. During this period, three of the most high-profile mediations took place in Yemen (2008–10), Lebanon (2008) and Darfur (2008–10). Doha also worked to resolve disputes between Sudan and Chad (2008), and Djibouti and Eritrea (2010). Immediately before the Arab Spring, Qatari policymaking was characterised by the high-level personal engagement of the emir and the prime minister, a small circle of elite decision-makers, and the commitment of significant financial resources to achieve mediatory outcomes. In June 2013, Tamim bin Hamad al-Thani came to power, continuing the political direction initiated by his father, while attempting to maintain the country's position as a regional mediator (Barakat, 2014).

The onset of the Arab Spring drastically influenced the foreign policy and aid trajectory of the small sheikhdom. After an initial period of caution in January 2011, Qatar decided to take a leading role in the 'direction of change', in contrast to other Gulf states that resisted the popular pressures unleashed by the Arab Spring. Doha pursued both direct and indirect interventions in Libya and Syria, advocating an Arab solution to Arab problems, while also mobilising economic assistance for Tunisia and Egypt. These factors converged in Qatar's close, yet controversial, relationship with the Muslim Brotherhood (Roberts, 2012), including the mobilisation of funds in support of Islamist movements.

However, Qatar's relationship with the MB goes beyond mere instrumental and strategic aspects, as illustrated in Chapter 2. This is a crucial point for explaining aid allocation in Egypt during Morsi's presidency and in Palestine, as well as in Somalia under Farmajo (2012–22) and Sudan under al-Bashir (1989–2019) (Donelli & Pericoli, 2024; Pericoli & Donelli, 2024). In absolute terms, the volume of Qatari governmental aid saw substantial growth in 2011 compared to 2010, and this trend has continued to increase. The efforts were aimed at supporting Arab countries in transition during troubled times, particularly Egypt, Syria, Palestine and Libya (Bashir & Abdelsalam, 2021). According to a study conducted by Kharas, based on internal data from the Ministry of Foreign Affairs, the top recipient countries of Qatari foreign development assistance from 2010 to 2012 were Egypt, Syria, Sudan, Tunisia, Palestine and Libya. All these countries shared the emergence of Islamist movements as an alternative to the *status quo*. For instance, in Egypt, during the Morsi era, Qatar allocated a USD 3 billion loan as financial assistance to the government but did not continue to support the country after President Morsi's deposition. However, until 2012, the aid was primarily channelled bilaterally, with a very substantial portion of it (about 40 per cent) provided in response to humanitarian crises (Kharas, 2015).

In late 2011 and early 2012, Qatar advanced two of its most ambitious mediation projects: facilitating unity negotiations between the rival Palestinian factions, Fatah and Hamas, and hosting historic talks between the United States and the Taliban (Barakat, 2014; Barakat, 2019). These efforts leveraged the country's strong traditions of offering refuge to controversial Islamist figures and providing a neutral space for negotiations (Barakat, 2012). In 2013, the Taliban established a diplomatic mission in the Qatari capital. Opened with America's support, the office was created to launch a peace process aimed at ending the American war in Afghanistan. Its goal was to offer a safe environment where international actors could engage directly with the Taliban. Analysing aid flow data from 2013 to 2020, the Qatari government contributed USD 20 million to the Afghan humanitarian crisis, mainly through the Qatar Red Crescent Society (QRCS) and the Afghanistan Humanitarian Fund, the country-based pooled fund established by the Office for the Coordination of Humanitarian Affairs (OCHA) in 2014. Before 2013, OCHA's Financial Tracking Service did not report any contributions from the Qatari government to Afghanistan. This highlights how Qatar's aid and diplomatic efforts in the conflict were tightly interlinked. In the Afghan case, Qatar applied its aid allocation criteria to include non-traditional aid recipients, allowing new interlocutors to be part of its aid policy during the Arab Spring.

In April 2016, Qatar became a participant in the OECD Development Assistance Committee (DAC) as a provider of sustainable concessional finance for development cooperation and humanitarian aid. This enhanced the country's involvement in the international aid landscape and multilateral channels. However, other factors have contributed to the shift in Qatar's foreign aid resource allocation. The Qatari embargo imposed by Saudi Arabia, the UAE, Bahrain and Egypt and the consequent accusation of backing terrorist organisations in the region had an influence on its role as a mediator and donor. Qatar denied these accusations, demanding that the Saudi-led bloc present evidence to the contrary, and refused to shut down the state-sponsored Al Jazeera, citing the right to freedom of the press. Since the start of the crisis, Qatar has taken significant steps to mitigate the impact of the international blockade (Zweiri, Rahman & Kamal, 2021).

Regarding the influence of the Gulf crisis on Qatar's humanitarian sector, the political and economic consequences have garnered much attention, but the effect on the humanitarian sector has been largely overlooked (Barakat, 2019). By focusing the spotlight on Qatar's activities, the blockade increased pressure on Qatari charitable organisations to demonstrate integrity and professionalism. Most Qatari foundations and philanthropic organisations were already active internationally in sectors like humanitarian aid, education, health and infrastructure. As a result of the Gulf crisis, several of these charities closed or scaled back their operations, though Qatar Charity and the QRCS remain major operational actors, and Qatar Foundation continues to play a role as a donor (Barakat, Milton & Elkahlout, 2020). Qatar Foundation is the largest not-for-profit organisation focusing on education, research and community development within the country and abroad (Alkubaisi, 2020). The Education Above All Foundation is the other entity in charge of financing education projects in third countries through the establishment of partnerships with state and non-state actors. Organisations such as the Sheikh Thani bin Abdullah al-Thani Foundation for Humanitarian Services or the Sheikh Eid bin Mohammad al-Thani Charitable Foundation scaled down their operations and restricted their activities mostly within the country.

Between 2016 and 2020, the funding trend remained fairly constant, except for 2017, when there was a noticeable increase in aid allocations. In 2020, Qatar provided USD 629 million, a figure that rose to USD 849 million in 2022 (data collected from QFFD Annual Reports). In terms of sectoral allocation during this period, significant investment was made in the infrastructure sector in 2017, while humanitarian aid steadily grew, starting in 2018 and peaking in 2019 (with 53.3 per cent of total funds allocated to humanitarian response). The primary recipient countries between 2016 and 2020 were Palestine, Syria, Sudan, Somalia and Yemen, particularly concerning humanitarian assistance. In 2021, Palestine (primarily Gaza) remained the top recipient, followed by Yemen, Afghanistan and Somalia.

Therefore, despite the 2017 crisis and the blockade, Qatar's role as a donor withstood both economic and political challenges. It also responded to the accusations of supporting terrorism through its aid interventions. While overall humanitarian contributions declined in 2018, Qatar's funding for response plan operations remained stable between 2016 and 2018 (Barakat et al., 2020).

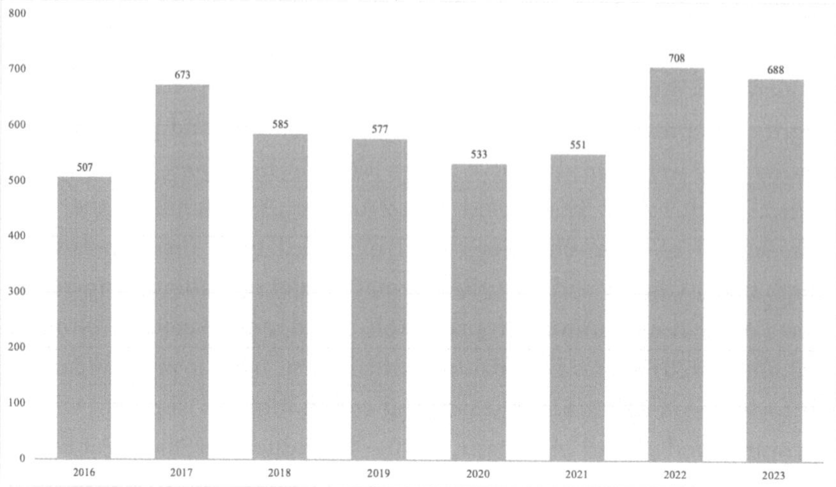

Figure 3.1 Total QFFD contributions from 2016 to 2023. Data for 2023 are preliminary. Source: QFFD Annual Reports.

In 2019, Qatar provided a greater portion of its official development assistance (ODA) bilaterally. Gross bilateral ODA accounted for 88.7 per cent of total ODA, with 4 per cent channelled through multilateral organisations (earmarked contributions) and 7.3 per cent allocated through core multilateral channels. In 2019, Qatar contributed USD 64.1 million in gross ODA to the multilateral system. Of this amount, USD 41.2 million was core multilateral ODA, while non-core contributions were earmarked for specific countries, regions, themes or purposes. Project-type funding earmarked for a specific theme and/or country represented 46 per cent of Qatar's non-core contributions, with the remaining 54 per cent allocated as programmatic funding (for pooled funds and specific-purpose programmes and funds). This trend of increased multilateral allocation continued in 2020, with 16.8 per cent of contributions earmarked and 8.4 per cent allocated through core multilateral channels. The earmarked contributions allow donors to maintain a certain space of decision in terms of resource allocation, maintaining their contributions in multilateral channels. Earmarked contributions (projects-type earmarking) continue to increase with 10.2 per cent in 2021 and 9.8 per cent in 2022. In 2021, the primary contribution remained bilateral (77.6 per cent), compared to 88.7 per cent in 2019 and 74.8 per cent in 2020, with a similar trend confirmed in 2022 (76.6 per cent bilaterally and 23.4 per cent multilaterally) (OECD, 2024).

Regarding recipient countries, Qatar shows consistency in geographical resource allocation, with the West Bank and Gaza, Yemen, Lebanon and Somalia as main aid destinations. The war on Gaza after 7 October 2023 will affect the region irreversibly, especially Gaza itself and the West Bank, and this will influence the efforts of donors like Qatar in terms of humanitarian aid and reconstruction process according to the future scenarios. Qatar's great effort in Gaza started in 2012 with the Reconstruction of Gaza Programme following the 2008–9 war, focusing on infrastructure, education and health sectors. The programme, financed by the QFFD and implemented by the Gaza Reconstruction Committee included roads and infrastructure construction, Sheikh Hamad bin Khalifa Residential City, Sheikh Hamad bin Khalifa al-Amal Residential City, construction of 600 housing units, the H. Sheikh Hamad bin Khalifa Hospital for the Rehabilitation of Artificial Limbs, and support to the Ministry of Public Works and Housing.

Figure 3.2 Lusail Marina Corniche, Qatar, November 2021. Photo by Guillaume Beaud.

The total amount pledged for this programme was USD 407 million disbursed in ten years with further integration into the budget. The Qatari Committee for the Reconstruction of Gaza was established in 2012, to carry out relief and reconstruction works in the Gaza Strip through an 'agency-driven approach' (Elkahlout, 2020).

Qatar's foreign aid policy

The Qatari National Vision (QNV) 2030 and the Third National Development Strategy (2024–30) represent the two main guidelines for the design of foreign aid. The QNV 2030 is based on five main objectives: (1) modernisation and preservation of tradition; (2) balance between the needs of present and future generations; (3) managing growth and uncontrolled expansion; (4) controlling the size and quality of the expatriate labour force and selecting the path of development; (5) promoting economic growth, social development and environmental management. To address these challenges, Qatar's government developed the National Development Strategy 2011–16 (NDS-1), the first comprehensive development strategy in Qatar aimed at achieving the QNV 2030 goals. In a similar vein, the second National Development Strategy (2018–22) (NDS-2) aimed to: sustain economic prosperity through the development of economic infrastructure, economic diversification, private sector growth and management of natural resources; promote human development through a comprehensive and integrated healthcare system, quality education and training, and an efficient and committed workforce; and foster social development through social protection, public security and safety, cultural enrichment and sports excellence. The Third National Development Strategy (2024–30) (NDS-3) recognises the gap between strategy and implementation existing in the two previous strategies, but the way to connect planning, budget and implementation remains vague. Human development and social development are the two main goals which include the effort of Doha as a mediator and donor. The QNV 2030 goals in the area of international cooperation emphasise the importance of

> an increased regional role economically, politically, and culturally, particularly within the framework of the Gulf Cooperation Council, the Arab League,

> the Organisation of Islamic Cooperation, and the UN system and its affiliated entities; [. . .] and contributing towards international peace and security through political initiatives and developmental and humanitarian assistance. (Government Communications Office, 2024)

For this reason, the NDS-2 includes a new chapter on international cooperation ('Global Partnerships for Development'), which aims to strengthen Qatar's regional and international role and status, enhance international partnerships, and contribute actively to regional and international peace and security.

Regarding international efforts, in a commitment to the Sustainable Development Agenda (SDA) 2030, the outcomes and targets of the NDS-2 were aligned with the SDA's goals and targets according to the sectors linked to this agenda. With this alignment, the goals and targets of the global SDA 2030 became a component of the NDS-2. Qatar's International Cooperation Strategy supports the goal of fostering greater economic and social development in low-income countries; aligns with the aforementioned SDA 2030 goals; promotes a global partnership for development to eradicate poverty, reduce inequality and advance economic development and environmental sustainability; and encourages the contribution of all stakeholders, including the private sector, NGOs, charities, academia, research centres and civil society.

QNV 2030 states: 'As a responsible member of the international community, Qatar will contribute to attaining international peace and security through political initiatives and developmental and humanitarian assistance.' Along with humanitarian and development assistance, there is a significant effort in conflict mediation and humanitarian diplomacy. The resolution of armed conflicts reflects a commitment to upholding ethical standards rooted in religious conviction and a dedication to peace and stability. Qatar's commitment to conflict mediation is enshrined in Article 7 of its 2003 Constitution, which states that 'the foreign policy of the State is based on the principle of strengthening international peace and security by encouraging peaceful resolution of international disputes' (Barakat & Milton, 2019).

Despite efforts in mediation remaining a strong component of the Qatari strategy, collaboration with regional organisations and regional cooperation, in general, remain limited. Additionally, while multilateral contributions have increased since 2019, they are still relatively modest compared to bilateral aid. This allows Qatar to maintain its autonomy and identity in foreign aid strategies, while core and earmarked contributions in multilateral channels provide it with the space to operate in collaboration with international organisations such as UN agencies (such as the World Food Programme, UNDP and OCHA). Therefore, these strategic documents should be considered general guidelines, with budgets and operations decided annually or according to emergencies and political priorities.

The institutional architecture of foreign aid

Observing the institutional architecture, the Department of International Cooperation, part of the Ministry of Foreign Affairs (MOFA), is responsible for promoting both bilateral and multilateral cooperation, working with other countries and collaborating with international and regional organisations to implement the ministry's development policy. Within this department, the Qatar Fund for Development (QFFD) was established by Law No. 19 of 2002, and Article 4 outlines its aim: 'The Fund shall aim at helping Arab countries and other developing countries to develop their economies and implement development programmes according to the rules established by the Council of Ministers upon the proposal of the Council.' The chairman of the board is the minister of foreign affairs, and the QFFD's vision aligns with NDS-3, QNV 2030 and SDA 2030. The decision to establish the institution arose from the intention to reform the aid system and make it more efficient. In practice, the QFFD was meant to assume the executive functions of the Department of International Cooperation and create a strategic framework for Qatari aid (Lestra, 2017). It became the primary public development institution responsible for allocating the governmental budget to projects aligned with its core strategy, which focuses on four main sectors: education, health, infrastructural development, and economic empowerment and humanitarian response. The humanitarian sector is primarily financed through the QFFD and implemented by charities, though in urgent cases, the minister of foreign affairs directly manages interventions during crises through other channels, such as international NGOs or UN agencies. The fund is committed to maintaining both predictability and flexibility in financing development and humanitarian interventions. Its mission is built around four strategic objectives: (a) providing humanitarian assistance to vulnerable communities during crises, (b) focusing on the four main sectors listed above, (c) strengthening partnerships with international donors to avoid duplication of efforts and enhance the impact of development and humanitarian funding, and (d) contributing to the Sustainable Development Goals and improving expertise to reduce the fragmentation of aid within Qatar's national context. Additionally, the QFFD is responsible for the monitoring and evaluation of projects both during and after their implementation.

Since its legal establishment in 2002, the process of structuring the QFFD encountered slowdowns and obstacles before its complete independence from MOFA. The institution was created to complement, rather than supersede, existing entities. The QFFD faced difficulties in operating within this fragmented environment. It was established in a context of state administration that was assumed to be centralised but, instead, was built upon a para-public charitable sector with various actors (Lestra, 2017). In 2015, the QFFD was transformed into an independent implementing agency with a strategy aimed at improving alignment with Qatar's organisations involved in foreign aid, including NGOs (of which there were around fourteen in 2015) and MOFA, which allocates funds for aid to foreign countries. One of the main goals of the QFFD was to bring together all parties involved in foreign aid under a unified vision and provide coordination among different actors, thus avoiding the fragmentation that characterised Qatari foreign aid before 2015, and filling the gap of institutional capacity.

Regarding the proliferation of objectives and recipients, since 2015, the QFFD has tried to concentrate more resources in fewer countries, with 85 per cent mostly allocated to eight countries. However, through partnership agreements, and governmental and non-governmental support, a large number of countries received Qatari aid in the form of grants and loans (seventy-eight in 2020 and sixty in 2022 according to annual reports). The QFFD has two main separate budget sections: one for humanitarian emergencies and one for development aid. In the approval process for funds and programmes in the development sector, sustainability is a key factor in decision-making and evaluation. One of the elements regarding sustainability is related to the identification of an 'owner' of the project beyond the project's life. Ownership can be handed over to an INGO, government or private sector agency to ensure the continuity of the project after its implementation.

Together with coordination and financing, the QFFD has the aim of monitoring projects during their implementation and evaluating their results once the projects are concluded. 'Before the creation of the QFFD, Qatar was doing a lot in terms of aid, a lot of money was spent, but little was reported and little was measured in terms of impact'.[1] This component of monitoring and evaluation is crucial for two main reasons: the improvement of aid efficiency and implementation, and also the image of Qatar as a donor in the international arena, where the evaluation of projects and funding can demonstrate how money is spent and how aid is truly impacting beneficiaries. The result of the monitoring and evaluation process is the impact assessment, which measures the results of the project at the economic, social and environmental levels, triangulating these three aspects to assess the project's success.

The Regulatory Authority for Charitable Activities

The second independent institution is the Regulatory Authority for Charitable Activities (RACA), created in 2014 (when QFFD started becoming independent from MOFA) by Emiri Decree No. 43 to improve coordination and enhance control over charitable operations. The authority is tasked with developing, supporting, encouraging, regulating and supervising charitable activities carried out by organisations in Qatar. Under the Regulation of Charitable Activities Law, all charities are monitored and must report to RACA. The law subjects the following to the supervision and control of RACA: charitable associations and institutions that existed at the time this law came into force, or those registered according to its provisions; other entities authorised to initiate charitable or humanitarian activities following this law; and individuals authorised to raise donations or carry out financial transfers for charitable or humanitarian purposes.

RACA is responsible for registering charities in Qatar, monitoring their work, maintaining records and overseeing financial control. All charitable associations and institutions are subject to rigorous audits and transparent accountability processes by RACA. In addition, individuals or entities involved in charity work must meet several legal requirements when establishing or operating a charity. RACA also has the authority to dissolve a charity if an individual or organisation violates the law. Moreover, the law prohibits any fundraising or foreign transfers for charitable or humanitarian purposes unless the charity has obtained prior authorisation from RACA (for a specific purpose and defined period). Under Circular No. (06) of 2020, there are fourteen organisations in the field of charitable activities under RACA, with the main two operating both within Qatar and abroad for humanitarian and development interventions: Qatar Charity and the Qatar Red Crescent Society.

Despite the existing regulations for monitoring and controlling the flow of funds to and from the country, the issue of the *hawala* system and cash transit remains unresolved. *Hawala* (an Arabic term meaning 'debt transfer') is one of many systems referred to as informal funds transfers (IFTs). These systems operate across various regions to transfer funds both domestically and internationally. *Hawala* differs from other IFTs in its reliance on strong religious and cultural beliefs. New technologies have sped up and streamlined the transfer of funds, further modifying the traditional *hawala* system and making private donations abroad difficult to track. A contemporary example of a *hawala* transfer might unfold as follows: the *hawala* agent receives money from a client, along with a commission fee (typically around 5 per cent), and provides the client with a code, often a random word or phrase from the Quran. The agent then contacts a partner in the recipient's area, shares the code and notifies them of the amount being transferred. The receiving agent then contacts the *hawala* dealer in their area, shares the code and releases the payment. At this point, all parties destroy any paper records that indicate the codes or transaction amounts. (In rare cases, paper records are kept, but in coded forms that only the dealer can decipher.) This leaves no paper trail of the transaction. *Hawaladars* (*hawala* dealers) typically settle any discrepancies in balances using a 'two-pot' system, where monetary exchanges continue as usual between partners unless there is an unusually high transfer request or an outstanding debt. At that point, goods such as gold or art, instead of cash, may be sent to settle the debt. The use of commodities makes it especially difficult for authorities to trace the goods back to their original financial transactions. The increasing prominence and globalisation of these transfers also poses greater challenges in tracking and regulating them (Razavy, 2005). This issue is particularly pronounced in Qatar, where the demographic composition (87.3 per cent non-nationals in 2018) (GLMM, n.d.) makes the system more likely to be used for money transfers among immigrants and non-nationals. Although Law No. 28 of 2002 aimed to regulate financial institutions and activities in Qatar to combat money-laundering, the semi-informal nature of the *hawala* system remains difficult to control.

Charitable organisations in Qatar

In Qatar, Law No. 2 of 1974 on the Establishment of Associations was the first law issued to regulate charitable work. It was amended by Law No. 15 of 2014, which regulates today's charitable activities. RACA differentiates implementing agencies which operate in the country and abroad into two categories: charities and private charitable foundations mostly related to the members of the al-Thani family. In 2022, the total number of charities and charitable foundations was fourteen, with Qatar Charity and the QRCS the main implementing agencies in third countries. Education Above All can be considered as a foundation operating in third countries (fifty-nine countries in 2024) through local partners in the education sector. It was created by Sheikha Moza bint Nasser, mother of the current Emir of the State of Qatar.

Qatar Red Crescent Society

Established in March 1978 as Qatar's first volunteer-based charitable organisation, the Qatar Red Crescent Society aims to assist and empower vulnerable individuals and communities inside and outside the country. It was registered with the Ministry of Labor and Social Affairs on 27 August 1981. The president of the organisation is Sheikh Abdullah bin Thamer al-Thani, a member of the al-Thani family. Despite the leadership being primarily Qatari, many of the employees are non-nationals. The QRCS is an active member of the International Red Cross and Red Crescent Movement, which includes the International Committee of the Red Cross, the International Federation of Red Cross and Red Crescent Societies, and a network of national societies across 193 countries. It is also a member of several regional and Islamic organisations, including the Islamic Committee of the International Crescent and the Arab Red Crescent and Red Cross Organization.

The QRCS's core mission is to provide a wide range of relief and development services both locally and internationally, leveraging its resourceful and specialist staff and volunteers. Throughout its long history, the QRCS has served as an auxiliary to the State of Qatar in its humanitarian efforts. In terms of strategy, it aligns with the Vision of the International Red Cross and Red Crescent Movement. It also ensures that its strategy is in line with QNV 2030, as well as the national strategies of the countries it serves. Additionally, the QRCS has a strategy for local interventions in Qatar and a strategy for international aid, both regulated by RACA.

The QRCS's core operations focus on health interventions (60 per cent), which include capacity-building initiatives and the provision of health services. The second major sector of intervention is water, sanitation and hygiene (WASH), which accounts for 20 per cent. The third sector is food security, also comprising 20 per cent, aimed at responding to urgent humanitarian needs and livelihood crises. Occasionally, the QRCS also provides educational support, such as in the case of Afghanistan, based on needs assessments and the specific requirements of the recipient country and the International Red Cross and Red Crescent Movement.

Regarding the source of funding, the largest portion (70 per cent) comes from public donations, which include individual donations, private corporations and some governmental institutions, such as the Ministry of Awqaf (*zakat* and *waqf* funds) and the Ministry of Health. If *zakat* comes from the government, it can only be used to finance projects within Qatar. The use of *zakat* is not tied to a specific programme but is allocated based on needs assessments conducted in the country. The funds are placed in the budget line according to the eligibility criteria for *zakat* usage. In other words, in multi-donor programmes, *zakat* is allocated following the conditions set by each donor, as well as the eligibility criteria associated with *zakat*. *Zakat* represents a secure source of funding for the QRCS, and, unlike government *zakat* funds, it can be used for interventions in third countries (after approval by RACA). For this reason, *zakat* is often used for rapid-response activities, such as food distribution and the provision of medical services. This enables the QRCS to address urgent needs in the affected populations.

The QRCS collaborates extensively with national and international organisations. It typically formalises partnerships through memoranda of understanding (MoUs) with the countries in which it operates. In some countries, the QRCS has established local offices and works closely with international organisations and civil society groups. However, the process of establishing partnerships is often lengthy and complex, requiring approval from the Qatari government.

In terms of its relationship with Qatari governmental institutions, the Qatar Fund for Development (QFFD) is the QRCS's primary institutional donor. There is no direct relationship with MOFA; their interactions are limited to Qatar's overall strategy in countries where the QRCS works (country-based strategy), which is implemented through Qatari embassies in those countries. One of the main challenges the QRCS faces in its dealings with Qatari institutions is navigating governmental decisions, particularly in countries experiencing political instability. The QRCS's operations are closely linked to Qatar's political stance in the regions where it operates, and it must adapt its interventions in line with the country's political priorities. This dependence on political considerations can sometimes limit the organisation's ability to respond quickly, especially during humanitarian crises.

Moreover, the humanitarian sector in Qatar is relatively new, and there are challenges in managing the relationship between institutional and non-governmental actors. The approval process and financial support by RACA have been subjects of internal debate. While the project approval process was modified in 2020 and is now faster than before, other bureaucratic challenges persist. For instance, partnership approval from RACA remains a lengthy and complicated process, which hampers the work of implementing organisations, especially during emergencies (for example in Sudan or Syria). Partnerships are crucial during the capacity-building phase and for follow-up at the end of a project. However, the bureaucratic restrictions imposed by RACA can undermine the sustainability and implementation of field projects. At the same time, RACA lacks the means to monitor the activities of NGOs on the ground.

A key problem is the absence of a sustainable aid strategy at the governmental level, a concern also highlighted by experts at the QFFD. In some cases, particularly in volatile or conflict-affected areas, the QRCS must align with the political stance of MOFA and RACA in the country where it is operating, which can detach interventions from the actual needs of the population. In such changing contexts, RACA may suspend financial support for programmes due to shifting political circumstances, which can have negative consequences on emergency responses, programme effectiveness and the reputation of organisations in the field.

Additionally, the process of coordination between RACA as a regulatory body and charities is still ongoing. Within the QRCS, the communications unit is responsible for reporting information to RACA and coordinating the organisation's interventions. However, this dialogue needs to be more closely tied to the programming and implementation units. The QRCS, as an implementing agency, needs to be able to respond to emergencies independently and with flexibility, using its funds to cover humanitarian needs as they arise. At present, the limitation of using only 10 per cent of public donations for indirect costs is insufficient to support the organisation's operational structure. The financial system, which has been undergoing transformation and scrutiny, remains a challenge in Qatar's charitable sector.

Qatar Charity

Qatar Charity (QC) was originally established in 1992 as the Qatar Charitable Society. It is the largest Qatar-based humanitarian organisation, with a global reach in Asia, Africa and Europe. QC implements development and humanitarian projects, and mobilises support and resources with specific objectives: providing a decent life for children and their families, alleviating the suffering of those affected by crises, contributing to inclusive and sustainable development, promoting peace and social cohesion, and promoting social development and charitable giving within the State of Qatar. The main sectors in which QC is involved include social welfare, water and sanitation, education, nutrition and economic empowerment. According to the 2019 Financial Report, QC has twenty-four branches worldwide.

Regarding sources of funding, 90 per cent of QC's income comes from individual donations, including *zakat* and *sadaqa*. There is no direct link between the Ministry of Awqaf and the organisation in *zakat* collection and management. The collaboration between UN agencies and local grassroots organisations remains a pillar of QC's strategy, enabling a more coordinated and integrated approach. This collaboration is carried out in three main ways: co-funding, funding or receiving funds. In the case of recipient countries,

QC has an MoU with the government in each country in which it operates, establishing the institutional relationship between the organisation and the respective country.

As highlighted by the QRCS, the financial aspect remains a significant limitation in Qatar's charitable sector. A key issue is the financial transaction process for project financing, which requires control and approval from RACA. Additionally, the lengthy process for obtaining licences to sign agreements or open new offices poses an obstacle to these organisations working in new contexts. The challenging relationship with RACA is a consequence of Doha's attempt to institutionalise aid through Law No. 15 of 2014. This law regulates aspects related to the registration and licensing of aid organisations and the collection of donations, ensures transparent reporting of overseas activities, and sets mechanisms for transferring funds to recipient countries and partners. It focuses on aid organisations and establishes strict procedures for their operations in the development and foreign aid sectors. This law is seen as a significant milestone in Qatar's foreign aid policy, especially concerning the non-governmental component of Qatari foreign aid and efforts to combat terrorism. It provides a solid foundation for the State of Qatar to reduce allegations of terrorism related to its organisations and aid funds (Bashir & Abdelsalam, 2021). From the implementing agency's perspective, however, this regulation is viewed as an obstacle to its work on the ground. As previously noted, the system is evolving, and the alignment between the government's political needs and the implementation of aid through charities remains a topic of internal institutional debate.

Zakat *management for aid and welfare*

Regarding the financial aspect of aid, Qatar is working to differentiate financing instruments for aid and implement anticipatory financing to improve disaster governance before a crisis occurs. The aim is to invest funds in disaster risk reduction (DRR) and minimise the impact of both natural and man-made disasters. The DRR department is part of the humanitarian response team, while the Department of Financial Products is responsible for developing new funding mechanisms, including microfinance. In terms of Islamic instruments, the QFFD does not have direct access to those funds, and there is no relationship between the fund and the Ministry of Awqaf and Islamic

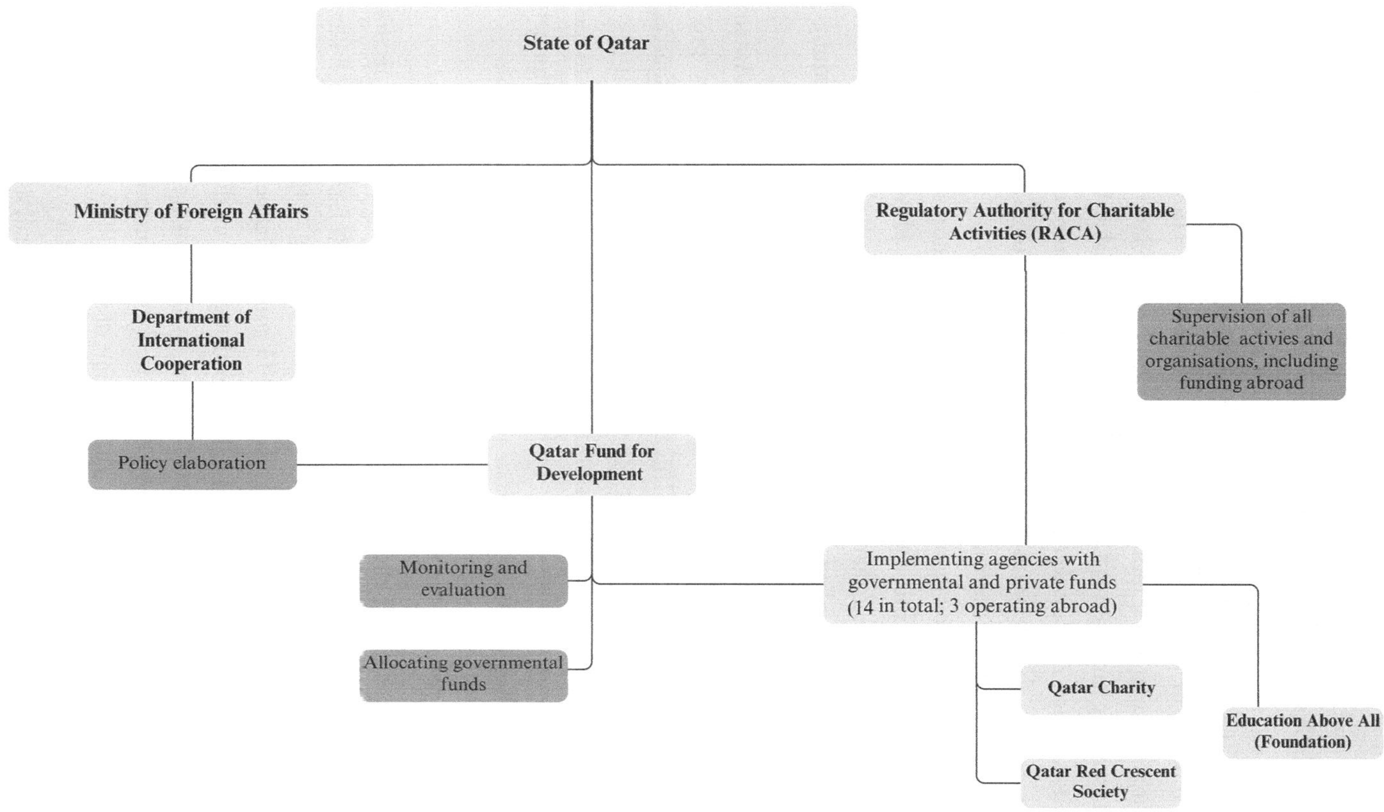

Figure 3.3 Qatari institutional aid structure.

Affairs for coordinating *zakat*, *waqf* or *sadaqa*. In this financial context, the partnership between the QFFD and the IsDB is particularly noteworthy, as they collaborate on various initiatives. For example, the Lives and Livelihoods Fund represents a joint initiative with both Western and Arab donors, in which the QFFD and the ADFD have participated since 2016.

However, in terms of Islamic instruments, *zakat* collection in Qatar occurs in three different ways: individually – through family relations of Qatari residents sending funds abroad, through the state via the Zakat Fund, or through charities. Since 2017, *zakat* management has come under extensive government control due to accusations that Qatari funds, including *zakat*, were being used to support terrorism (Alkahlout, 2023).

Zakat received directly by charities from private donors is used to finance programmes both within Qatar and in third countries. However, all projects established under the Zakat Fund must be approved by RACA, and projects abroad are officially linked to the State of Qatar, balancing religious requirements with political considerations.

On the other hand, *zakat* collected by the state is managed by the Awqaf Ministry, which uses *zakat* and religious donations to finance welfare programmes primarily within Qatar. This aspect is connected to the tribal-resources paradigm discussed in Chapter 2. Through this mechanism, the central government seeks to define and control the limits of resource expenditure in the country, to improve social welfare. In this context, *zakat* becomes an additional source of funding for the rentier state to provide services to its population.

The path forward: a system in transition

In 2021, six years after the QFFD began operations, one of the most recurrent discussions among bureaucrats and charity employees regarding the internal structure of aid in the country focused on building better coordination and dialogue between the MOFA, the QFFD and charitable organisations – particularly Qatar Charity and the QRCS –through the mediation of RACA. This highlights how the institutional process is still evolving in the country, with potential changes and improvements to the aid bureaucracy, especially in terms of internal coordination. The creation of the QFFD has significantly reshaped the image and structure of aid both within Qatar and abroad. However, some weaknesses and challenges emerge from the analysis of this donor.

The first issue concerns fragmentation and proliferation. Fragmentation refers to the various actors involved in aid bureaucracy and strategy, while proliferation concerns objectives and recipients (Lestra, 2017). In terms of fragmentation, the number of charities in the Qatari aid space has remained unchanged since the establishment of the QFFD and RACA (with fourteen organisations registered by RACA in 2024). However, both institutions centralise the coordination of their activities, and, particularly since 2017, QC and the QRCS have become the most active implementing organisations in third countries. Therefore, although the number of actors remains the same, the new regulatory framework probably prevents the creation of new agencies and concentrates the majority of efforts abroad on two main implementing bodies.

Regarding proliferation, it is generally considered to hinder aid efficiency, as it assumes that the more dispersed the aid a donor provides, the less likely the donor will act efficiently (Bürcky, 2011). The QFFD aimed to address proliferation, reducing the number of objectives and countries for resource allocation. As emerged during an interview with a QFFD employee, 'we wanted to focus our support on specific parts of the world to make a meaningful impact, rather than simply distributing support and funding, which could jeopardise resources'. When examining the number of targeted areas, a small group of countries receive the majority of resources, with some variation over the years but consistent top recipients, such as Gaza and the West Bank. However, according to annual reports, Qatar covers several countries through foreign aid interventions, either directly or indirectly through partners, confirming the proliferation of objectives and recipients in its strategy.

Despite the institutionalisation of the aid system, the personalistic aspect of the decision-making process still appears to be part of it. Some decisions regarding project implementation and resource allocation across the region result from negotiations between elites in both the donor and recipient contexts, especially when there are strong or well-established relationships between the two. This aspect is linked to a weak needs assessment process before planning and implementation, which can undermine the effectiveness of aid in addressing the actual needs of the targeted community and increase the risk of exposing aid to political influences. The centralisation of the decision-making process by the elite, with limited space for technical considerations and needs assessment, could undermine the effectiveness of aid, responding to perceived needs that align with political objectives, rather than the real needs of the targeted population. This aspect demonstrates why the conceptual framework of the top-down evaluation of foreign aid incorporates both the elite decision-making process and elite relationships in donor and recipient countries as key variables for understanding aid dynamics (see Chapter 2, 'From the Gulf to the Umma'). However, to move in this direction, the QFFD, as an institution, launched a 'needs assessment mission' in 2021, initially in five countries, with plans to expand to five more. The aim was to reduce political decision-making and enhance the technical evaluation and impact of resources through institutionalisation.

Furthermore, at the heart of institutional development is the creation of the Risk and Compliance Department, which is responsible for overseeing partnerships and eligibility criteria, and controlling fraudulent activities to ensure that funds are protected. Most of the Qatar Fund's projects and programmes are implemented in countries where institutional governance, bureaucracy and overall business practices pose significant financial and operational risks. For this reason, the Risk and Compliance Department focuses on monitoring, managing and mitigating these risks to ensure compliance with national and international laws, regulations and best practices. In partnership with RACA, the department has worked in recent years to enhance the accountability and transparency of aid transactions.

However, the attempt to centralise and control the aid system and implementing agencies in the country has had both positive and negative implications. The first concerns the relationship between RACA and local charities. The coordination and control by RACA aim to improve the internal management of various actors and their aid activities abroad, while also enhancing efficiency, particularly during crises. This includes reducing the overlap of efforts and facilitating the work of charities on the ground. The control over funding and aid activities implemented by charities could, however, create obstacles to flexible implementation. That said, the rapid and ongoing transformation of institutional capacities – and the existing constructive dialogue among different actors in the system – enables institutions and implementing agencies to shape the aid structure within a space still dominated by the government's political agenda in the decision-making process.

United Arab Emirates Aid Structure: Decentralising Implementation to Optimise Interests

Compared to Qatar, the UAE exhibits different features in terms of aid structure and resource allocation, which have characterised the country as a key donor in the MENA region and the Horn of Africa.

Historical evolution of the UAE as a donor

The UAE was established as an independent state in 1971 and the volume of foreign aid started increasing in line with fluctuations in oil prices during 1973–4, contributing to the support of Arab countries and Muslim communities. Since then, both governmental and non-governmental institutions and charities have proliferated in the country (Almezaini, 2017). From 1973 to 1978, UAE aid represented an average of 4.8 per cent of GNI (justified by the rapid rise in oil prices), and 1.5 per cent from 1974 to 1994.

As noted earlier in the discussion of the Qatari aid strategy, the Arab uprisings marked a turning point in the aid policies of Gulf countries, including the UAE. After 2011, with changes in the regional order, aid allocation became increasingly politicised and tied to strategic alliances in the region. In contrast to Qatar, the UAE viewed the Muslim Brotherhood as a threat to both domestic and regional stability. Since the 1990s, the UAE has sought to limit the number of immigrants and expatriates with links to the Brotherhood, and the spread of this movement prompted a securitisation of its foreign policy. In 2013, after the Egyptian military ousted Islamist president Mohamed Morsi, the UAE offered USD 3 billion to support Egypt's economy, in a package that included a USD 1 billion grant and a USD 2 billion loan (Almezaini, 2017). This illustrates how the UAE's aid was intended not only to support Egypt's stability under the al-Sisi regime but also to counter the influence of the Muslim Brotherhood.

Starting in 2011, alongside its development aid, the UAE significantly increased its humanitarian aid efforts. In 2013, the UAE provided USD 90 million for humanitarian emergencies, and the annual rate of official development assistance (ODA) increased by 113 per cent that same year. A large portion of this aid was geographically allocated to Yemen and Egypt, where the UAE, initially in alignment with Saudi foreign policy, took advantage of specific windows of opportunity to stabilise ideologically aligned governments (Cochrane, 2021).

In 2015, development aid to Egypt declined in favour of countries in the Horn of Africa such as Somalia and Sudan (Donelli & Pericoli, 2024), as well as to multilateral organisations and multi-country programmes that combined both development and humanitarian aid (Gökalp, 2020). At the same time, foreign aid to Yemen increased steadily, while Jordan and Syria also received substantial aid. About 82 per cent of the UAE's humanitarian aid in 2018 was directed to these three countries, according to the foreign aid report published by the UAE Ministry of Foreign Affairs and International Cooperation (MOFAIC).

In Yemen, since 2015, the UAE has been part of the regional coalition in the ongoing war and has become one of its largest humanitarian donors, providing financial and technical assistance. In April 2015, the UAE, along with Saudi Arabia and other regional coalition forces, decided to intervene militarily against the Houthi rebels. Successively, the UAE empowered new actors in the conflict such as the Southern Transitional Council (STC) and the National Resistance Movement, influencing the dynamics of control in certain parts of Yemen (Elayah & al-Awami, 2024) and increasing the fragmentation within the coalition (Brehony, 2020). The military involvement was accompanied by a consistent allocation of aid resources in the country as top recipient of the UAE's ODA from 2018 (OECD, 2020).

Starting in 2011, alongside its development aid, the UAE significantly increased its humanitarian aid efforts. In 2013, the UAE provided USD 90 million for humanitarian emergencies, and the annual rate of official development assistance (ODA) increased by 113 per cent that same year. Overall, humanitarian assistance has shown a marginal but growing trend in resource allocation. In 2018, 36 per cent of total bilateral ODA was allocated to fragile and conflict-affected contexts, although this proportion decreased to 22 per cent in 2019. Compared to Qatar, the amount of resources allocated to humanitarian interventions is higher for the UAE in absolute terms. However, when observing aid dedicated to humanitarian assistance as a percentage of the total, Qatar's effort is much more significant (53 per cent in 2019, and this trend continued to grow until 2022). Therefore, despite the increase in resources, the UAE continues to be characterised by its development priorities.

Humanitarian interventions in the UAE are directly coordinated and financed by MOFAIC, with a notable correlation with military and security operations in terms of geographical allocation. Much of the relief assistance is coordinated through Dubai Humanitarian (DH), founded in 2003 by Sheikh Mohammed bin Rashid al-Maktoum through the merger of Dubai Aid City and Dubai Humanitarian City. It is the largest humanitarian logistics hub in the world and a free-zone authority. DH hosts UN agencies, NGOs and commercial firms involved in the management, storage and global distribution of aid (Ziadah, 2019). It can respond to crises by providing the essential logistics infrastructure, facilities and services that enable international humanitarian organisations to fulfil their objectives worldwide. In addition, DH plays a pivotal role in facilitating efficient first responses to crises on a global scale. DH was founded as a global humanitarian aid hub with a mandate to facilitate and develop efforts to provide both local and international humanitarian organisations with logistics facilities and services. The government of Dubai established an independent free zone where DH is based, positioning Dubai as a key player in the international logistics of humanitarian aid (Younis & Sundarakani, 2010).

Beyond the logistical aspects of humanitarian aid, when considering country allocations of aid alongside military expenditure and interventions, a relationship between these two spheres can be observed. The UAE ranks among the top fifteen defence spenders in the world, according to Business Monitor International, and was the fifth-largest arms importer globally between 2009 and 2018, according to the Stockholm International Peace Research Institute (SIPRI, n.d.). UAE defence expenditure as a percentage of GDP has remained comparatively high in recent years. In 2020, the UAE is estimated to have spent USD 19.8 billion on defence, or 5.6 per cent of its GDP, making it the second-largest spender in the region.

In 2019, the top five recipient countries of UAE aid were Yemen, Sudan, Eritrea, Mali and Egypt – all of which had a UAE military presence, underscoring the connection between security and aid interventions. In addition to Yemen, Sudan and Mali, the UAE also operated in humanitarian settings in Jordan, Lebanon and Syria. In some cases, such as the Syrian crisis, the humanitarian response extends regionally, reaching neighbouring countries like Jordan, Iraq, Lebanon and Egypt. The UAE's humanitarian response to the Syrian crisis in Jordan, in particular, accounts for almost 68.9 per cent of the total UAE aid to Syria, reflecting the massive support directed to Syrian refugees in Jordan (UAE MOFAIC, 2019).

Since 2019, the UAE's aid flow has been decreasing in absolute terms, with an inconsistent trend in humanitarian efforts. From 2020 to 2022, general programme assistance, which includes direct budget support and multilateral core and earmarked contributions to multilateral organisations, was the leading sector in terms of resource allocation, followed by health and social services. Along with development assistance, bilateral aid remains a constant trend in the UAE's foreign aid strategy, accounting for around half of the total foreign assistance in this channel (58 per cent in 2020, 41 per cent in 2021 and 56 per cent in 2022). Furthermore, the percentage of resources allocated as earmarked contributions to international organisations is higher than core contributions, as seen in the Qatari case, with a peak of 12 per cent in 2021 (when humanitarian contributions also increased).

In analysing the UAE's role as a donor in the region, its emerging influence in the Horn of Africa – especially in Sudan and Somalia – presents

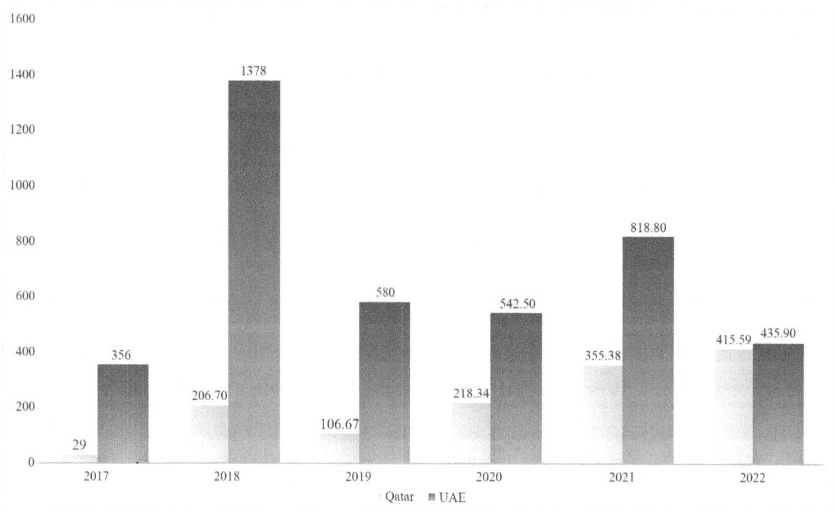

Figure 3.4 Qatar and UAE contributions in humanitarian sector from 2017 to 2022. Source: OECD, QFFD and UAE MOFAIC Annual Reports.

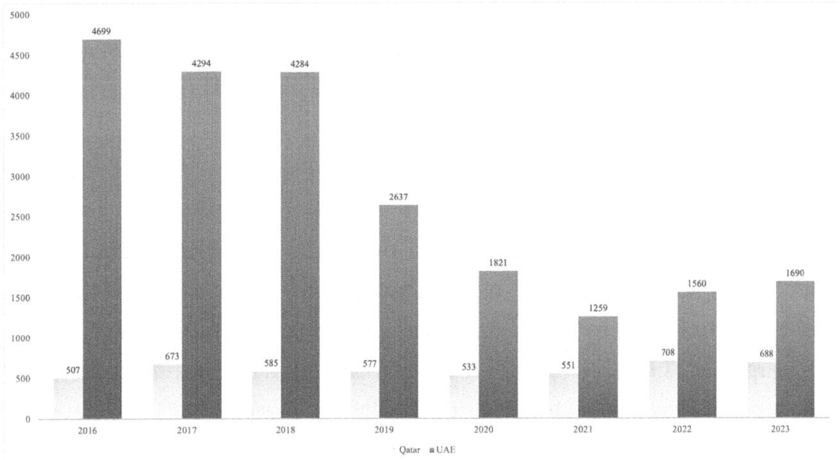

Figure 3.5 Qatar and UAE aid contributions from 2016 to 2023.
Source: OECD country profile data (2024) and QFFD Annual Reports.

an interesting case for evaluation, particularly in comparison with Qatar. The competition between the two countries following the Qatari blockade is especially relevant in the context of Sudan and Somalia, where both the internal and external characteristics of donors and recipients have influenced aid allocation and competition.

Observing the flow of foreign aid to Sudan, the UAE allocates most of its resources to development interventions rather than humanitarian relief. Compared to Qatar, the amount allocated by the UAE to Sudan is higher in absolute terms, with peaks in funding observed in 2016, 2019 and 2020. The decrease in funding in the period 2017–18 was likely related to the neutral position taken by President al-Bashir in the Gulf Cooperation Council crisis. In 2019, Sudan underwent a regime change and entered a transitional period. In response, the UAE increased its foreign aid disbursements in 2019 by more than eight times compared to 2018, reaching USD 543.2 million. In terms of targeted sectors, over 99 per cent of the UAE's foreign aid to Sudan in 2019 was allocated to development sectors, including a contribution of USD 250 million to the Central Bank of Sudan, while the remainder was used for humanitarian and charitable aid. In 2021, however, the total amount provided to Sudan decreased to USD 78.9 million

(100 per cent in grants), with a significant increase in the percentage allocated to humanitarian assistance (27 per cent). The three sectors receiving the most funding were food crop production, social welfare services and emergency health (UAE MOFAIC, 2021).

The shift from development to humanitarian interventions may be linked to the strategy of supporting the transitional government in delivering services and maintaining control over various regional states. Additionally, the aid resources and investments in agriculture and food security might be connected to the UAE's strategy of transforming Sudan into a 'food supplier'. GRAIN (2024), a small international non-profit organisation, reports that two Emirati firms are farming over 50,000 hectares in northern Sudan, with agricultural products being shipped through the Red Sea. In late 2022, Sudan signed a preliminary agreement with the UAE's AD Ports Group and Invictus Investment to build and operate the Abu Amama port and economic zone on the Red Sea, with a USD 6 billion investment. This project, located about 200 kilometres north of Port Sudan, includes a road to connect Abu Amama with the agricultural area of Abu Hamad in Sudan's River Nile state (Reuters, 2022). After 2021, a new military coup and ongoing instability in Sudan led to a reduction in UAE funds (Donelli & Pericoli, 2024).

UAE foreign aid policy

The UAE foreign aid policy is the main document developed by MOFAIC to provide guidelines to all state and non-state actors involved in the aid landscape regarding the main policy directions. Along with the UAE foreign policy, there is a foreign aid strategy, which serves for the technical implementation of these policy directions. The current foreign aid policy (2022–7) is based on four main pillars: (1) to promote regional stability, peace and prosperity; (2) to improve lives and reduce poverty in less fortunate communities; (3) to build closer relations with other nations; and (4) to foster mutually beneficial economic ties with developing countries.

Trade and mutual economic benefits are crucial elements of the foreign aid policy. For developing countries, the UAE has created Country Partnerships for Development, which scale up the asymmetrical relationships between the donor and the recipient, establishing a development agenda based on the recipient country's strategies. The UAE selects partner countries for this programme according to their relevance as potential economic partners, creating 'trading and investment bridges'. This helps the UAE expand its trade space and build relationships one by one with developing countries. Unlike the Western approach, the UAE's economic approach to foreign aid does not involve any conditionality or institutional reforms in recipient countries with fragile or conflict-affected contexts. As stated in its policy document, 'activities are designed in such a way that they strengthen institutions and alleviate conflict, and are vetted to ensure that they do not inadvertently worsen fragile situations' (UAE MOFA, 2022: 12). The modalities of alleviating conflict and strengthening institutions are not described in the document, but the final objective remains the stability and prosperity of the region. Most of the recipients are, indeed, Arab countries, due to the mutual benefits of a stable regional context, security and economic growth, as well as the cultural proximity to these countries, which facilitates interventions and interactions.

The institutional architecture of foreign aid

Regarding the institutional ecosystem of aid in the UAE, the Founding Father of the UAE, Sheikh Zayed bin Sultan al-Nahyan, institutionalised UAE aid as early as 1971, the year the Union was formed, with the creation of the Abu Dhabi Fund for Development (ADFD) as the country's principal development agency. Civil society joined the effort to deliver aid overseas in the late 1970s with the emergence of organisations such as the Dar El Ber Society and the Dubai Charitable Society. The nation's leadership further supported this momentum during the 1980s and 1990s by creating and sponsoring aid organisations and charities in every emirate. These included the Zayed Bin Sultan Al Nahyan Charitable and Humanitarian Foundation, the Khalifa Bin Zayed Al Nahyan Foundation, the Sheikh Mohammed Bin Rashid Al Maktoum Foundation, the Al Maktoum Foundation and Sharjah Charity International among others (Almezaini, 2012).

The creation of the Emirates Red Crescent in 1983, as the country's principal humanitarian agency, was the only attempt to centralise the implementation level. In 2008, the Cabinet of the UAE established the Office for the Coordination of Foreign Aid (OCFA), signifying the government's commitment to supporting the transformation of the UAE's aid sector. OCFA was assigned the responsibility of documenting and coordinating UAE foreign aid, assessing its impact and supporting capacity-building in UAE organisations. In 2013, OCFA's mandate evolved, necessitating the creation of the Ministry of International Cooperation and Development (MICAD), which continued OCFA's responsibilities, in addition to developing the UAE Foreign Assistance Policy. In 2016, MICAD merged with the Ministry of Foreign Affairs to become the Ministry of Foreign Affairs and International Cooperation (MOFAIC). In 2017, the UAE Foreign Assistance Policy was launched to ensure the effectiveness of this assistance.

Within this aid architecture, the ADFD represents a governmental entity responsible for allocating funds for aid according to the policy and strategy. In terms of regulation, the administration of aid remains centralised, with the strategic direction set by MOFAIC. The ADFD maintains autonomy in designing its strategy for financing aid in third countries, which, in the long term, aligns with the general objectives established in the Foreign Assistance Policy. This autonomy provides space for the development of specialised sectors and innovation, particularly in terms of financial tools. In terms of sectors, the ADFD's primary focus is on infrastructural development and renewable energy.

When comparing this institution to the QFFD, several differences emerge. In the case of the ADFD, it is responsible solely for developing and financing development interventions through grants and soft loans, whereas the QFFD has dual mandates in both development and humanitarian interventions. Furthermore, the ADFD has more flexibility than the QFFD in its relationship with its ministry of foreign affairs and has no direct relationship with UAE charities, as the ADFD's main channels are governments (bilaterally) and UN agencies (multilaterally). However, in both countries, aid policy development remains highly centralised. For the case of the UAE, the project is tailored around two main points: the donor strategy and the government recipient strategy. Concerning the coordination level, the work of implementing agencies is controlled and regulated directly by MOFAIC at the federal level, without any intermediary authority between the federal government and implementing organisations or foundations.

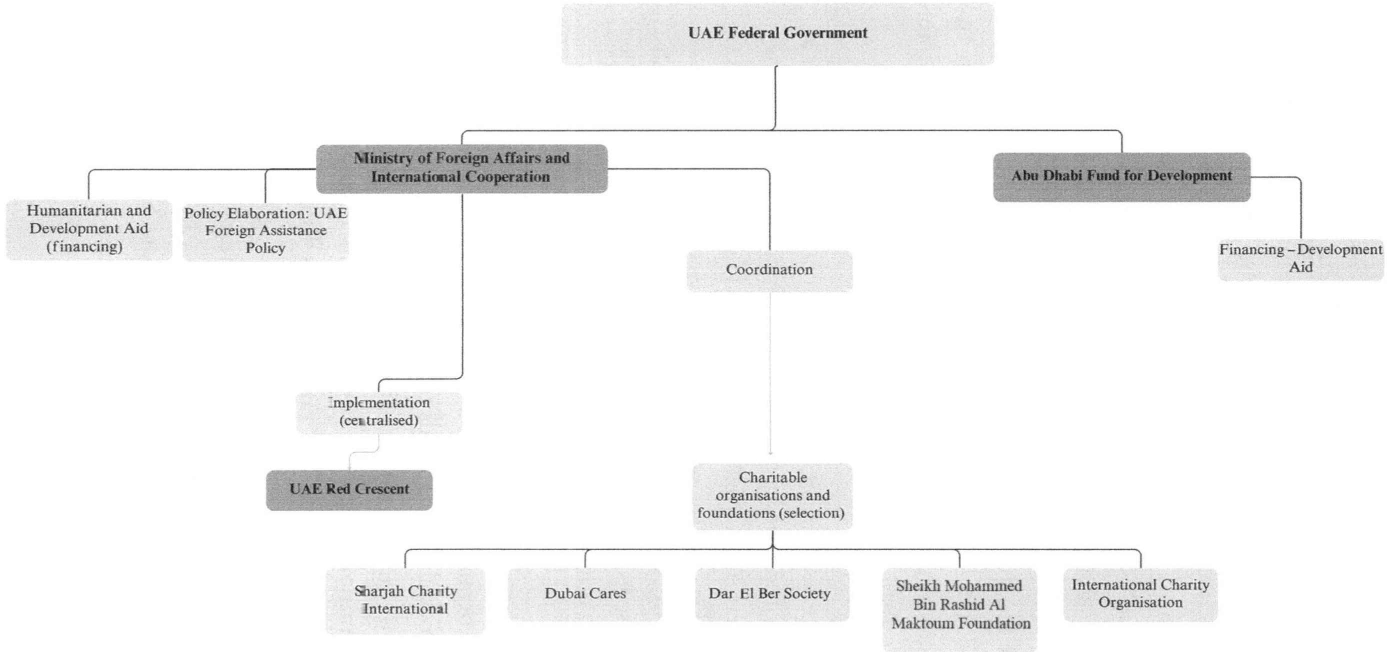

Figure 3.6 UAE institutional aid structure.

Charitable organisations in the UAE

Regarding the implementing agencies of development and humanitarian aid in third countries, the Emirates Red Crescent Authority is the only organisation operating under MOFAIC, while all the other organisations operate under each emirate's law and policy. Regarding federal and local regulations for these organisations, the Federal Council of Ministers recognised 'non-profit' entities through Cabinet Decision No. 41 of 2020, which amended the list of charities annexed to Cabinet Decision No. 55 of 2017. This amendment was an attempt to establish a comprehensive legal and regulatory framework for the third sector in the UAE. In 2008, Federal Law No. 8, concerning public welfare associations, differentiated between two types of 'third sector organisations', public welfare associations and professional associations. Article 2 defines a public welfare association as

> any group that represents an organisation with a continuous capacity for a specified or unspecified period. This association is formed of natural or juristic persons to achieve social, religious, cultural, scientific, educational, professional, female services, creative, or technical activities, or any of the purposes of charity or solidarity, whether through material or moral assistance, or technical expertise. It seeks, in all its activities, to serve the public interest only, without generating material profit.

By contrast, professional associations are defined by Article 1 as 'any group that represents an organisation with a continuous capacity for a specified or unspecified period, allocating funds to achieve any of the purposes mentioned in Article 2 of this law, without aiming for material profit.'

As per the definitions, they are similar in terms of being non-profit organisations and carrying out the same activities listed under the law. While the public welfare association consists of a group pursuing the approved activities, the professional association is created by its founder(s) and is based on the allocation of a sum of money to carry out those activities. Considering this definition, we can differentiate between charitable organisations (or charities as implementing agencies) intended as public welfare associations, and foundations intended as professional associations (funding entities).

However, it should be noted that free zone areas in the UAE, such as Dubai Humanitarian and the Dubai International Financial Centre, are not governed by either federal or local laws (Al Kaabi, Yaaqeib & Bin Touq, 2023).

Table 3.1 UAE Charitable organisations and foundations implementing and/or financing humanitarian and development aid in third countries (selection per relevance in terms of countries and resources). The table does not include organisations operating only within the country for charitable purposes.

Organisation	Emirate	Type of organisation	Year of establishment
Emirates Red Crescent Authority	UAE Federal Government	Charity	1983
Khalifa Bin Zayed Al Nahyan Foundation	Abu Dhabi	Foundation	2007
Zayed Bin Sultan Al Nahyan Charitable and Humanitarian Foundation	Abu Dhabi	Foundation	1992
Sheikh Mohammed Bin Rashid Al Maktoum Foundation	Dubai	Foundation	2007
Mohammed Bin Rashid Al Maktoum Global Initiatives	Dubai	Charity	2015
Al Maktoum Foundation	Dubai	Foundation	2015
Dubai Charity Association	Dubai	Charity	1994
Dubai Cares	Dubai	Charity	2007
Noor Dubai	Dubai	Foundation	2008
Dar El Ber Society	Dubai	Charity	1979
Dubai Humanitarian	Dubai	Independent authority – logistics	2003
Dubai Foundation for Women and Children	Dubai	Foundation	2007
Sharjah Charity International	Sharjah	Charity	1989
International Charity Organisation	Ajman	Charity	1984

Source: UAE MOFAIC and Annual Reports.

Zakat *management for aid and welfare*

The UAE established the Zakat Fund in 2003 to collect *zakat* for internal distribution. In most high-income Muslim countries, including Qatar and the UAE, there is an attempt to centralise *zakat* management, even though it remains in some cases a voluntary donation to the state. Non-governmental institutions are also involved in managing *zakat* and *waqf*, depending on each country's national regulations. Except for Saudi Arabia and Kuwait, all other *zakat* governance bodies are administered by the Ministry of Islamic Affairs.

In terms of services provided to *zakat* payers and beneficiaries, Oman and the UAE are the most advanced and transparent in their governance (Muhammad, 2019). Recognising the importance of online platforms in reaching society across a country, the Bahrain Ministry of Justice and Islamic Affairs, the Oman Zakat Department and the UAE Zakat Fund provide multiple channels for *zakat* payers to contribute, such as online banking and mobile apps through their e-government facilities.

In the UAE, some Islamic banks, such as Dubai Islamic Bank (DIB), act as intermediaries between donors and the government for *zakat* collection and distribution to charitable organisations. The bank evaluates projects and beneficiaries, directly donating *zakat* to activities implemented within the country, particularly in the education and health sectors. The charitable organisations that receive *zakat* from the bank are all accredited by the UAE government, including Mohammed Bin Rashid Al Maktoum Global Initiatives, Emirates Red Crescent and Dubai Cares. In 2020, DIB became a partner of the Community Development Authority and donated *zakat* through the Social Solidarity Fund, contributing USD 2.7 million out of a total of USD 4.3 million donated that year.

Regarding financing mechanisms for aid in third countries, there is no direct relationship between the General Authority of Islamic Affairs or the Zakat Fund and the ADFD. For instance, the ADFD does not use any Islamic social welfare instruments to support aid. Although there are no restrictions on the use of resources such as *zakat* or *waqf*, these funds are generally limited to enhancing social welfare within the country. This is similar to the case in Qatar, where the Ministry of Awqaf does not channel *zakat* to the QFFD for welfare projects abroad. Concerning funds collected by governmental institutions, the Kuwaiti Zakat House is the only one distributing funding abroad, particularly to those affected by conflict.

Some contributions are provided by the ADFD through the IsDB, such as the Lives and Livelihoods Fund (LLF), which collaborates with other Muslim and non-Muslim donors in the form of grants and loans. The LLF is the largest development initiative of its kind in the Middle East and serves thirty-three IsDB member countries. Moreover, in 2021, the IsDB and Dubai Cares committed USD 202.5 million towards the Global Partnership for Education's 2021–5 'Raise Your Hand' financing campaign, with the IsDB pledging USD 200 million and Dubai Cares contributing USD 2.5 million. These pledges – the first from the Middle East region – use innovative financing approaches to help transform education in lower-income countries.[2]

The path forward: security, economy and foreign aid

The observation of the UAE's foreign policy strategies across different contexts, along with the evolution of its characteristics, reveals the factors that guide its policy, with security concerns and threat perception being central drivers (Almezaini, 2024). As Guéraiche (2022) notes, 'security, and more precisely the awareness of potential threats to the federation', has significantly shaped the UAE's behaviour, particularly as a donor state. The rising influence of the Muslim Brotherhood as a political force, potentially capable of dominating revolutionary movements in several countries, prompted the UAE to counterbalance these threats to both its internal security and the regional stability of the status quo after the Arab Spring. This shift marked a pivotal moment in the UAE's foreign policy approach, particularly after 2013. Furthermore, this factor can explain the significant allocation of resources to the Horn of Africa, particularly Sudan and Somalia, Yemen, Egypt and Jordan for bilateral aid, as well as to Yemen, Sudan and Jordan for humanitarian interventions. In 2022, Afghanistan and Ethiopia were added among the main recipients of humanitarian assistance.

Looking at the technical aspects of the aid environment, as with Qatar, needs assessment plays a marginal role compared to political considerations in resource allocation. Additionally, there is no established mechanism for responding to humanitarian crises or adapting to changing contexts. The UAE's aid system lacks flexible and adaptable financing instruments to address crises in fragile and conflict-affected settings, as well as a dedicated unit for coordinating such interventions. However, the rising humanitarian needs in the MENA region and the increase in bilateral ODA allocated to humanitarian interventions highlight the need for strategic regulation and better coordination of UAE aid efforts during emergencies.

Charitable Organisations under Control: Spaces and Limitations

The study of aid, focusing on the donors' strategies, involves multiple levels of analysis. This book is dedicated to the top-down evaluation of foreign aid provided by Qatar and the UAE, examining their internal bureaucratic structures and the variables that influence their behaviours and policies. However, between the top-down formulation of policies and the implementation of aid on the ground, which is marginally part of this book, there exists an intermediate level within this structure: the implementing agencies or charities. These organisations operate on the ground but are embedded within the broader institutional framework and regulated by governmental laws.

As mentioned earlier, charitable organisations and their relationship with the government exhibit distinct characteristics in Qatar and the UAE. In both cases, control over charities and their operations is accompanied by a certain degree of flexibility. There is, indeed, a non-state involvement in foreign aid in the Gulf States that has been shaped in different ways and by different actors. This includes charities and foundations created by the members of the ruling families as well as grassroots and religious organisations, and transnational organisations, some of them rooted in the culture of Islamic humanitarianism. The largest 'private' charitable foundations in GCC states have been established by, or otherwise connected to, members of the ruling families (Coates Ulrichsen, 2024b).

Factions within the ruling elites have created opportunities for the emergence of entities that, while partially autonomous, remain closely linked to prominent figures in each country. This is evident in Saudi Arabia, where internal rivalries among senior princes have allowed for such entities, and in the UAE, due to the decentralised nature of the relationship among the seven emirates. Similarly, in Qatar, the fractured nature of the ruling al-Thani family has facilitated the growth of charitable organisations connected to them. These dynamics highlight how the Gulf's power structures, rentierism and tribal networks can influence the bureaucracy and organisation of foreign aid. However, despite these decentralised origins, all three countries have moved towards centralising foreign aid, as demonstrated by the establishment of RACA in Qatar and the centralisation of foreign aid under MOFAIC in the UAE.

In Qatar, following the establishment of RACA in 2014, the scope for independent charitable organisations to allocate funds abroad or carry out activities has been significantly restricted. Nevertheless, the institutionalisation of dialogue between implementing non-state agencies (charities) and the governmental level (the QFFD and the ministry) has created spaces for negotiation, allowing for advocacy aimed at aligning aid practices with technical needs rather than political objectives. In December 2024, during the Doha Forum, the Center for Conflict and Humanitarian Studies signed an agreement with Qatar Charity to collaborate on scientific research related to humanitarian work (Center for Conflict and Humanitarian Studies, 2024). This partnership highlights the growing cooperation between civil society and non-state actors in the humanitarian field, both during emergencies and for long-term development initiatives. However, increasing government control over charitable organisations has led to a reduction in the number of entities operating abroad, with Qatar Charity and the Qatar Red Crescent Society emerging as the primary implementing agencies. Two prominent non-state organisations – the Eid bin Mohammed Charitable Association and the Sheikh Thani bin Abdullah Foundation for Humanitarian Services – faced significant government pressure, which resulted in a shift towards domestic operations. The Eid charity and the Sheikh Thani bin Abdullah Foundation (RAF) ceased operations abroad entirely (Barakat & Milton, 2019; Coates Ulrichsen, 2024b).

In the UAE, the centralisation of foreign aid was further strengthened by the establishment of MOFAIC in 2016, which enhanced central oversight and control across all levels of the foreign aid sector. Unlike Qatar, the UAE does not have a separate coordinating entity for foreign aid; instead, all charitable organisations are monitored by both the federal government and the individual governments of each emirate.

However, in both countries, the degree of autonomy of these organisations varies, as state control has increasingly been used as a tool for rebranding donors' images and overseeing fundraising activities, as well as managing the allocation of resources abroad. In the UAE, the decentralised federal structure has led to the fragmentation of implementing agencies, with each emirate pursuing distinct political objectives, which, nevertheless, must ultimately align with federal government strategies. In Qatar, ongoing negotiations and dialogue between the government and charitable organisations help mitigate the political connotations of institutionalisation, thereby creating space for greater flexibility in the relationship between the government and implementing agencies in the management of foreign aid.

Conclusion

The institutionalisation of foreign aid in Qatar and the UAE reflects a complex interaction between historical developments, political ideologies and shifting geopolitical dynamics. As this chapter has shown, Qatar's transformation from a modest donor to a key regional and global humanitarian actor is closely linked to its internal political changes and strategic reactions to external events – particularly the Arab Spring and the 2017 Gulf crisis. The development of a more structured aid system, including increased bureaucratisation, professionalisation and alignment with international standards, has strengthened Qatar's dual role as both a humanitarian donor and a diplomatic mediator. Additionally, ideological factors – especially the influence of the Muslim Brotherhood movement – have played a central role in defining the direction and nature of Qatari aid, setting it apart from other Gulf donors. This analysis contributes to a deeper understanding of how these two Gulf states can use foreign aid not only as a tool of soft power but also as a means of building and projecting their identity in the regional and international arena. Qatar's experience highlights the need to consider political, religious and institutional dimensions when analysing aid practices in the Gulf and beyond.

By contrast, the UAE's foreign aid system is based on a dual structure: centralised oversight through federal institutions such as the Ministry of Foreign Affairs and International Cooperation and the Abu Dhabi Fund for Development, combined with decentralised implementation by emirate-specific agencies and foundations. This mixed model allows the UAE to pursue an aid policy that is both flexible and aligned with its broader geopolitical and economic interests. Unlike Qatar's ideologically driven approach, the UAE's aid strategy is shaped primarily by security concerns, economic diplomacy and the goal of regional stability, especially following the Arab Spring. The close link between military involvement and aid distribution, particularly in fragile states like Yemen, Sudan and Somalia, illustrates the securitisation of foreign aid strategies. Although the UAE has increased its humanitarian assistance, development aid remains its primary focus, often used to strengthen trade ties and extend influence.

The differing internal structures and identities of Qatar and the UAE are reflected in their aid policies and implementation in the Syrian context, particularly in light of the distinct positions each country adopted during the conflict. The following chapter is dedicated to the Syrian humanitarian response from the period following the Arab Spring until 2023.

Notes

1. From an interview with a QFFD employee.
2. Islamic Development Bank News (6 April 2021). Retrieved from https://www.isdb.org/news/the-islamic-development-bank-and-dubai-cares-commit-2025-million-to-the-global-partnership-for-education-through-innovative-finance

4

AID AND POWER: QATAR AND UAE RESPONSE IN SYRIA

It was 7 December 2024 when my friend Giulia left Syria with other humanitarian workers, as Hay'at Tahrir al-Sham and other opposition groups gradually moved forward to the capital. On 8 December, Al Jazeera wrote: 'Celebrations in Damascus as Syrian declares end of al-Assad rule' (Al Jazeera, 2024a). At that time, I was completing this chapter, while all the lines and geographical delimitations between Assad-controlled and non-controlled areas did not exist anymore. It was a new beginning for Syria, although the narrative of liberation was not completely convincing for everyone. But there was a fact, the twenty-four-year rule of President Bashar al-Assad had come to an end after thirteen years of war. Despite the changing and volatile dynamics, analysing the management of humanitarian aid and the involvement of Qatar and the UAE as donors was probably more relevant than before for understanding future scenarios and challenges in the country.

The analysis of aid dynamics leads me to several reflections: How did the rebels survive, and in what ways did aid dynamics help them maintain power or expand control? Additionally, what aid dynamics are likely to emerge in the 'new' Syria, considering the inclusion and exclusion of the population from the reconstruction plan under al-Assad's regime and the access to aid in rebel-held areas?

The aim of this chapter is, in part, to explore these dynamics related to the central topic of the book. But we need to take a step back to examine

Figure 4.1 Al-Hamidiyah Suq, old Damascus, November 2024. Photo by Giulia de Cesaris.

the conflict in which aid interventions were implemented, along with the involvement of the Gulf States – particularly Qatar and the UAE – as key actors and donors in the Syrian context.

Foreign Aid and Contested Sovereignty

The Syrian uprising, which began as a peaceful protest movement advocating political reforms and social justice, quickly escalated into a sectarian civil war. Looking at events before December 2024, the military dynamics of the civil war favoured al-Assad's regime, with few attempts at negotiations between the conflicting parties and the regime, as in the case of southern Syria (Al-Jabassini, 2024). Consequently, Syria's early recovery did not follow the typical model of international financial institutions, which are based on comprehensive, nationwide programmes with central planning and management of international funding (Asseburg, 2020).

The Syrian government began planning the reconstruction phase in 2017, focusing its efforts on cementing demographic changes, rewarding loyalty and compensating international allies (Said & Yazigi, 2018). The regime had not undertaken any meaningful processes to address the crimes committed during the conflict, facilitate reconciliation among population groups or implement structural reforms to promote inclusion. These steps were essential not only for rebuilding the country's socio-economic structures but also for reinforcing sovereignty comprehensively.

Many regional and international powers mobilised financial resources to engage in the Syrian conflict, while the humanitarian response remained a secondary priority. Moreover, the Syrian government sought to control aid delivery from Damascus, imposing restrictions on United Nations agencies, the International Committee of the Red Cross and other international organisations authorised to operate in the country. These restrictions often prevent such organisations from freely crossing front lines to reach the most vulnerable populations. Other organisations, unable to operate officially in Syria – including those linked to the Syrian diaspora – began delivering aid across neighbouring borders into areas controlled by opposition groups, without the permission of the Syrian government. No organisations operating in opposition-controlled territories had the authorisation to operate in Assad-controlled areas (Bseiso et al., 2021).

Some studies have explored the relationship between humanitarian aid and sovereignty, particularly how the former can impact state sovereignty – not through conditionality, but from a social cohesion perspective. In their study of the Syrian case, Leenders and Mansour (2018) demonstrate that during the conflict, humanitarian aid, state sovereignty and the maintenance of the authoritarian regime became closely intertwined. The Assad regime, in particular, sought to assert control over UN-led humanitarian aid efforts, which operate in various parts of the country, to prevent aid from reaching areas outside its control. In this way, (contested) sovereignty and external resources became part of the conflict dynamics.

Therefore, a reflection on the concept of sovereignty, both in the Middle East more broadly and in Syria specifically, is necessary to contextualise the control over foreign aid by state and non-state actors during conflicts. There is an ongoing debate about whether sovereignty represents a stable, essential notion or a concept that is more fluid and context-dependent. One widely accepted definition of sovereignty, rooted in early modern Europe, is that it refers to supreme authority within a given territory. Each element of this definition underscores a crucial aspect of the concept. First, the holder of sovereignty possesses authority – not merely coercive power, but the right to command and the right to be obeyed. This 'right' implies that sovereignty derives from a legitimate source of power. The second component, territoriality, specifies that community membership is tied to residence within defined borders. A sovereign state's borders may not necessarily correspond to a 'people' or a 'nation' and may encompass multiple identities, as demonstrated by national self-determination and irredentist movements. It is within these geographic boundaries that modern sovereigns assert supreme authority (Philpott, 2020).

However, given that this definition has been applied and imposed in contexts that may lack the same historical features and prerequisites as European states, it is worth questioning whether this concept is universally applicable. This discrepancy may explain why, in some contexts, the traditional notion of sovereignty may no longer be suitable and may need to be rethought. Following the Arab uprisings, the concept of sovereignty in the Middle East has revealed critical aspects of both fragility and resilience.

The outcomes of the Arab uprisings included destabilisation and challenges not only to regimes but also to the sovereignty and territorial integrity of states. However, according to Fawcett, despite the upheavals of the Arab Spring, the Middle Eastern system of states and borders is likely to remain largely intact in the medium term. This does not imply that these states are strong in a Weberian sense, or that sovereignty at various levels is not contested; rather, it suggests that continuity – specifically the preservation of power and borders – will prevail over major change (Fawcett, 2017). The Arab Spring produced phenomena that went beyond regime change, evolving into multifaceted dynamics where multiple players, both state and non-state actors, as well as regional and extra-regional forces, intervened to support different factions and either rebuild or maintain the regime. The Syrian case exemplified the failure to establish a new, more legitimate and inclusive government, with the old regime emerging victorious in the name of territorial unity in a formal, legal sense. Yet the integrity of Syria's borders, along with sources of internal authority, remains contested and fragmented. This was true before opposition groups took control of the country at the end of 2024, but it is too soon to define which direction this regime change is going to have. The concept of sovereignty has been contested, particularly in its legitimacy and territoriality components. To re-establish control, al-Assad focused on the attributes of 'Westphalian sovereignty', especially territorial integrity. In a 2016 interview, he stated that the primary goal was for the state to 'take control of every part of its land' and pledged that the fight would continue 'until we capture the whole country, Syria gains its independence, and every part of its territory gets liberated' (DanishSyrian, 2016). The restoration of territorial control had, over the years of war, justified the regime's use of violence against both internal and external 'enemies' (Menshawy, 2019).

The modern Syrian state was 'invented' by the post-World War I settlements, with the Ba'athist party, under Hafez al-Assad, solidifying the 'territorial state' for decades. This consolidation involved the construction of a centralised state, based on an administrative, political and security hierarchy (Vignal, 2017). Sovereignty in Syria has served both as a stabiliser and as a legitimiser (Menshawy, 2019). A key feature of the Syrian case was the regime's inability to project state power and assert authority within its borders – central attributes of sovereignty. This incapacity left parts of the country 'governmentally empty', with only the 'state shell' remaining.

The regime's attempt to pursue a centralised system created what Yazigi (2016) describes as a 'legal façade of sovereignty'. This façade served as the foundation upon which both internal and external actors played a role in the potential reconstruction plan of the country. The reconstruction process was shaped through external funding, in the form of either foreign aid or investments, with the regime attempting to steer this process to its advantage.

The legal framework for reconstruction, put in place by the regime, prioritised the strengthening of its power over genuine reconstruction efforts. This framework did not address key issues such as infrastructural damage, the provision of essential social services to war-affected populations or the economic recovery of devastated areas. Instead, it focused on consolidating al-Assad's power and legitimising his position as president of Syria. To achieve this, the regime tried to reward its supporters in the business and military sectors. For instance, loyal business and military figures had been re-engaged in rebuilding damaged infrastructure and had been allowed to acquire confiscated properties at favourable prices (Said & Yazigi, 2018).

Within this legal framework, the Syrian government's reconstruction plan was likely to further entrench the despotic nature of the regime, using reconstruction as a tool to punish or discipline rebellious populations. An illustrative example of this selective and exclusionary reconstruction is Decree No. 66 of 2012, amended in 2018. The decree allowed the Damascus governorate to expel the populations of two large areas in Damascus.

In April 2018, the Syrian government issued Decree No. 10, which expanded upon the earlier decree. In September of the same year, the Damascus Governorate Committee released a report outlining the destruction and planned reconstruction of the Tadamon district in Damascus under the new law. Other areas in Damascus, such as Jobar, Barzeh and Qaboun, were also slated for evaluation for reconstruction under Decree No. 10, a process that was expected to begin in early 2019 (Daher, 2018). It is likely that the law also served as a tool for consolidating both old and new power networks within Syria, potentially leading to shifts in the social and demographic structure of the affected areas (Said & Yazigi, 2018).

An example of these challenges can be found in the returns of internally displaced persons (IDPs) and refugees to their homes. A 2018 study by Costa and Macmillan on the case of Aleppo highlights several barriers that prevented IDPs from safely returning. These barriers included the post-conflict environment and the political imbalance related to the regime's control over the city. Specifically, challenges included issues of physical safety, such as the presence of military and intelligence services, limited transportation options and the fear of checkpoints. Economic limitations further exacerbated the situation, with the destruction of infrastructure, looting of homes and businesses and the collapse of local industry. In addition, there were concerns about persecution, the inadequate scale of reconstruction effort, and the challenges of social reintegration within the city.

Post-conflict Aleppo has seen a significant shift in its social fabric. A clear divide has emerged between those who opposed the regime and those who did not, which had the potential to fuel rising tensions and discriminatory policies. The selective reconstruction of the city has further discouraged many Aleppians from returning (Costa & Macmillan, 2018). This situation illustrates that the issue is not merely one of physical reconstruction but one of sovereignty and control.

The resilience of the Syrian regime had come at a considerable cost – especially in terms of human lives and physical destruction, but also politically. In addition to growing dependence on foreign states and actors, the regime's patrimonial features were strengthened, while its authority diminished. Crony capitalists and militia leaders gained considerable power, while the clientelist, sectarian and tribal characteristics of the regime, particularly its Alawite identity, were reinforced. The war also facilitated the rise of new businessmen closely linked to the regime. In contrast, the majority of Syrian entrepreneurs in the diaspora remained hesitant to return and invest under those conditions (Daher, 2018).

Reconstruction has historically been used as a political tool to re-establish and consolidate political power, often benefiting certain segments of society while economically rewarding individuals allied with the government. Instead of a unified, national reconstruction plan, powerful figures tend to shape reconstruction projects in specific areas of the cities according to their interests. As a result, the process was less focused on recovery and renewal and more on consolidating political power (Aldassouky & Hatahet, 2020).

This had been true until Hay'at Tahrir al-Sham (HTS) took control of Damascus in December 2024, revealing the fragility of al-Assad's sovereignty over Syrian territory and its dependence on external powers for survival. The rebel governance of the non-state armed group, which began in northwest Syria over the civilian population, must now readapt and redesign its strategy to exercise power in the entire country and build its sovereignty in terms of territorial control and both internal and external recognition. The intention of Ahmad al-Sharaa to pursue international legitimacy and external support from the international community is a clear sign of its shift away from jihadism to a more mainstream and less ideological approach to governance (Drevon & Haenni, 2025). However, how HTS consolidates control and reconfigures sovereignty in a fragmented context will depend on many factors, particularly its ability to rebuild the country through inclusion rather than exclusion of all the Syrian groups and minorities.

Aid Management in Government- and Opposition-held Areas

Another important aspect to consider is how aid has been managed differently in government- and opposition-held areas. A study conducted by Meininghaus in 2016 explores how, in intra-state conflict, the presence or absence of humanitarian aid plays a largely unrecognised role in the prospects for post-conflict state-building. In the specific case of Syria, the distribution of aid between government- and opposition-held areas significantly affected population movements and local governance. This factor is particularly relevant when analysing the aid strategies of Qatar and the UAE, which allocated resources according to a geographical dimension, namely aid distributed in relation to the regime's or the opposition's control over territory, as the empirical analysis will show later.

Humanitarian aid in intra-state conflicts has two interdependent effects: it influences population movements, and it shapes local governance processes. Therefore, understanding the availability and modalities of aid provision is crucial – not only for mitigating current risks but also for fostering greater awareness of the long-term consequences of post-conflict reconstruction.

In terms of the official response, humanitarian aid within Syria has been planned, structured and monitored through successive Syrian Humanitarian

Assistance Response Plans (SHARPs) since June 2012. The primary coordinating body on behalf of the UN in this regard is the Office for the Coordination of Humanitarian Affairs (OCHA).

In parallel, Regional Refugee and Resilience Plans (3RPs) were established to address the Syrian refugee crisis in neighbouring countries, each implementing its national response strategy under the guidance of UNHCR. In 2015, SHARP was replaced by the Syria Strategic Response Plan (SRP), following the newly developed Whole of Syria approach, linking internal and external relief operations within a single strategic framework, alongside the 3RPs. SHARP was a joint plan issued by the Syrian government in collaboration with several UN agencies, the International Organization for Migration and international non-governmental organisations (INGOs). However, with the introduction of the SRP, the Syrian government was only mentioned as a source of consultation, marking a shift in the approach.

From the outset, and in line with international humanitarian law, SHARP was committed to respecting national sovereignty. It explicitly stated:

> Humanitarian action will be conducted following UN General Assembly Resolution 46/182 and the Guiding Principles contained in its Annex, under the overall leadership of the Government of the Syrian Arab Republic, and in full respect of the state sovereignty and territorial integrity, alongside the recognised principles of humanity, impartiality, and neutrality.[1]

In this context, SHARP emphasised the prerogatives of the Syrian government in representing and protecting the state, further underlined by its explicit request for humanitarian organisations to assist in 'the rehabilitation and reconstruction of critical infrastructure and vital public services affected by the current events through rapid response'.

By February 2015, the Syrian government under al-Assad and its allied militias controlled only about half of the country. Despite this, the government maintained the authority to regulate aid deliveries across Syria. Administratively, any INGO wishing to operate in Syria had to gain approval from the Syrian authorities – a procedure that existed even before the conflict. INGOs intending to provide relief were required to collaborate closely with the Syrian Arab Red Crescent and coordinate their activities with the relevant

Syrian ministries. Direct support to these ministries formed part of long-term programmes such as the maintenance of water supplies. Moreover, collaboration with local NGOs also required government permission, with Syrian security services continuing to closely monitor civil society activities where possible. In government-controlled areas, the Syrian authorities carefully framed aid distributions as a reflection of their domestic efforts. For example, in February 2014, they claimed at the UN that 'Syrian domestic efforts account for 75 per cent of the humanitarian aid needed by the Syrian people, as opposed to barely 25 per cent provided by international organisations' (Leenders & Mansour, 2018).

In practice, the Syrian government retained the right to determine which geographic areas were accessible to INGOs and had the power to grant or deny visas for every member of staff, based on extensive security checks. Moreover, no organisations operating in regime-controlled areas were allowed to deliver aid across borders into other areas controlled by opposition groups, as these operations were considered a violation of the regime's sovereignty. Given these significant obstacles and the urgent need to reach areas cut off from aid, UN Resolution 2139 was passed in February 2014, calling for the free and safe passage of humanitarian convoys and workers, including to hard-to-reach areas. To facilitate this, a joint committee was established, composed of officials from the Ministry of Foreign Affairs, the Ministry of Social Affairs, security personnel, the Syrian Arab Red Crescent and the United Nations. This committee was tasked with negotiating access to such locations on a case-by-case basis.

In 2013, a coordination system was established to oversee cross-border operations from Türkiye into northern Syria, as part of the annual Syria Humanitarian Response Plan (HRP) across the entire country. The OCHA office responsible for managing these cross-border operations was based in Gaziantep, in southern Türkiye, while the one responsible for operations in territories controlled by the regime was based in Damascus. In 2014, the Syria Cross-Border Humanitarian Fund was created, following UN Resolutions 2139 and 2165. This multi-donor, country-based pooled fund aimed to expand and facilitate humanitarian assistance in Syria. Therefore, in Idlib and northern Aleppo, there were two ways of delivering aid: cross-border (from outside Syria, over the Turkish border) and cross-line (from regime-controlled areas to opposition-controlled ones).

Subsequently, in 2014, UNSC Resolution 2165 allowed cross-border deliveries to require only notification to the Syrian government rather than its prior approval (Global Centre for the Responsibility to Protect, 2014). This provision was extended by Resolutions 2191 and 2258 for another year each. However, deliveries and outreach programmes to opposition-controlled or contested areas, including besieged regions, remained highly sensitive. Requests for access to these areas were often declined or left unanswered, and efforts to protect humanitarian aid workers from attacks continued to be hampered. The Syrian government justified these procedures by asserting that areas under its control were 'safe to access', while characterising territory outside its control as insecure, thus justifying the denial of aid to opposition-held regions. Withholding aid to opposition-held areas became a strategic tool for the Syrian government, aimed at defeating what it termed 'terrorists' – a perspective that conflated the lives of combatants with those of civilians. This strategy tried to force opposition armed groups into submission, without regard for the consequences faced by civilians in these areas. Where local governance structures were in place, aid was often channelled through local administrative councils (LACs) or local coordination committees (LCCs). These bodies emerged in opposition-held areas at the start of the conflict, and their structures, tasks and relationships with armed groups vary widely. In addition to their political and social functions, LACs and LCCs took on a wide range of responsibilities, from documenting the war and organising protests to maintaining basic services like electricity and waste collection, and even distributing exam papers for students in closed schools. Their decision-making processes remain largely informal (Meininghaus, 2016).

In July 2020, the UN Security Council's (UNSC) resolution to extend cross-border operations was reduced from four border crossings to one: Bab al-Hawa (from Türkiye). In July 2022, the UNSC resolution allowing the delivery of humanitarian aid across Türkiye's border into northwest Syria – without the permission of President al-Assad – expired, as diplomats failed to reach a new agreement due to a Russian veto. Russia, which consistently opposed the cross-border aid operation as a violation of Syrian sovereignty, used its veto to block a one-year renewal. The Russian proposal for a six-month extension was also voted down by the United States, the United Kingdom and France. While the UN and its partner NGOs have been significant providers of aid to the northwest, other aid groups, such as the Turkish Red Crescent, also operate in the region.

Due to the complexity, informality and often clandestine nature of aid deliveries in opposition-held areas, comprehensive figures on actual aid flows throughout Syria are unavailable for the period analysed (2015–23). Some of the data available are related to the humanitarian access in each region and sub-region of the country. UN OCHA humanitarian partners produce an Access Severity Overview that measures the impact that humanitarian access constraints have on (a) the ability of humanitarian partners to reach people in need and (b) the ability of people in need to reach humanitarian assistance across the three humanitarian response modalities identified by OCHA: the Humanitarian Country Team, the Humanitarian Liaison Group and the Northeast NGO Forum in all 270 sub-districts of Syria (OCHA, 2024). The Damascus area registered low access severity in 2022 and 2023 and moderate access severity in 2024, while Idlib varied from very high to high access severity in 2022 and 2023 and low access severity in 2024, showing a gradual improvement in aid access in opposition-controlled areas (MDX, n.d.).

Figure 4.2 Two men on a motorcycle with destroyed buildings in the background in Deir ez-Zor, eastern Syria, September 2020. Photo by Giulia de Cesaris.

Aid in northwest Syria: mapping the actors, understanding dynamics

Regarding aid management and distribution in opposition-held areas of northwestern Syria, the two primary institutions responsible for coordinating with donors and overseeing aid after 2018 were the Syrian Salvation Government in Idlib and the Syrian Interim Government in northern Aleppo.

The Syrian Salvation Government

In Idlib, the non-state armed group Hay'at Tahrir al-Sham (HTS), formerly known as Jabhat al-Nusra or the al-Nusra Front, provides a prominent example of local governance in the Middle East following the Arab uprisings. This group was founded by former al-Qaeda commanders who defected from Islamic State in Iraq in 2013. Initially pledging allegiance to al-Qaeda, they later asserted their independence and severed ties with the organisation in July 2016 (Keser & Fakhoury, 2025). In 2016, the movement declared independence from al-Qaeda, rebranding as Jabhat Fateh al-Sham, to survive and concentrate its efforts on the local project of the Syrian opposition. From 2017, the group became Hay'at Tahrir al-Sham and controlled significant areas of Idlib province after a military takeover, which included clashes between itself and other factions such as Ahrar al-Sham and the Nour al-Din Zenki movement in Idlib and western Aleppo from February to April 2018. The fighting concluded in January 2019, leaving HTS with control over much of Idlib (Solomon, 2022).

Before this military consolidation, a form of local governance was established in 2017 as a civilian technocratic administration. The Syrian Salvation Government (SSG) was formed through three primary mechanisms: the centralisation of governance bodies, delegation of authority to an educated urban elite, and outsourcing of specific public services to third parties independent of the formal administrative structure (Drevon & Haenni, 2021). The SSG adopted a top-down approach, with HTS, acknowledging its limited capacity to govern directly, delegating authority to segments of the educated urban elite and outsourcing certain public services. HTS used the creation of an 'independent administration' to facilitate humanitarian aid and international recognition without being officially under HTS control (Drevon, 2024).

In terms of its interaction with aid organisations, the centralised structure of the SSG facilitated coordination between these organisations and the administration, as emerged in an interview with OCHA Gaziantep. In 2022, OCHA coordinated 1,480 camps for IDPs in Idlib province, 80 per cent of which were directly controlled by the SSG, which maintained authority over both the territory and the population.[2]

In Idlib and western Aleppo, the SSG operated through various ministries and sub-entities including the Ministry of Health, which managed healthcare services in collaboration with local NGOs and medical unions; the Ministry of Education, which collaborated with education-focused NGOs; and the Ministry of Local Administration and Services, which coordinated early responses, reconstruction and the relation with humanitarian actors. The SSG established an Emergency Response Committee, a Directorate of Social Welfare and a Directorate of Housing and Reconstruction to manage aid distribution. After the earthquake in February 2023, the Emergency Response Committee launched a public donation campaign and facilitated access to foreign press and humanitarian actors in the areas affected. After that, a new Directorate of Earthquake Victim Affairs was established to oversee the aid distribution (Hatahet, 2023).

The politicisation of HTS and the bureaucratic transformation of rebel governance through the creation of the SSG helped the movement maintain relationships with external actors, including donors, while providing services to the population and working on its image for normalisation and external recognition. In his book *From Jihad to Politics*, Drevon effectively illustrates the evolution of HTS and Ahrar al-Sham from jihadist groups to political actors:

> The choices of armed groups like Ahrar al-Sham and HTS in Syria suggest the existence of other strategic choices, including their potential normalization. These groups' repositionings during the Syrian conflict reveal important social movement dynamics that delineate the conditions in which Jihadi groups can politicize, become more mainstream, and perhaps even start to engage the international community. (Drevon, 2024: 200)

The events following December 2024 indicate that HTS and its leader, Ahmad al-Sharaa (formerly Abu Mohammed al-Jolani), have advanced the movement's transformation, positioning it to play a key role in shaping Syria's post-Assad future.

Figure 4.3 A group of children in rural Aleppo, northern Syria, August 2024. Photo by Giulia de Cesaris.

The Syrian Interim Government

The Syrian Interim Government, by contrast, appeared more decentralised and fragmented than the SSG. The SIG is a Turkish-backed non-state actor that controlled part of northwestern Syria until December 2024. In November 2012, the Syrian National Coalition for Revolutionary and Armed Forces, a coalition of opposition groups formed with the support of international actors, was established. In 2013, it formed the SIG, based in Azaz. The SIG's armed forces consist of the Syrian National Army, the second-largest opposition group after HTS, which was established at the end of 2017 (Adamczyk & Doumit, 2023).

The SIG had an official mandate from the Syrian National Coalition to administer early response and aid assistance through three ministries: Health, Education and Local Governance. These entities oversee healthcare and education services, while local councils manage daily administration within their regions, coordinating with humanitarian actors to assist affected communities. The SIG established mechanisms to regulate aid distribution, one of which is the Humanitarian Relief and Assistance Committee. This committee aimed to coordinate the activities of humanitarian organisations with relevant ministries and to influence decisions through the Health and Education directorates, in partnership with the Syria Recovery Trust Fund.

The Turkish administration of the region, coupled with the competitive struggle for control of the security sector, led to decentralisation, fragmentation and inefficiency within the SIG. Local councils, managed by Turkish provincial governments, operated independently with a lack of coordination, resulting in confusion and a decline in trust among aid organisations. The international community rarely provided direct financial support to the SIG, citing concerns about its capacity to govern effectively and independently, as well as issues surrounding transparency and accountability (Hatahet, 2023).

The Political Involvement of the Gulf States in Syria

The observation of aid distribution in both regime- and opposition-controlled areas provides a general framework for understanding how different donors operated in response to humanitarian needs and recovery programmes, whether within or outside UN coordination mechanisms. The analysis of Qatar and the UAE as donors in Syria has been traced from the understanding of their position in the conflict, to find an answer to one of the questions posed in this book. Specifically, when evaluating the Syrian humanitarian response and considering the inherent political dimensions of aid, do the sectarian approaches to the conflict and the fragmentation of the opposition – shaped by these two external supporters – reflect how Gulf states implement their aid policies?

The post-conflict recovery of Syria provides a case where Qatar and the UAE have pursued different approaches to humanitarian assistance intervention in general. After a decade of war, widespread destruction made reconstruction one of the most debated issues in both academic and policy-making circles. With the sources of foreign financing for reconstruction still uncertain and following the regime change in December 2024, potential investments from the Gulf monarchies could represent a crucial source of funding, shaping the country's infrastructure rebuilding and overall recovery (Daher, 2020).

From a political perspective, Qatar responded to regional opportunities by becoming a key external funder of the Syrian regime's opposition. Saudi Arabia and Qatar funded different groups, which fragmented the armed opposition and created separate structures within it. Saudi Arabia formed the National Coalition for Syrian Revolution and Opposition Forces, while Qatar sponsored the Syrian National Council. In this context, the GCC crisis created obstacles to inter-Gulf coordination in the Syrian crisis (Khatib, 2021).

Riyadh used the uprising to settle geopolitical scores and attempt to topple Bashar al-Assad's regime. Saudi Arabia's determination to reorient Syria away from 'the axis of resistance' and towards the Saudi–US camp evolved into a complex regional and international geopolitical contest. The struggle over Syria thus took on open sectarian connotations, aiming to replace an Alawi regime with a Sunni protégé (Salloukh, 2013). For the first two years, Saudi Arabia and the UAE supported the more secular segments of the opposition, including former Ba'athists like Riad Hijab and Mustafa al-Assad, secular intellectuals such as Michel Kilo (rooted in the Christian community) and secular-leaning representatives of the Free Syrian Army (FSA) like Lu'ay Miqdad. Logistical and military support was primarily directed towards nationalist and secular armed groups, aiming to bypass jihadist factions whose roles in the conflict alarmed both Western and regional powers. It was not until September 2013 that Saudi Arabia began funding Islamist groups, such as Liwa' al-Islam (which later became part of Jaish al-Islam, the Army of Islam) in Damascus and the Army of the Sunnis in Deir ez-Zor. These groups were supported to counter the influence of ultra-radical factions like the Nusra Front (later known as Fatah al-Sham) and ISIS, as well as to potentially create a network of Islamist groups loyal to and dependent on the Saudi regime and unwilling to challenge the region's national borders (Colombo, 2017; Khatib, 2019).

At the macro level, Qatar sought to push for dialogue and mediation among the various groups, continuing its efforts even after the end of 2024, when the rebels took Damascus. Initially, Doha supported other Sunni Islamist groups, challenging the regional positions of the UAE and Saudi

Arabia. However, Qatar was not always opposed to the Syrian regime. The Gulf country had once been a close ally of the al-Assad family, playing a key role in easing Bashar al-Assad's relations with France after the 2005 assassination of Rafiq Hariri in Lebanon (in which the Syrian regime was suspected of involvement). Additionally, Qatar invested heavily in Syria's infrastructure and economy during the 2000s. Following the Arab Spring, however, Qatar became a significant external funder of the opposition and attempted to influence events as the Syrian uprising became increasingly militarised (Khatib, 2019). In March 2013, Qatar inaugurated a new Syrian embassy representing the Syrian opposition and lobbied the Arab League to hand over Syria's seat to the representatives of the opposition. In the northwest, Qatar supported Ahrar al-Sham in cooperation with Türkiye. This decision was based on the group's evolution from a coalition of military brigades into a political movement between 2012 and 2013. During this period, the movement began engaging with international figures, such as US ambassador Robert Ford and other Western diplomats, to become an 'acceptable' recipient of foreign military support. This was particularly important for Qatar, as it did not want to appear to be supporting a listed 'terrorist' group (Drevon, 2024).

Ahrar al-Sham largely originated as an offshoot of the Syrian Islamist Social Movement (ISM). Its strong ties to the ISM played a key role in its growth, allowing it to expand more effectively than other opposition groups that lacked a structured organisation, due to the fragility of Syrian civil society before 2011. This connection to the ISM has influenced Ahrar al-Sham's ideological trajectory and helped shape its decentralised organisational framework, which then constituted a weakness in the process of politicisation. In December 2012, Ahrar al-Sham established the Syrian Islamic Front, which included groups like the Al-Haqq Brigades in Homs, the Al-Fajr Islamic Movement in Aleppo, Ansar al-Sham in Latakia, Jaysh al-Tawhid in Deir ez-Zor and the Hamza ibn Abd al-Muttalib Brigade in Damascus. This alliance paved the way for these groups to later unify, except for the Al-Haqq Brigades, under the banner of the 'Islamic Movement of Ahrar al-Sham'. Ahrar al-Sham explicitly distanced itself from al-Qaeda's legacy, adopting a more inclusive approach towards other groups and the broader population. This strategy played a crucial role in the group's efforts to gain legitimacy and secure external support (Drevon, 2021).

Figure 4.4 Destroyed buildings in the city of Aleppo after the recapture of the area by the Syrian Army from rebel fighters in 2016. Aleppo, October 2019. Photo by Giulia de Cesaris.

Since the onset of the Syrian uprising in mid-March 2011, the UAE has taken a distinct stance on the situation, initially supporting the Syrian opposition while maintaining various ties with the Assad regime in Damascus (Daher, 2019). After Saudi king Abdullah bin Abdulaziz al-Saud condemned al-Assad's 'killing machine' and called for an end to the violence in August 2011, the UAE aligned with other GCC members in denouncing the Syrian regime's actions against protesters by the end of that summer.

In March 2012, along with the other GCC states, the UAE shut down its embassy in Syria and reiterated its support for the 'legitimate aspirations' of the Syrian people to restore security and stability. The UAE also became part of the 'Friends of Syria' coalition at its first meeting in Tunis in February 2012, joining other countries opposed to the Damascus regime. Within Syria's political and armed opposition, the UAE consistently supported figures and factions that were either opposed to or critical of the Muslim Brotherhood's policies. While the UAE's role in supporting the opposition was less significant than that of Saudi Arabia, Qatar and Türkiye, it did provide backing to armed groups – particularly non-Islamist units of the FSA – between 2012 and 2018. These groups were carefully vetted to ensure they were both anti-Brotherhood and anti-jihadist.

However, the UAE's position began to shift in 2018, reflecting a broader regional realignment. In the summer of 2018, the UAE and Bahrain both reopened their embassies in Damascus, signalling a move towards normalising relations with the Assad regime. This shift was influenced by regional dynamics, particularly developments in 2014 and 2015. The UAE's intervention in Libya – supporting the Libyan National Army, led by Khalifa Haftar, with airstrikes against Islamist factions backed by Türkiye and Qatar – played a role in this change. Additionally, the UAE's involvement in the Saudi-led war in Yemen, which began in March 2015, further shaped its foreign policy (Daher, 2019).

Qatari Aid in Syria: Interventions in Opposition-held Areas

Qatar's efforts towards Syria during the years of conflict were characterised by a dual approach, primarily through multilateral channels such as the Humanitarian Response Plan (HRP) and the implementation of projects through Qatar Charity (QC) and the Qatar Red Crescent Society (QRCS). Overall, the major sectors supported from 2015 to 2023 in different parts of the country were food security, education, health and IDP assistance.

In 2015, data available from the OCHA Financial Tracking Service (FTS) showed a modest allocation in the Humanitarian Response Plan (HRP) by Education Above All (USD 1.3 million). However, due to limited funding data in the annual reports and on the OCHA FTS, it is difficult to track funds allocated outside of multilateral channels.

In 2016, the Qatar Fund for Development (QFFD) funded ten projects in Syria, including the Qatari Initiative to Educate and Train Syrian Refugees (QUEST). The initiative was designed as a rapid response to address the urgent educational and training needs of Syrian children and youth displaced by the ongoing crisis. In collaboration with Education Above All, the Sheikh Thani bin Abdullah Foundation for Humanitarian Services, Reach Out to Asia (ROTA) and Silatech, QUEST provided training and education to approximately 400,000 displaced Syrians inside Syria, as well as Syrian refugees in Jordan,

Lebanon, Iraq and Türkiye. QUEST was funded for five years at a total cost of over USD 150 million. The initiative aligned with the strategies outlined in the 'No Lost Generation' initiative, the Syria HRP and the 3RP. In 2018, the Qatari government expanded QUEST, transforming it from a rapid response initiative into a development programme. The QFFD enhanced the programme to include health and economic development interventions. These interventions specifically targeted youth and women – particularly Syrian refugees in neighbouring countries – by providing technical skills training and employment advice, and facilitating access to finance and higher education. Regarding the response to urgent needs, in 2016, the QFFD pledged USD 10 million for humanitarian relief in the country, in particular in the Aleppo area, and USD 5 million for refugees in Türkiye to the Joint Humanitarian Trust.

In 2017, the QFFD Annual Report registered a multi-sector donation through the HRP of USD 12 million and a reconstruction effort in Homs through the QRCS. In 2018, aid allocation was directed along three main lines. In partnership with Education Above All, the QFFD allocated USD 21.4 million to improve access to education in Idlib, Aleppo, Hama, Homs, Dar'a, Quneitra, Damascus and Rural Damascus. Additionally, it funded the QRCS and QC to intervene in emergency response efforts in Dar'a and eastern Ghouta. Several agreements were signed by the QFFD for emergency response projects through Qatari NGOs aimed at assisting displaced populations in those two areas. The relief provided included food and emergency health services within Ghouta, shelter and non-food items, health services for those displaced from Ghouta to northern Syria, and shelter and medical assistance for those displaced from Dar'a. These interventions were carried out before the recapture of these areas by pro-government forces in March 2018.

In the same year, through the QRCS, the agency financed projects for IDPs in Syria with a budget of USD 7 million. The projects covered operations in eleven health centres, support of community health services and mental health support, housing for displaced Syrians, and restoration of houses in the city of al-Bab, in the Aleppo district. In 2018 the city was under the control of pro-Turkish militias, as part of the Turkish occupation of northern Syria.

The 2019 Annual Report highlights that the majority of the QFFD's funds for the Syrian crisis were allocated to addressing the refugee issue in neighbouring countries – Türkiye, Jordan and Lebanon. In Türkiye, for example, the QFFD partnered with the Dutch NGO SPARK to finance a project that implemented agronomic courses for Syrian refugees in southern Türkiye. Additionally, QC allocated a grant of USD 51.3 million to the HRP, with a significant increase (USD 68.8 million) in resources allocated through multilateral channels compared to the previous year (see Figure 4.5).

In 2020, the QFFD provided USD 2 million in support to UNHCR for Syrian refugees in Lebanon and allocated USD 20.7 million to the United Nations Relief and Works Agency (UNRWA) for Palestinian refugees in Syria. Additionally, it funded a four-year project in partnership with SPARK, aimed at supporting IDPs in northern Syria and refugees in Türkiye and Jordan, with a total allocation of USD 10 million.

In 2021, the QFFD provided significant financial support for various humanitarian efforts aimed at assisting vulnerable populations in Syria and neighbouring regions. In partnership with the UK Foreign, Commonwealth & Development Office, the QFFD allocated USD 1.6 million to support education in Syria. Major interventions were also implemented in northern Syria to support IDPs and refugees in Lebanon.

A similar trend can be observed in 2022, with a total allocation of USD 9.8 million for Palestinian refugees in Syria through UNRWA, Syrian refugees in Jordan and Lebanon and IDPs in northwest Syria. Additionally, the QFFD pledged USD 10 million to the World Health Organization (WHO) to support the Access to COVID-19 Tools Accelerator, thereby contributing to global efforts to combat the pandemic. In 2023, the QFFD allocated USD 98 million, as the most consistent contribution to the infrastructural project in northwest Syria for the Euphrates Basin Project in collaboration with the Türkiye Disaster and Emergency Management Authority (QFFD, 2016–23).

Regarding multilateral contributions through the Syria HRP, Qatar's involvement in the allocation of resources steadily increased from 2015 to 2023, reaching its peak in the latter year. This includes contributions to the earthquake response. For the 2023 earthquake flash appeal, Qatar allocated USD 10.7 million through OCHA, with QC serving as the implementing agency.

The increase in multilateral allocations for Syria is closely linked to Qatar's efforts following the GCC crisis in 2017, and the desire to 'legitimise' its role as a donor within the international community (Barakat, 2019). However, most contributions remained earmarked, with interventions carried out in opposition-controlled areas through Qatar's state-based charities. The operations of QC and the QRCS in these areas were not only a political choice by the donor but also a response to structural impediments imposed by the Assad regime, which sought to prevent organisations from operating in both opposition- and regime-controlled areas simultaneously.

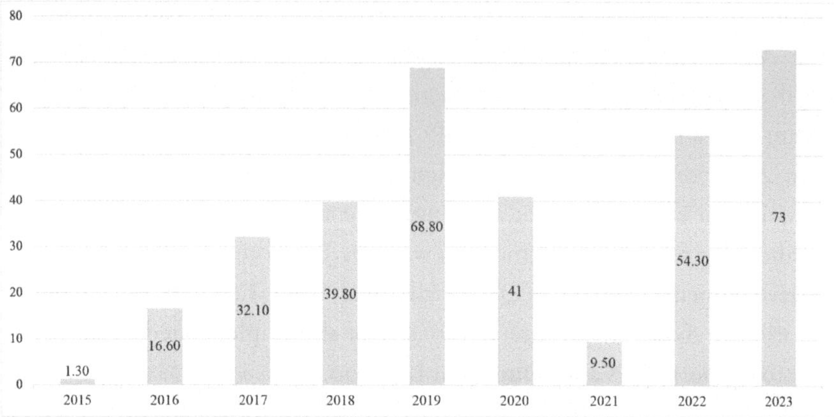

Figure 4.5 Qatar's contributions to the Syrian Humanitarian Response Plan from 2015 to 2023.

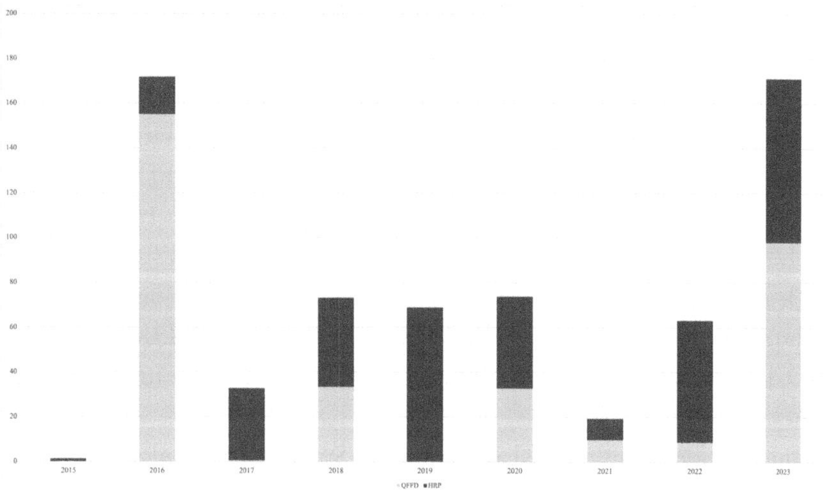

Figure 4.6 Total funds allocated by QFFD through bilateral and multilateral channels in Syria, as well as the Syrian Humanitarian Response Plan, from 2015 to 2023.

Charitable organisations and humanitarian negotiations

One of the most important aspects of the Qatari response in Syria through multilateral channels and its organisations is the geographical allocation of resources, which occurs in opposition-controlled areas. The QRCS established the office in Gaziantep in 2012, while QC had its office in Türkiye and operated cross-border in Idlib and northern Aleppo.

Most of the funds were distributed to emergency areas in rebel enclaves, where regime control and statehood were completely absent. This was the case in Dar'a and eastern Ghouta before 2018, when pro-government forces launched military campaigns to reconquer these areas and imposed a nearly five-year siege, allowing only a limited supply of food and nutritional aid, and exclusively in Idlib and northern Aleppo after 2018.

The Qatar Red Crescent Society

The QRCS has been active in seven Syrian governorates – Aleppo, Idlib, Hama, Lattakia, al-Raqqah, Deir ez-Zor and al-Hasakeh – since 2011. From 2015 to 2022, it implemented a variety of projects related to the Syrian crisis, with primary donors including the Qatari government, UNICEF, private donations, the Syria Cross-Border Humanitarian Fund (SCHF) and the Silatech Organization. In 2021, the QRCS financed projects under the Syria HRP in sectors such as nutrition, shelter, livelihoods, education, food security, agriculture and WASH (water, sanitation and hygiene). Aid allocation was primarily focused in northern Syria, particularly in the Idlib governorate (including Darkosh, Zardana, Bennsh, Fos-Zuf, Ein el-Bayda, Haranbush, Qah, Harim, Ma'arrat Tamsrin and Salqin) and rural Aleppo (especially al-Bab), with a particular emphasis on IDP camps.

The main donors and partners involved in financing the QRCS's long-term programmes in Syria included OCHA, UNICEF and WHO. The QRCS also worked to strengthen its relationships with local organisations to ensure the sustainability of the projects it funded. To better adapt to the ever-changing context of Syria, the QRCS established a Unit for Impact Monitoring in 2020. This unit is responsible for ensuring sustainability in conflict-affected areas and identifying best practices to inform future planning.

Qatar Charity: food security and early recovery in northwest Syria

In 2015, QC opened an office in Ankara to respond to the Syrian crisis and had been operating through the Turkish border for eighteen months prior. Data available on the OCHA FTS show that starting from 2017, major donors to the organisation included the Qatari government and the SCHF. Moreover, with funding from the QFFD, QC established four primary healthcare centres in 2020, benefiting 144,000 people in Idlib governorate. These centres operate in coordination with local and international organisations, including the Health Cluster, WHO and UNICEF.

In 2020, QC, with funding from the SCHF, initiated a project aimed at supporting the self-reliance of the crisis-affected population and enhancing socio-economic services in northern Syria. The project, which concluded in January 2023, addressed urgent humanitarian priorities outlined in the 2021 Needs and Response Strategy. It focused on two main sectors: food security and livelihoods, as well as early recovery. The project aimed to create job opportunities for individuals affected by the crisis and expand small businesses through integration with value chain support in targeted areas: al-Dana in Idlib governorate, and Afrin and al-Rai in Aleppo governorate.

The main activities of the project included:

- Rehabilitating two irrigation stations in Afrin, with both main and secondary canals extending 40 kilometres, to ensure access to irrigation services for approximately 2,000 hectares of agricultural land.
- Providing job opportunities for nearly fifty workers in the beneficiary areas and establishing three medium-sized food-processing workshops in Afrin, al-Dana and al-Rai, aiming to create job opportunities for 165 beneficiaries.
- Distributing agricultural inputs to 200 farmers in al-Dana, Afrin and al-Rai.
- Supporting 114 small business owners to scale up their businesses through small grants, and building their capacity in business management with 30 hours of training and six coaching visits throughout the project. This activity targeted shop owners in two markets newly established by QC in al-Rai (39 shops) and al-Dana (50 shops), as well as twenty-five beneficiaries outside the markets.

It is worth noting that QC had implemented numerous food security projects in the same areas, including wheat and vegetable value chain support, small grants, and the rehabilitation of silos and agricultural structures. From 2019 to 2020, in partnership with OCHA and the World Food Programme, QC supported the wheat value chain in northwest Syria, marking the first such initiative in the region. The project aimed to renovate silos to store up to 12,000 tonnes of wheat, build a new mill with a production capacity of 50 tonnes of flour per day, train mill and silo staff, procure over 1,000 tonnes of wheat, distribute subsidised bread and provide farmers with essential inputs for wheat cultivation, along with technical support through awareness-raising sessions.

The project improved food security for 24,510 people in Marea (northern Aleppo) and surrounding areas, with indirect benefits for more than 267,000 people in rural northern Aleppo. QC also provided 200 agricultural baskets, each containing fertilisers and pesticides for farmers cultivating 1 hectare of wheat, and distributed 278,000 litres of diesel to power irrigation pumps (Qatar Charity, 2020–2).

Local partners in the northwest: Ihsan Relief and Development Organisation

The operations in opposition-controlled areas, in particular in Idlib and northern Aleppo, were carried out by Qatar either directly by QC and the QRCS, or in collaboration with local organisations or organisations created by the Syrian diaspora in third countries. One of the organisations present in northwest Syria, operating in Idlib and northern Aleppo, is the Ihsan Relief and Development Organisation (IRDO), which collaborates with Qatari organisations, the UN and other international donors. The organisation was started in 2012 in Doha by a group of Syrians based in Qatar, originally called Syrian Business Forum, and was formally established in 2014. Initially, in 2012, after Qatar raised about USD 50 million to respond to the crisis, the organisation offered to distribute and implement projects with those funds in areas that were most in need such as Homs, rural Damascus and Darʿa.

The organisation (interviewed in 2023) operated through two offices in Idlib and one in the northern Aleppo area. It worked in the sectors of protection, education, food security, livelihoods, WASH and shelter. The organisation received funding from international donors, governmental institutions and private donations and was part of the UN OCHA clusters for cross-border aid coordination in both regions.

Regarding the relationship with Qatar, following the creation of RACA, the only two organisations authorised to spend and implement funds abroad are QC and the QRCS, as illustrated in Chapter 3. Collaboration between IRDO and Qatar occurred exclusively through these two charities after RACA approved funding and projects. Education Above All, on the other hand, can disburse funding and implement projects through partnerships but does not have any direct implementation activities. This partnership and the practical aspects of the collaboration reflect the centralisation and control of foreign aid by Doha, as part of an attempt to legitimise transparent operations in areas controlled by non-state armed groups, such as HTS, which are listed as terrorist organisations.[3]

The aid distribution process in opposition-controlled areas was based on two primary components: the needs assessment conducted by aid workers on the ground and consultations with local authorities, including the SSG (Idlib) and the SIG (northern Aleppo). However, the relationship with the SSG appeared to be more structured and centralised compared to the SIG. Aid distribution was the result of negotiations with local authorities, who also provided a list of beneficiaries. This list was double-checked (verification and validation process) by the organisation and donors, who made the final decision, to ensure alignment with the needs assessment, avoid political implications – such as beneficiary selection based on political considerations – and maintain the neutrality of the aid implementation.

The entire negotiation process with the SSG and the SIG can be considered a form of bottom-up humanitarian diplomacy. In this context, implementation agencies are the key actors in securing access to areas, identifying beneficiaries and facilitating aid distribution in collaboration with non-state armed groups. At times, permission to operate in these areas was contingent upon certain conditions, such as the selection of and access to recipients, despite their complete dependence on external aid. This process remains one of the most challenging aspects of humanitarian work, particularly in conflict zones that are fragmented and where non-state armed groups are labelled as terrorist organisations (Khadhraoui, 2019).

Humanitarian Diplomacy and Non-state Armed Groups

The distribution of aid in Idlib and northern Aleppo, where Qatar and other international organisations have been involved, is key to understanding both the practices of aid negotiations and whether – and how – aid distribution in opposition-controlled areas has, in some cases, helped rebels survive, or at least maintain a form of control in these areas.

Cross-border and cross-line operations in Syria have long been debated by the international community, humanitarian workers and scholars as part of the broader discussion on how humanitarian aid should be organised. The UN response was based on multiple access hubs in different regions, including Jordan, Lebanon and southern Türkiye. Since 2014, UN resolutions have allowed aid to be delivered cross-border without the explicit permission of the government of Syria, with these resolutions being periodically renewed every six to twelve months. The resolutions prevented the central government from controlling aid (and territories) through the cross-border mechanism, 'raising questions about its legitimacy as the sole UN-recognised state authority inside Syria' (ACAPS 2023: 3).

The approach of Qatar in the opposition-controlled areas, together with other international organisations, raises some aspects that are beyond the Syrian case and part of the ongoing debate in the international aid community. Firstly, the localisation of aid response through partnerships and collaboration with local actors, as demonstrated by the case of IRDO, shows how access to those areas was implemented by Qatar in a hybrid mode: through the direct presence of Qatari organisations or implementation via Syrian organisations eligible for funding (after RACA's registration and approval). This process of localisation has been discussed by scholars and practitioners as 'good practice' to improve humanitarian response (Elkahlout, Milton, Yaseen & Raweh, 2022), especially when complex emergencies create barriers for internationals to distribute and manage aid directly. The case of Yemen, for instance – analysed by Elkahlout et al. (2022) – presents evidence of increased funds granted to local NGOs and progress in empowering local actors to lead and manage international aid. However, there is still a significant disparity between the funding received by international NGOs and local NGOs in Yemen, as there was in the case of northern Syria.

Moreover, the case of Syria highlights the different levels of humanitarian diplomacy when aid is delivered in conflict zones, fragmented contexts or areas controlled by non-state armed groups or groups labelled as terrorist organisations. In general terms, definitions of humanitarian diplomacy vary according to the actors and levels at which humanitarian efforts are implemented. De Lauri (2018) frames it as 'persuading decision-makers and leaders to act, at all times and in all circumstances, in the interest of vulnerable people and with full respect for fundamental humanitarian principles'. However, this process of negotiation can occur at different levels, such as the multilateral or state level (top-down), or between implementing agencies and local actors or non-state authorities who control the area where aid needs to be distributed (bottom-up). In the case of Syria, particularly in Idlib and northern Aleppo, these three levels occurred and implied different dynamics.

The first one is the multilateral negotiation of aid in the Security Council and through UN Resolutions for cross-border access, as explained before. At the state level, in the case of Qatar, the modalities of the direct political negotiation between state institutions and non-state actors, such as the SIG and SSG, have never been disclosed during my interviews or official statements. However, this is not the first time Qatar has operated through its organisations to deliver aid more flexibly compared to other donors in the international community, and the relations with part of the Syrian opposition were probably helpful in this process. The cases of Darfur (Donelli & Pericoli, 2024), Gaza and Afghanistan after the Taliban takeover in August 2021 (Milton & Elkahlout, 2025) are examples of how the humanitarian diplomacy of Qatar (Milton, Elkahlout & Tariq, 2025; Barakat, 2024) has been characterised by a 'blend of balance, strategic foreign policy, and synergistic operation between non-governmental organisations and government agencies' (Elkahlout & Hedaya, 2024: 1828), making this donor more flexible and capable of intervening in contexts where the international community was paralysed, unable to respond (as in Darfur) or limited by the domestic necessities of its donors (as in the cases of Afghanistan or Gaza).

The third level of humanitarian diplomacy is carried out by implementing agencies, such as Qatari organisations or their local partners, and consists of the everyday practices of aid distribution and management between the implementing agencies, local authorities and donors. The selection of beneficiaries has been described by IRDO as one of the most challenging negotiations between the local authorities and the donors. The SSG or the SIG is used to select beneficiaries according to their parameters, while the implementing agencies select the targeted groups based on a needs assessment. To strike a balance between political and humanitarian needs, the implementing organisation cross-checks the selected beneficiaries against its criteria, the final decision resting with the donors.[4]

Despite their complete dependence on foreign aid and external resources, opposition groups attempted to politicise aid distribution to maintain control and exert power. In Idlib, all service delivery and resources were outsourced to cross-border foreign aid, relying on it while simultaneously claiming legitimacy for providing services. NGOs operating in the region were registered with the SSG's Ministry of Development and Humanitarian Affairs and were required to obtain a permit for each project. Typically, NGOs must sign a memorandum of understanding with local councils in the areas where they operate. They may also be obliged to appoint representatives to attend regular coordination meetings with the SSG (Hall, 2022). In areas under Turkish control, organisations had to secure a permit from the Turkish government to operate, and only NGOs registered in Türkiye could mobilise employees from Türkiye to Syria for cross-border operations. Once permission was granted, NGOs had to continue coordinating with the relevant Turkish provincial government or Syrian municipal council departments for project implementation (Hall, 2022).

The distribution and management of aid in both opposition- and government-controlled territories was entirely a political process, shaped by contrasting power dynamics with specific and differing political objectives. It is difficult to assess to what extent the aid process contributed to the survival of the rebel groups in the northwest. However, due to the externalisation of service delivery and the reliance on foreign aid to meet basic needs in the areas under their control, it is reasonable to assume that foreign aid played a double role in assisting the population and ensuring the governance of the rebel groups. This is likely to remain one of the unresolved dilemmas for the donor community, as it must choose between assisting the civilian population and negotiating aid access with political entities, whether state and non-state actors or formal and informal authorities.

UAE's Aid in Syria: Interventions in Government-controlled Areas and Refugee Response

As previously mentioned, the UAE's stance on the Syrian conflict evolved, and with this shift came a change in its approach to aid interventions in the country. Initially, Abu Dhabi supported the Free Syrian Army (FSA) but later aligned with Russia and re-established relations with al-Assad's government. However, the UAE's approach remained more cautious compared to that of its regional neighbours. Emirati support for FSA groups was channelled through programmes operated by the CIA, particularly in southern Syria, via the Military Operations Center based in Jordan. Nevertheless, there were no reports of the UAE supplying Syrian rebels with weapons; its support was limited to financial assistance (Katzman, 2014). The UAE also participated in the fight against ISIS, contributing to its air force capabilities. From 2011 to 2015, the UAE was actively engaged with the Syrian opposition, assisted Syrian refugees and maintained limited relations with the Syrian government (Almezaini, 2021).

By the end of 2015, the UAE began to shift its policy towards Syria. After nearly five years of conflict and a lack of stability, this change was influenced in part by Russia's growing involvement. By December 2018, the UAE had moved away from its opposition support, restored diplomatic relations with Damascus and began collaborating with Russia to counter Türkiye's role in Syria (Almezaini, 2021).

All these dynamics are somehow reflected in the implementation of aid strategies and resource allocation looking at the periods 2015–17 and 2018–23. In 2016, the UAE government disbursed a total of USD 130 million, primarily for humanitarian assistance in Syria (USD 40.5 million, provided bilaterally) and for refugee support in neighbouring countries (USD 89.5 million). In Jordan, the Emirates Red Crescent managed the UAE–Jordanian Mrajeeb al-Fahood refugee camp, as well as another camp in Iraq. In 2017, the UAE government continued its humanitarian efforts, providing aid to beneficiaries in the de-escalation zone in southern Syria as part of its commitment to the Brussels donor conference for Syria in April.

The UAE allocated a total of USD 64.3 million for humanitarian assistance in the country, with USD 22.4 million directed specifically to Syria.

From 2018 to 2023: aid in government-controlled areas, Kurdistan and Jordan.

The period from 2018 to 2023 is characterised by a reduction in resource allocation within Syrian territory, while greater efforts were focused on addressing the refugee crisis, particularly in Jordan, Lebanon and Iraq. In 2018, the UAE continued its interventions in both the humanitarian response in Syria and refugee assistance in Jordan and Lebanon, with the latter two countries being the main recipients. That same year, the UAE pledged USD 50 million to support stabilisation and early recovery programmes in Raqqa, following the city's recapture by the Syrian Democratic Forces. This pledge signalled the UAE's support for the Kurds and its attempt to counter Turkish influence in northern Syria. However, according to data from OCHA FTS, it remained a pledge and was never actually disbursed.[5]

Starting in 2019, humanitarian assistance efforts in Syria began to decrease, with only USD 5.8 million allocated for the country's humanitarian response. At the same time, the UAE continued to prioritise the refugee crisis in Jordan, allocating USD 38.7 million, which accounted for 68.9 per cent of its total contribution to the Syrian crisis. Lebanon followed with USD 11.2 million, and Iraq received USD 4 million.

In 2020, Syria, along with Iraq, became part of the UAE's regional stabilisation efforts. The UAE used the Syria Recovery Trust Fund (SRTF) as a platform to engage with international donors on the country's future and development approach. It also provided USD 2 million to the Agency for Technical Cooperation and Development (ACTED), a French NGO, for interventions in the Kurdish areas of northeastern Syria. The trend of prioritising neighbouring countries to address the refugee crisis over direct support to Syrian territories continued in 2020, with USD 22.2 million allocated bilaterally to Syria and USD 38.3 million allocated to Jordan.

This trend was confirmed in 2021, when the allocation of resources for responding to the refugee crisis in Jordan was higher than that for Syria, with USD 56.7 million allocated to Jordan and USD 30.5 million to Syria. Jordan is the third country, after Yemen and Afghanistan, to receive humanitarian aid from the UAE. In 2022, USD 30 million was allocated in Syrian territory (Assad-controlled areas) and USD 10 million in Jordan for the refugee response.

In 2023, a total of USD 281.3 million was allocated in Syria for earthquake response and humanitarian needs, with USD 277.7 million specifically for earthquake relief – representing a 778 per cent increase compared to 2022. The majority of the funding came bilaterally from the UAE government (89 per cent), followed by contributions from the Emirates Red Crescent and the Mohammed bin Rashid al-Maktoum Global Initiatives. In terms of sector allocations, emergency multi-sector aid and budget support ranked first and second, respectively, followed by projects for reconstruction and rehabilitation (UAE MOFAIC, 2016–23).

The efforts in multilateral channels: HRP and the Syria Recovery Trust Fund

In contrast to Qatar, the UAE's contributions to the OCHA HRP from 2015 to 2023 have been relatively smaller and inconsistent. The UAE's only donations through this multilateral channel were in 2015 (USD 1.1 million), 2020 (USD 9.5 million), 2022 (USD 7 million) and 2023, when it allocated USD 15 million for the earthquake flash appeal.

The UAE has allocated funds through other multilateral channels outside the UN, such as the Syria Recovery Trust Fund (SRTF), a multi-donor trust fund established by the Group of Friends of the Syrian People and the Working Group on Economic Recovery and Development. The SRTF aims to channel grant funding from the international community in a transparent and accountable manner. The fund was launched in 2013 with three original donors: Germany, the UAE and the United States, along with the National Coalition of Syrian Revolutionary and Opposition Forces (SOC) as the legitimate representative of the Syrian people, and the German Development Bank (KfW) as trustee. Over time, other donors – including Denmark, Sweden, Finland, Japan, the UK, Kuwait, France, Italy and the Netherlands – joined the fund. In 2014, Türkiye became a permanent member and host country for operational management, followed by Jordan in 2015. From 2013 to 2024, the UAE contributed to the SRTF with USD 19.4 million. However, based on these data, the UAE's multilateral

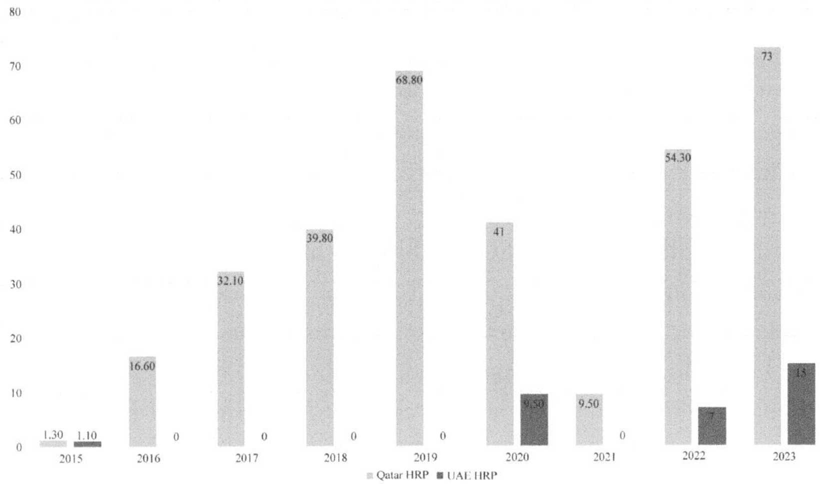

Figure 4.7 Qatar and the UAE's paid contributions to the Syrian Humanitarian Response Plan from 2015 to 2023.

contributions in Syria remained relatively small, with a greater emphasis on bilateral interventions.

The 'Tyranny of Emergency': Aid after the Earthquake

In February 2023, a 7.8 magnitude earthquake struck southern Türkiye and northwestern Syria, resulting in 4,500 fatalities and 10,400 injuries in the latter region (Reliefweb, n.d.). The expression 'tyranny of emergency' was used by Minear (2002) to indicate the allocation of funds for the latest crises where 'adhocratic' forms of humanitarianism – ruling by improvisation – provide solutions to immediate needs without addressing long-term responses or perspectives (Dunn, 2012; Carpi, 2023: 159). Aid interventions after the earthquake in February 2023 in opposition-controlled areas exemplify this concept, showing how a complex emergency occurred in precarious conditions where donors were already dealing with political obstacles to humanitarian aid distribution.

At that time, due to Russian and Chinese vetoes, only one border crossing, Bab al-Hawa, was accessible for aid delivery. The Assad government attempted to exploit the crisis by calling for the lifting of sanctions, while also claiming, without evidence, that these sanctions impeded the relief efforts, all the while continuing to bomb northwestern Syria (Tharoor, 2023). Initially, the government requested aid to be channelled solely through Damascus but, under international pressure, later agreed to open additional border crossings to the northwest.

Both the SIG and the SSG established institutions responsible for managing resources from external aid for the response efforts. The SSG created the Directorate of Earthquake Victims Affairs under the Ministry of Local Administration and Services, while the SIG established the Central Committee for Damage Assessment. As highlighted by Hatahet (2023), there was a significant contrast between the approaches of the SSG and the SIG in addressing the aftermath of the earthquake. The SSG concentrated on managing its image and asserting control, while the SIG faced challenges related to coordination and concerns over authority. The SSG adopted a hands-off approach towards humanitarian organisations, prioritising leadership, centralising response efforts and striving to overcome international isolation. The SIG delayed aid from Kurdish-controlled northeast Syria for two days, supposedly awaiting clearance from Türkiye.

Both the Assad government and opposition militant groups were reportedly involved in diverting aid. However, the main response came from civil society. No fewer than 2,600 volunteers of Syria's Civil Defence, or White Helmets, reached the sixty most affected sites within 10 hours of the earthquake, rescuing around 2,900 survivors from the rubble with minimal equipment, much of which came from local communities and businesses.

Finding more survivors required specialised equipment and expert search teams, which only the UN or other countries could provide. Unfortunately, none arrived. Despite having the capability to deploy modern search-and-rescue resources, the US refrained from intervening. The EU activated its Civil Protection Mechanism at the Assad government's request, but this excluded northwest Syria. Regional responses were also inadequate. Türkiye initially closed the Bab al-Hawa crossing for 48 hours, likely due to the chaos caused by the disaster and the absence of international pressure for access. Initially, only Qatar, Saudi Arabia and Iraqi Kurdistan sent aid to northwest Syria.

The UN's response was widely criticised for failing to send search-and-rescue teams or specialised equipment to northwest Syria during the critical first three days. The UN cited logistical and road challenges, yet the Gaziantep-based logistics cluster's interactive map indicated no major obstacles to aid arriving from the UN hub near Reyhanli, just 5 kilometres from the Syrian border. The UN's delay in acting, particularly in waiting for al-Assad's approval to open two nearby border crossings, was both politically and legally unnecessary. This delay, occurring six days after the earthquake during a visit by the WHO director general, resulted in unnecessary loss of life and granted al-Assad leverage he had lost in 2014 under UNSC Resolution 2165, which authorised cross-border assistance without government consent. The Assad government's delay was reportedly intentional, aimed at politicising the disaster (Jabbour et al., 2023: 802–3).

The response of the Gulf States

Both Qatar and the UAE played a consistent role in providing resources for the earthquake response, with some changing dynamics compared to the previous years. Qatar's response was twofold: through the OCHA Syria Earthquake Flash Appeal, Doha contributed USD 10.7 million, while the UAE donated USD 15 million, marking the largest multilateral contribution from Abu Dhabi to Syria since 2015. However, among the Gulf States, the largest contribution was made by Saudi Arabia, with USD 24.7 million.[6] In terms of bilateral contributions, Qatar allocated USD 98 million for northwest Syria, coordinating with the Türkiye Disaster and Emergency Management Authority, primarily for shelter and infrastructure reconstruction. In contrast, the UAE allocated USD 281.3 million in 2023 for earthquake-affected areas under government control, directing funds either to the government or through interventions carried out by the Emirates Red Crescent (ERC).

Qatar's presence in the northwest, through its charities and local partners, enabled it to respond to the emergency more quickly and efficiently. This was due to its direct relationships with local authorities and its established presence in the two areas. In contrast, OCHA, before the earthquake, lacked direct access to Idlib and northern Aleppo, which, among other causes, limited its ability to respond promptly.[7]

The UAE's response to the emergency demonstrates a significant increase in resources allocated compared to previous years, highlighting its intention to maintain, and potentially strengthen, its ties with Damascus. By using the emergency as an opportunity to deliver aid to government-controlled areas, the UAE appears to be leveraging this crisis to solidify its relationship with the Assad regime. President bin Zayed al-Nahyan initiated the 'Chivalrous Knight 2' operation to provide extensive support. This operation involved various UAE entities, including the Armed Forces, the Ministry of Interior, the Ministry of Foreign Affairs, and the ERC. The UAE sent two search and rescue teams, comprising 134 members, and established two field hospitals with 250 beds and seventy-five medical staff. The country also launched the 'Bridges of Goodness' campaign, deploying forty-four aircraft carrying 1,660 tonnes of aid to Syria, including shelter tents for 20,000 people. Additionally, the UAE contributed to Türkiye's relief efforts by sending a 42-person search and rescue team and 34 aircraft with 447 tonnes of supplies, including 70 tonnes of medical aid. It also set up field hospitals in the Islahiyah region and Hatay, providing medical care to thousands (Emirates News Agency – WAM, 2023).

The 'revival' of the emergency, amid the ongoing humanitarian crisis, shaped new forms of aid management and strategies for humanitarian actors to negotiate access. However, the response of both international and regional actors to the emergency deserves some consideration. Emergencies in protracted crises can affect aid management in a given context, creating new opportunities for donors and organisations or opening up spaces for rethinking previous approaches.

In the case of Syria, the tyranny of emergency and the humanitarian response by international actors were hindered by political circumstances in opposition-controlled areas and by al-Assad's stance on cross-border aid operations. These political circumstances, which characterised aid distribution in the northwest, further reinforced their negative impact on aid management, without rethinking a shift in the aid approach with a long-term perspective.

Figure 4.8 A young girl observes the informal camp of IDPs created in rural Homs after the earthquake in February 2023. Photo by Giulia de Cesaris.

Syrian Refugees and the Gulf States' Response

Alongside efforts directed at Syrian territory (including both regime- and opposition-controlled areas), both Qatar and the UAE, through different approaches and at varying levels, incorporated responses to the Syrian refugee crisis in neighbouring countries, particularly Jordan, Lebanon and Türkiye. Their response to the refugee issue highlights several key aspects that characterised the Gulf States' approach, not only in their political choices but also in their value-based approach to humanitarian interventions in crisis responses.

Addressing the refugee crisis: foreign aid to neighbouring countries

The assessment of contributions to Syrian refugees is primarily based on two sets of data and channels: bilateral interventions (or through charities) as reported in the MOFAIC and QFFD Annual Reports, and contributions through multilateral channels, specifically about the OCHA Syria Regional Refugee and Resilience Plan (3RP).

Based on available data, the UAE's contributions to neighbouring countries, particularly with a larger allocation of resources to Jordan, are considerably higher than those of Qatar. In certain years, these contributions even surpassed the grant allocations for Syrian territory. Regarding interventions within Syria, the approach remains consistent: the UAE primarily engages through bilateral channels, while Qatar tends to focus more on multilateral efforts. Regarding the multilateral channel of 3RP, the coordination of interventions has occurred through the UN's leading role, while no coordination mechanism has been implemented among the Gulf States for the refugee response in neighbouring countries (Fakhoury, 2019).

Beyond the data analysis and the top-down political decisions regarding fund allocation to neighbouring countries as part of the Gulf States' response to the Syrian crisis, interesting insights emerge from ethnographic studies of the states' interventions in addressing the refugee issue (Carpi, 2020; Facon, 2023; Facon, 2024; Berg, 2025; Facon-Salelles, 2025).

The ethnographic study conducted by Berg in Jordan in 2023 highlights how the UAE has reimagined humanitarian responses in refugee camps by creating what could be described as 'five-star basic human needs' (Berg 2025). One of the key projects initiated by the UAE in Jordan through the ERC is the Mrajeeb al-Fhood camp, which opened in 2013 to alleviate the pressure on the largest Syrian refugee camp, Zaatari. Located 30 minutes from Jordan's second-largest city, Zarqa, and halfway to the Azraq refugee camp (which opened a year later), Mrajeeb al-Fhood was designed to host up to 25,000 Syrian refugees on an area of 250,000 square metres, in five gradual stages. It is also referred to as the Emirati Camp or the 'five-star camp', and it earned this reputation due to its abundant resources – electricity, hot water, three hot meals per day delivered directly to residents' shelters, street lighting, and the distribution of brand-new clothes for both everyday wear and special occasions (Carpi, 2015). This concentration of resources sets it apart from other crowded refugee camps governed by the UNHCR throughout Jordan (Rasmi, 2013).

Analysing the role of the Gulf States in the refugee response in northern Lebanon, Carpi (2020) challenges the concept of neutrality in humanitarian efforts, introducing the idea of 'operational neutrality'. This concept highlights how 'politics is discussed in humanitarian language and how it is also entangled in humanitarian practices' (Carpi, 2020: 418). To interpret the approach of the Gulf States, she utilises the concept of political realism, through which the Gulf States' aid is analysed by discarding 'neutrality as a moral standard while making the political moral' (Carpi, 2020: 424). This perspective is exemplified in programmes explicitly targeting Syrians politically active in opposition to the regime, among other actions. In other words, 'the political realism of assisting in situations of conflict and displacement' is presented as 'morally desirable', while the 'overt politicisation of aid is legitimised by declarations of good intentions, based on philanthropic acts' (Carpi, 2020: 423).

This perspective has been incorporated into the ethnographic studies conducted by Facon-Salelles in Lebanon, where she examines the legitimisation and narrative surrounding Gulf donors' involvement in the refugee response. According to her analysis, religious humanitarianism plays a crucial role in the legitimisation process of these donors, driven by moral imperatives, the identification of the legitimate symbols of 'the local', and 'pragmatic' legitimisation that emphasises the efficiency and visibility of Gulf aid on the ground (Facon, 2024; Facon-Salelles, 2025). To describe their aid model, she draws on the concept of *adhocracy*, defined as an intentional institutional set-up that grants policy actors a certain degree of flexibility and 'autonomy from bureaucratic hierarchy to address a specific issue and adapt to complex, rapidly changing circumstances' (Natter, 2023: 678).

Since this book does not include direct ethnographic experiences in Lebanon and Jordan, the scope of this analysis is to gather and (indirectly) observe empirical data and studies to evaluate the Gulf States' approaches to the same crisis (the refugee crisis related to Syria). What emerges from the literature and ethnographic studies is the flexibility, or adhocracy (Facon-Salelles, 2025), in their aid model compared to other actors, which is tied to a value-based process of legitimisation and the perception of recipients. This model can also be identified in Syrian territory, particularly in areas where aid is negotiated with non-state armed groups.

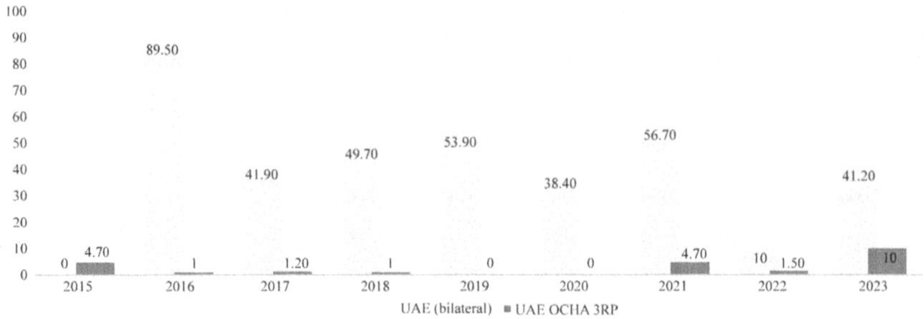

Figure 4.9 The UAE's contributions through bilateral and multilateral (OCHA 3RP) channels from 2015 to 2023 to neighbouring countries for the Syrian refugee response.

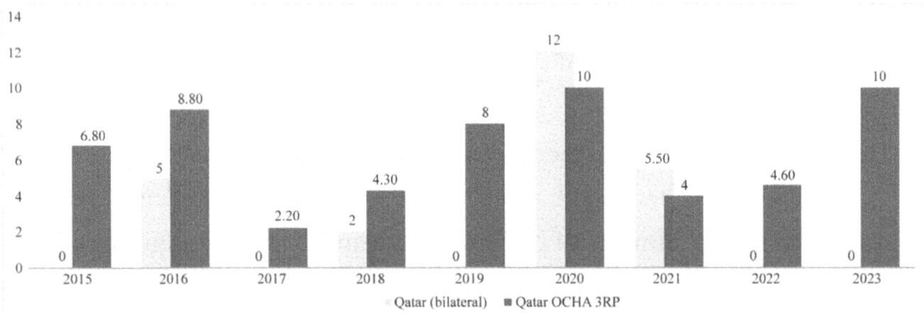

Figure 4.10 Qatar's contributions through bilateral and multilateral (OCHA 3RP) channels from 2015 to 2023 to neighbouring countries for the Syrian refugee response.

Externalisation of migration and foreign aid

Despite their significant humanitarian aid contributions, the Gulf States have been criticised for not accepting larger numbers of refugees and using foreign aid to neighbouring countries as a tool for controlling migration. As the migrant crisis escalated at Europe's borders, the Gulf States were accused of offering 'zero resettlement' to Syrian refugees fleeing the conflict (De Bel-Air, 2015). This discourse, however, should be framed within a legal context and recognition of refugee status. The GCC states are not signatories to the 1951 Convention Relating to the Status of Refugees and its 1967 Protocol, and therefore, do not recognise 'refugee' as a legal category. Moreover, expatriates in the region are typically considered 'guests' on short-duration visit visas or temporary contract workers, and only a fraction of them are eligible for family reunification.

The UAE has allowed Syrians and other vulnerable populations to remain within its existing migration framework, the *kafala* system (Maestri, 2021), utilising temporary visas offered under this labour migration system as a form of 'asylum policy by proxy' or 'quasi-asylum policy' (Charles, 2021). The *kafala* sponsorship system regulates labour migration in the GCC states and requires one party (*kafil*) to provide a legal guarantee on behalf of another party (*makful*), undertaking his legal responsibilities in case the latter is unable to (AlShehabi, 2019).

Regarding the UAE, there are no data available on foreign nationals' stocks and flows by country of citizenship since the early 2000s. As a result, it is difficult to estimate the number of Syrians who entered the country after 2011 (De Bel-Air, 2015). While the exact number remains unknown, the UAE government estimates that there were approximately 140,000 Syrians in the country before the onset of the crisis in 2011. These Syrians initially migrated as economic migrants, and as the situation in Syria worsened, they became mixed migrants. They were later joined by approximately 100,000 more Syrians who arrived after the crisis began (AP, 2015). The majority of these newcomers were relatives of Syrian migrant workers who had already established themselves in the country (Charles, 2021). Therefore, access was granted to Syrians who had first-degree family members in the UAE for up to three months. Moreover, since 2011, UAE authorities have expelled Syrians on several occasions for security reasons, particularly related to their support for the Syrian opposition or their commercial ties with Qatar, especially during the embargo (Hitman, 2019).

In the case of Qatar, the similarity of its demographic structure to that of its neighbours makes the social context fragile and 'delicate for absorbing a massive group of refugees' (Hitman, 2019: 93). In 2013, the number of Syrians registered in the country as foreign workers was 18,474 (Babar, 2014),[8] and there is no available database with updated information on foreign workers by nationality. In September 2018, Qatar made a huge step towards the recognition of refugee rights with Law No. 11/2018 on Organising Political Asylum[9] and other laws regulating residency in the country. One abolished exit permits for most migrant workers, and the other allowed people for the first time to apply for permanent residency. However, according to Human Rights Watch, the law is not fully aligned with international human rights law, due to the limits it imposes on participation in political activities (Human Rights Watch, 2018). Despite its weaknesses and limitations, it represents the only domestic refugee law in the GCC.

The humanitarian efforts towards Syria's neighbouring countries, as a strategy to externalise migration management – a practice also familiar to the European Union – have dominated the narrative surrounding the relationship between refugees and the Gulf States during regional crises. Nevertheless, the lack of formal recognition of refugee status within the GCC and the data available do not imply that there are no individuals who could be categorised as refugees, because an overemphasis on legal normative categories leads to the invisibility of *de facto* refugees (Lysa, 2023: 272).

Regional Organisations: Political *Impasse* or Structural Inability?

As a regional crisis involving both regional and international actors, with significant consequences for neighbouring countries, the Syrian conflict has witnessed a lack of involvement from regional organisations such as the Organisation of Islamic Cooperation (OIC) in mediation efforts and humanitarian diplomacy, alongside the Islamic Development Bank (IsDB) in supporting post-conflict recovery. The reasons for this lie in the political involvement of their member states in the Syrian conflict, as well as the structural limitations of these organisations to act as supra-state actors within regional and international dynamics.

Initially, in 2012, the OIC decided to suspend Syria, citing President Bashar al-Assad's suppression of the Syrian revolt. The OIC secretary general, Ekmeleddin İhsanoğlu, described the decision to suspend Syrian membership as 'a message to the international community, that the Islamic community stands with a politically peaceful solution and does not want any more bloodshed' (Alsharif, 2012).

This decision was primarily driven by Saudi Arabia's efforts to diplomatically isolate Syria and support calls for the arming of the Syrian rebel opposition (Alsharif, 2012). Before the 2012 OIC decision, the Arab League had already suspended Syria's membership in 2011. This marked the first time the OIC had taken such a dramatic measure against a member state. Some scholars have interpreted Syria's suspension as a boycott of Iran's influence in the region. In this context, Saudi Arabia sought to transform the OIC into a tool for its anti-Iran agenda, a move that escalated tensions within the organisation and came to a head at the 2016 summit in Istanbul. During this summit, a resolution was adopted calling on Iran to refrain from interfering in the affairs of other states (Akbarzardeh & Ahmed, 2018).

In 2014, the future OIC secretary general Iyad Ameen Madani led a three-member delegation to attend the Geneva Conference on Syria, commonly known as Geneva II, on 22 January. This marked the beginning of a 'promising process' that, for the first time, saw the participation of both the Syrian government and the opposition. During the meeting, Madani reiterated the OIC's policy on the Syrian crisis as outlined in the resolutions of the OIC summit. This policy emphasised the preservation of Syria's sovereignty, independence and territorial integrity; adherence to the Islamic values of peace, justice and equality; respect for human rights; and the necessity of taking all possible measures to prevent the conflict from escalating into a fully fledged civil war. Madani also stressed the Syrian government's responsibility for the tragic deterioration of the situation. Furthermore, the Resolutions on Humanitarian Affairs, adopted in 2013, called upon the UN Security Council to take additional steps in response to the worsening humanitarian crisis in Syria (OIC, 2013).

In April 2016, the OIC strongly condemned airstrikes that targeted areas controlled by the Syrian opposition in Aleppo, including residential neighbourhoods, mosques and healthcare facilities such as al-Quds Hospital. Madani labelled these attacks as war crimes, calling for the Syrian regime to be held accountable and for those supporting the regime to be held responsible for the ongoing violations (OIC, 2016). Following the 2018 eastern Ghouta attack, the OIC General Secretariat demanded an immediate halt to such assaults and called for the unrestricted delivery of humanitarian and medical aid to the city. The OIC reiterated its commitment to the Geneva Declaration and the relevant UN resolutions, which emphasised the preservation of Syria's territorial integrity and the need for a peaceful resolution to the conflict.

When the regime collapsed and various rebel groups took control of the country, the OIC did not immediately react or take any stance on the political transition. At the regional level, Jordan hosted a meeting of the Arab League with Saudi Arabia, Iraq, Lebanon, Egypt, the UAE, Bahrain and Qatar on

14 December 2024. The meeting resulted in a joint statement in which the donor countries expressed their support for an all-inclusive transition (Ministry of Foreign Affairs (Iraq), 2024). In March 2025, the OIC restored Syria's membership after thirteen years of suspension, highlighting the 'readiness' of the organisation – and its members – to fully cooperate with the new government (SPA, 2025b).

The Syrian crisis posed a significant challenge for the OIC and IsDB in terms of their role in conflict resolution and post-conflict recovery. It highlighted the regionalisation of an intra-state conflict, where various member countries, each with differing interests, contribute to supporting both state and non-state actors, leading to a fragmentation of the conflict. In this context, the diverse interests of member countries and their commitment to its Charter have hindered the OIC's ability to act as a cohesive supranational entity and mediate effectively. Additionally, Syria's suspension from the OIC has limited the IsDB's interventions since 2012, restricting the bank's activities to neighbouring countries focused on addressing the Syrian refugee crisis, as well as interventions for IDPs in opposition-controlled areas (Pericoli, 2024). Ideological and political rivalries among the member states were part of the OIC's inability to play an active role in conflict mediation, along with other factors related to the institution itself.

The first of these factors concerns the institutional structure and the lack of a rule-enforcing body. As a result, the OIC's weakness stems from the limited mandate of its executive organs. Moreover, apart from the absence of an executive body, there is no mechanism for the imposition of sanctions, as the OIC's framework does not contain any express provisions for such measures (Bacik, 2011). However, the UN system has also shown weakness and inability to 'maintain international peace and security' in many cases, including Syria. The veto power of the five permanent members of the Security Council has been one of the main constraints on UN action. Russia's veto in July 2023, blocking cross-border aid to northern Syria without the central government's authorisation, risked compromising aid access in the opposition-controlled areas. In this instance, Russia emphasised that Syria was the only country where cross-border aid was implemented with the Council's authorisation instead of the government's, adding that, following the earthquake, the Syrian government opened the Bab al-Salam and al-Rai crossings, showing its willingness to remove barriers to humanitarian assistance – but under its control (United Nations, 2023). Therefore, the limits of multilateralism have emerged at both the international and regional levels in a region with relatively low economic and political integration, where international multilateralism is contested and, in some cases, perceived as part of the conflict (Makdisi, 2019).

Secondly, the protection of sovereignty seems to be one of the fundamental principles of the organisation above all other issues. This sometimes contrasts with two elements: the clash between the state system and the transnational logic of Islamic solidarity, and the preservation of sovereignty over regime change. State sovereignty is a central principle of international relations in the modern system, based on sovereignty and territorial states. Therefore, any other identity-constructive forms, such as religion or ethnicity, are incompatible with the spirit of the modern international system. In this sense, sovereignty, as an organising principle, determines borders in the international system of states and authority not according to function, but geography (Thomson, 1995). The point is that Islamic solidarity, emphasised in the OIC's Charter, and the concept of *Umma* contain transnational elements that go beyond the concept of sovereignty itself. So, on the one hand, the OIC tries to promote religious identity in international cooperation and a sense of belonging; on the other hand, OIC member states are primarily driven by their national interests and territorial integrity (Bacik, 2011).

Concerning the approach of the IsDB in the Syrian case, the decision-making process of the bank and the dominant role of Saudi Arabia in the allocation of funds are key factors. Studies on aid allocation by the IsDB (Mustafa & Razak, 2012; Hernandez & Vadlamannati, 2017) highlight some critical aspects. First, the limited number of studies on aid allocation by Arab donors agree that predominantly Muslim countries are their main beneficiaries. This observation extends to the IsDB, which was established with the specific purpose of providing development assistance only to countries affiliated with the OIC and facilitating their access to *shariʿa*-compliant financial resources (Warde, 2000).

Saudi Arabia, as the largest donor to the bank, pays particular attention to the various Islamic denominations in forging political alliances within the Islamic world, and this is reflected in IsDB lending patterns

(Clark, 2012a). The analysis by Hernandez and Vadlamannati of IsDB aid allocation to its fifty-six members during the 1976–2007 period reveals a bias towards Sunni countries, with Shi'a countries receiving aid on exceptional occasions, while non-Muslim countries are the least favoured. These lending patterns closely mirror Saudi Arabia's political stance in the Islamic world. Specifically, the IsDB allocated, on average, 78 per cent more resources to member countries where the head of state is Sunni-affiliated. Member countries with Shi'a-majority populations saw significant increases in lending from the bank only when religious tensions with non-Muslim communities were high.

Interestingly, along with country size, religious affiliation is a core driver of IsDB aid commitments (Hernandez & Vadlamannati, 2017). However, two main trends within the IsDB might help mitigate the polarisation and manipulation of aid: the introduction of the Development and Financial Assessment Index to ensure the systematic and transparent allocation of resources among member countries, and increasing cooperation with UN agencies and other international organisations in programming and implementing projects (Pericoli, 2020).

Against this backdrop, the decision to suspend Syria's membership in the OIC in 2012 limited the IsDB's capacity to intervene directly in the country. This decision reflected Saudi Arabia's position in the early stages of the conflict, a stance that was strongly criticised by Iran.

From the Old to the New Syria

The fall of Bashar al-Assad's regime marked a crucial turning point, leaving Syria grappling with both old and new challenges, including post-war reconstruction and the rebuilding of the social contract between the government and its citizens. Under Ahmad al-Sharaa, Hay'at Tahrir al-Sham entered a new phase, evolving its ideology and strategic objectives, as well as adopting a new approach towards regional and international actors, including the Gulf States, which had varied reactions. In January 2025, the Emir Tamim bin Hamad al-Thani became the first Arab leader to visit Damascus since the overthrow of al-Assad. Moreover, Doha reopened the Qatari embassy, which had been closed since July 2011 (Al Jazeera, 2025a). Earlier in the same month, Syrian foreign minister Asaad al-Shaibani, along with the minister of defence and the intelligence chief, made his first overseas visit to Riyadh, signalling a shift towards openness. In an interview with Saudi-owned Al Arabiya television, Syria's *de facto* leader emphasised that Riyadh would 'certainly have a large role in Syria's future' and highlighted the 'significant investment opportunities for all neighbouring countries' (Al Jazeera, 2025b). It is not surprising that the new leader sought to attract external funds and both new and old allies, given the immense need for resources and funding for post-conflict reconstruction. The UAE, instead, adopted a more cautious approach.

The recovery and stabilisation of Syria represent some of the primary challenges in the region. During the years of conflict, the approach to aid distribution and the provision of social services to the population have followed two parallel lines. On one side, the regime has sought to defend itself by maintaining its prerogative to either deny or provide social services, using them as a tool of power and a means of safeguarding sovereignty. On the other side, the opposition has aimed to challenge the state's legitimacy by offering its services, relying on external resources through foreign aid (Dewachi, Marei & Whittall, 2021). This is because, in Syria, as in other postcolonial nation-states, the delivery of social services has played a crucial role in establishing and maintaining state control – control that is central to the government's assertion of sovereignty (Dewachi et al., 2021:14).

When Bashar al-Assad assumed power, the Syrian government brought associations and charitable organisations under its control. Although these organisations were shaped by the authoritarian regime, they retained some degree of autonomy. The primary objective was to outsource the delivery of social services to private or non-governmental entities, which, ultimately, remained under the regime's influence. However, the services provided by charities were insufficient to fill the vacuum left by the state's partial disinvestment, signalling the decline of the state-organised social welfare system (Ruiz de Elvira, 2024: 263).

This weakness in the capacity to deliver services and the outsourcing of welfare to private or government-organised non-governmental organisations (GO-NGOs) was further exacerbated during the war. This may explain why, during the conflict, the regime began outsourcing service delivery to external humanitarian organisations and foreign aid, while also enabling GO-NGOs to attract international funding, with both remaining under its control. These dynamics allowed loyalist charities to provide services through aid financed directly or indirectly by UN agencies, targeting loyal communities in a framework of inclusion and exclusion based on loyalty to the regime (Aldassouky & Hatahet, 2020).

In this complex scenario, both Qatar and the UAE followed two parallel lines of aid action through their assistance. On one hand, Qatar aligned its efforts with cross-border operations, directing aid to opposition-controlled areas through its organisations and contributions to the Syria Humanitarian Response Plan. On the other hand, the UAE's aid allocation remained focused on areas controlled by the regime, especially after 2018, demonstrating continuity in its strategy even before official normalisation.

A comparative analysis of foreign aid

The analysis and comparison of Qatar and the UAE's foreign aid strategies in Syria reveal several significant implications. The most notable considerations include: (a) the contrasting approaches in terms of the geographical distribution and channel allocation of resources, and (b) the lack of regional coordination in crisis response between these two Gulf donors. Regarding resource allocation, the funding trends for both donors appear consistent, except for 2017, with an increase in contributions in 2023, largely driven by the response to the earthquake and the related emergency. However, the

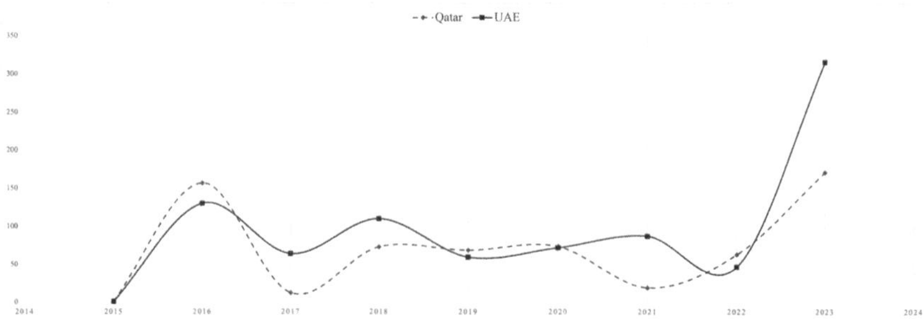

Figure 4.11 QFFD and UAE foreign aid allocation in Syria through multilateral and bilateral channels (including HRP and funds for refugees in third countries) in the period 2015–23. Source: QFFD Annual Reports, UAE MOFAIC Annual Reports, Syria OCHA HRP Financial Tracking Service.

allocation of resources differs between the two, both in terms of geographical areas and in terms of delivery channels.

In the case of Qatar, the primary channels of aid were its charitable organisations – Qatar Charity and the Qatar Red Crescent Society – as well as the UN multilateral channel (the Syria Humanitarian Response Plan). Their efforts were focused exclusively on cross-border operations in Idlib and northern Aleppo after 2018. Before 2018, resources and projects had been implemented in Dar'a and Quneitra, before the regime's recapture of these two areas. As a result, Qatari aid efforts were concentrated in opposition-held areas, where state authority was either absent or severely limited, particularly in the case of areas that had been reconquered. Since this study does not include the beneficiaries' perspective and given the lack of monitoring and evaluation data on the implemented projects, it is challenging to assess the precise impact of Qatar's aid on local governance dynamics. Nevertheless, it is reasonable to assume that, by financing projects in opposition-held regions, Doha, along with other international donors, contributed to the provision of resources and services in areas where state authority was either non-existent or weak, thereby assisting *de facto* authorities in meeting the basic needs of the population. The decision to allocate funds exclusively to opposition-held areas was influenced by two key factors: Qatar's political stance towards the Assad regime and the operational challenges posed by the regime's ban, which restricted activities in Assad-controlled areas for organisations operating in opposition-controlled ones.

The allocation of resources through multilateral channels began to increase in 2017 (see Figure 4.6), when Qatar intensified its engagement with UN channels as part of its broader strategy, extending beyond the Syria context. As previously discussed, this shift was prompted by the Gulf crisis and Qatar's need to enhance its image as a donor and credible actor within both the regional and the international contexts. However, through earmarked contributions, donors can retain a degree of manoeuvrability in terms of project selection and the geographical distribution of resources. This allows them to exercise their preferences and assert their positionality within multilateral frameworks.

When examining aid parameters concerning the variables outlined in the conceptual framework (described in Chapter 2), it is revealing to observe how Qatar's identity as a donor emerges, shaped by transitional, internal and external dynamics. Qatar's Islamic identity and its position on political Islam reflect an alignment with Islamist movements within the opposition to al-Assad in the Syrian conflict. This alignment partially explains the political and foreign aid strategies of Doha and its consequent geographical allocation of resources. The centralisation of Qatar's aid system enabled the country to operate cohesively through its two charitable organisations, managing operations with local partners under RACA's supervision. This structure not only enhanced localisation and flexibility but also allowed Qatar to maintain a centralised approach in terms of policy formulation and implementation. This cohesive approach, along with Qatar's independence in foreign policy and aid strategies, has provided Doha with the capacity to negotiate with non-state actors and armed groups to facilitate access to aid. Qatar's independence is further influenced by both internal and external factors, including geopolitical events such as the Gulf crisis of 2017 and the subsequent reconciliation in 2021. In 2021, funding to Syria saw a decrease, which can be attributed to the emergence of other regional crises, including the situation in Afghanistan and the post-war reconstruction efforts in Gaza. In these contexts, there was a significant reallocation of resources to address what were perceived as new phases of emergency.

On the other hand, the UAE's approach followed three main strategies: (a) implementing foreign aid in government-controlled areas through bilateral channels or the ERC; (b) providing significant contributions to neighbouring countries, particularly Jordan, in response to the Syrian refugee crisis; and (c) allocating resources multilaterally through the SRTF and the OCHA HRP. The amount allocated multilaterally for both the Syrian response and the refugee crisis was smaller compared to Qatar, representing a relatively minor proportion of the total annual allocation. The decision to channel aid bilaterally rather than multilaterally, both for Syria and the refugee response, demonstrates the UAE's commitment to maintaining autonomy in its aid strategy. By prioritising political relations and its strategic positioning, the UAE can direct aid through bilateral channels.

The geographical allocation of aid in Syria holds significant meaning also in the case of the UAE. Between 2016 and 2018, in southern Syria, often referred to as the 'cradle of the revolution', al-Assad's forces, with

Russian air support and, in many cases, backing from Iran and pro-Iranian forces, recaptured numerous opposition-held areas, including the southern governorates of Darʿa and Quneitra (Tokmajyan, 2020). Supporting the government in this region entailed opposing the opposition and enabling the regime to distribute aid based on its priorities. Similarly, the allocation of aid to Raqqa provides another example of how aid distribution in the country was shaped by the conflict's historical context and the vested interests of the involved actors.

The UAE's substantial efforts in Jordan regarding Syrian refugees served a dual purpose. By adopting a 'quasi-asylum policy', where vulnerable Syrians were integrated into the existing migration framework, the UAE accepted a limited number of Syrian refugees into the country. At the same time, the considerable resources allocated to neighbouring countries, with Jordan as the primary recipient, align with the concept of the 'grand compromise' (Cuéller, 2006; Arar, 2017b). This approach entails states in the Global North paying to contain refugee populations outside their borders, thereby safeguarding their sovereignty. More importantly, within the framework of the grand compromise, some states are not reliant on UNHCR for aid (Arar, 2017a) and thus avoid the domestic involvement of international institutions in refugee governance, particularly the UNHCR (Kagan, 2011; Charles, 2021).

As in the case of Qatar, transnational, internal and external variables help explain the UAE's approach to Syria, as well as in other contexts. The 'securitisation' framework adopted in the region led the UAE to marginalise Islamist movements, viewing them as threats to both internal and external stability. The centralisation of aid policies and bureaucracy limits the fragmented implementation on the ground, with bilateral grants or the ERC serving as the main agency. While other organisations operated in Syria, their budgets were relatively small compared to those of the bilateral or ERC-led efforts. As part of its securitisation approach, the UAE sought to contain the migration flow of Syrians into the country, allocating resources to support neighbouring countries in hosting refugees.

One of the UAE's priorities in Syria was to counter the growing influence of Türkiye and Iran, despite their differing positions towards the regime. This strategy aimed to prevent the expansion of Iranian influence on one hand, and the spread of Islamist movements within the opposition on the other, thereby reinforcing the counter-revolutionary narrative in the region (Bakeer, 2019). After the fall of al-Assad, the UAE has to transform its securitisation approach towards new political actors.

Conclusion

In addressing one of the questions posed in this book, regarding the relationship between sectarian approaches to conflict and foreign aid, the analysis indicates a positive correlation between these two factors. The varying interests within the Syrian context are reflected in how Gulf states implemented their aid policies, particularly in terms of aid distribution in either government-controlled or opposition-held areas (Pericoli, 2023a). The initial response of Saudi Arabia and Qatar to the transitional phase of a post-Assad government has included diplomatic and financial support. Saudi Arabia and Qatar plan to pay off Syria's debt to the World Bank (SPA, 2025a), which would allow the financial institution to approve new funds for the country's reconstruction, and provide financial support to state employees (Ministry of Foreign Affairs (Qatar), 2025).

The alignment between Qatar and Saudi Arabia in Syria's post-war reconstruction reflects the initial cooperation between the two GCC countries on bilateral and regional agreements aimed at facilitating Syria's stability and enhancing their respective influence. In April 2025, the Syrian and UAE presidents formally met in Abu Dhabi, marking the beginning of diplomatic relations between the two countries after the fall of Bashar al-Assad. The UAE, however, has shown greater caution in providing initial financial and aid support during the reconstruction phase.

Looking ahead to the future post-conflict reconstruction, with new and old political actors involved, aid policies need to be reimagined to align with the actual needs of the affected communities, and be accompanied by an inclusive political agenda.

Notes

1. UN General Assembly Security Council, A 68/958 – S/2014/547. Retrieved from https://docs.un.org/en/A/68/958
2. From an interview with an OCHA employee, 2023.

3. The revocation of HTS's designation as a Foreign Terrorist Organization by the United States entered into force in July 2025. Retrieved from https://www.state.gov/releases/office-of-the-spokesperson/2025/07/revoking-the-foreign-terrorist-organization-designation-of-hayat-tahrir-al-sham
4. From an interview with an IRDO representative, 2023.
5. OCHA FTS, Syrian Arab Republic 2018, Country Data UAE. Retrieved from https://fts.unocha.org/countries/218/flows/2018
6. OCHA FTS, Syria Earthquake Flash Appeal 2023, per donor countries. Retrieved from https://fts.unocha.org/plans/1149/summary
7. From an interview with a UN OCHA Gaziantep representative, May 2023.
8. Qatar Ministry of Labour data for August 2013.
9. Al Meezan Qatar legal portal. Retrieved from https://www.almeezan.qa/LawPage.aspx?id=7738&language=ar

CONCLUSION: IMAGINING A NEW HUMANITARIANISM

This concluding chapter begins by acknowledging something that should have been clarified in the introduction of the book. However, as I progressed in this journey, I gradually recognised this fact. We need to distinguish between humanitarianism and humanitarian aid, just as we distinguish between principles and practices, as this book has attempted to do. I began searching for Islamic principles that inspire humanitarianism, defined as 'the active belief in the equal value of all human life and the consequent action to assist others and protect their rights' (Aloudat & Khan, 2022: 1).

The intent was to challenge the idea of universality and the predominance of the Western aid structure – and values – and demonstrate that something can be universal only when it is expressed within its historical context, culture and multidimensionality. I then proceeded to examine whether and where these values are present in actors and donors who come from a different background than the Western one, such as the Gulf States, concluding that humanitarianism and humanitarian aid – defined as the formalised system of governments, agencies and organisations operating and assisting people in need – cannot be analysed as the same phenomenon. Therefore, the book argues that behavioural norms (in the Islamic understanding or any others) represent the foundations for plural humanitarianism, while the structure of humanitarian aid and foreign aid is built upon the state's logic when the state is acting as a donor, or implementing agencies' logic when it comes to the implementation level.

And if it is true that the humanitarian space today is characterised by the coexistence of different actors and donors bringing in varying values and practices, it is also true that the system itself exerts pressure on those actors. To survive, they tend to align with the 'universal' and 'secular' spirit of humanitarianism, as conceived by Western norms. This trend can be seen in the process of institutionalising the aid system and aid implementation by the Gulf States, as these countries seek to legitimise themselves in the international arena while maintaining centralised control over aid policies and funding, in line with their internal political structures.

But how can humanitarianism evolve? Does the Gulf States' foreign aid follow the hegemonic approach to humanitarian interventions, or does it present an alternative model?

These questions, posed in the Introduction, bring us back to the main argument of this book. The humanitarian space can no longer be perceived as universal and driven solely by Western values, due to the multipolarity of its current structure and the presence of actors with different backgrounds and approaches. Recognising the added value of donors and agencies with varying political and cultural approaches is probably the first step towards the harmonisation of the humanitarian space, which currently rejects multipolarity in the name of universality. The Gulf States' tendency to align their approach with the international system as a form of survival and legitimisation has both limits and potential. Despite the predominance of state logic in the decision-making process, which makes these actors similar to any Western states, their approaches appear to be more flexible in some cases, as Syria has shown, and capable of adapting or negotiating in contexts where they are perceived as different from others.

On 4 February 2025, while this book was still in the making, the United States Agency for International Development (USAID), the world's largest aid donor, was shut down by the new Trump administration, which planned to place the autonomous agency under the control of the State Department (Lindstaedt, 2025). This political decision could have a profound impact on the development and humanitarian aid sector worldwide. However, where a power and resource vacuum emerges, new actors may step in to fill the gap in financing, strategies and soft power, particularly China and potentially the Gulf States. If the dominance of resources and actors from the Western world has been one of the primary drivers of the aid space as we have come to understand it, it may be time to envision a new form of humanitarianism, where new values, practices and adaptive strategies would emerge.

From Principles to Funding

The analysis of the Islamic social welfare instruments has demonstrated that the principles that inspire the Islamic understanding of humanitarianism can be seen as complementary rather than an alternative approach to the international framework. The exploration of Islamic social financing tools brings attention to ongoing debates about the gap in conventional humanitarian financing. While humanitarian needs continue to rise, traditional financing methods are in decline. In regions such as Asia, the Middle East and Africa, Muslim populations are disproportionately affected by disasters and conflict. In response, faith-based organisations, as well as international and regional actors, are addressing these needs through different financial tools.

In 2016, following the World Humanitarian Summit, a call to action was published to discuss the major challenges of the humanitarian landscape, including the gap between needs and response. This report, titled *Too Important to Fail*, recognised for the first time the relevance of Islamic social finance in bridging the gap in conventional humanitarian financing (High Level Panel on Humanitarian Financing, 2016). The high number of conflicts and crises occurring in the OIC countries made the use of Islamic social finance both urgent and relevant. Since then, numerous partnerships and initiatives have been launched to channel Islamic instruments in humanitarian responses.

The case analysed in this book presents several important considerations. UNHCR, as a non-Muslim international organisation, began operating as a 'mediator' between donors and recipients to distribute *zakat* and *sadaqa* to Muslim refugees worldwide. Following the eligibility criteria for *zakat*, the agency developed a mechanism to address the growing gap between the required budget and donor contributions. In 2013, the funding gap was approximately USD 2.4 billion out of a total budget of USD 5.3 billion, while in 2022, the requested budget had risen to USD 10.7 billion, with a gap of USD 4.5 billion.[1] In 2022, Syria recorded the highest number of people displaced within their own country, totalling 6.8 million. Additionally, Lebanon, Jordan and Türkiye were among the leading countries hosting the largest number of refugees worldwide.

These data highlight the need for sustainable and predictable solutions to address the refugee crisis with a long-term approach. However, the use of *zakat* and *sadaqa*, along with the structure of the Refugee Zakat Fund (RZF), has limitations. *Zakat* and *sadaqa* are not predictable, as they are dependent on the donors' intentions to continue allocating their resources to the organisation or elsewhere. Moreover, the structure of the RZF and the nature of *zakat* itself – where the donor retains the power to decide how and to whom resources should be allocated – pose a risk of compromising the distribution of resources following the needs of the most affected communities. As most contributions come from the Gulf States and state-related foundations, political considerations may influence the allocation of resources, as well as the fluctuations in *zakat* or *sadaqa*. The case of Lebanon, for instance, illustrates a fluctuation in resources between 2019 and 2023, which is linked to the political considerations of donors more than a decrease in the budget requested (Pericoli, 2025a).

As this work argues, principles differ from practices when they are put into action due to external inputs and the structure in which they are implemented. In this case, the 'politicisation' of Islamic social welfare instruments occurs when the act of giving is influenced by the political considerations of donors in the allocation of resources, rather than being directed to where they are most needed. However, a gap between principles and practices also exists between the Islamic moral economy and Islamic Banking and Finance (IBF), with the latter created to fulfil the aspirations of the former. The social failure of the IBF system – often framed as the tension between 'form versus substance' or '*shari'a*-compliant finance versus Islamic-based finance' – is primarily driven by IBF's need to survive and adapt within the conventional monetary system (Asutay, 2012). This adaptation has led to a neglect of the goal of promoting societal equilibrium by ensuring equitable access to resources (Asutay, 2025).

The collaboration between the Islamic Solidarity Fund for Development and UNHCR, which includes both cash *waqf* and cash non-*waqf* components, creates opportunities for sustainable financing for refugees. In this model, the decision-making process for resource allocation is primarily based on the technical evaluations of the two organisations, rather than on the intentions of donors.

Identities and Legitimisation

The top-down analysis of two Gulf donors, Qatar and the UAE, and the elaboration of their aid policies and practices, reveals that the politicisation and institutionalisation of aid across all levels – charities and NGOs, as well as national and regional organisations – are evolving in the same direction.

As the historical excursus illustrates, the process of institutionalising the aid space in the Gulf States resulted from their willingness to operate within the same system as other international humanitarian actors, rather than as 'other' or 'parallel' entities. This process of institutionalisation interacted with the political conditions of aid both within the internal structure and externally, at the implementation level.

In the case of Qatar, the strong centralisation of aid strategies and the increasing efforts to institutionalise the administrative framework of aid – emphasising transparency, coordination with the central government and charities through RACA, and the allocation of resources through multilateral channels (with a growing number of funds beginning in 2017) – has driven key dynamics within the aid system. First, the centralisation of aid has reduced the fragmentation of actors involved at the implementation level, with two main organisations operating as implementing agencies. This phenomenon has made Doha a more cohesive actor, enabling it to be more flexible and efficient in its aid response. However, this flexibility is tied not only to the institutional structure but also to the identity of the donor, which, independent of its neighbours in terms of foreign aid decisions, has established relations with non-state armed groups such as the Taliban, Hamas and factions of the Syrian opposition. The response to the earthquake in February 2023 provides evidence of how flexibility and ability to interact with informal authorities and non-state armed groups can facilitate more efficient aid delivery during emergencies.

The second aspect concerns Qatar's control over its implementing agencies in terms of funds and operations. This control aims to enhance its transparency and credibility as a donor within the international community while maintaining the relevance of political choices over technical considerations.

However, despite limitations imposed on Qatar Charity and the Qatar Red Crescent Society, the institutionalisation of this form of control through RACA has created a 'negotiation process' between charitable organisations and the state, fostering a space for these actors to improve aid dynamics under authoritarianism. Therefore, in the case of Qatar, the institutionalisation of aid practices has both positive and negative implications. On one hand, at the implementation level, it enhances the capacity for negotiations with formal and informal authorities on the ground; on the other hand, internally, it has created a space for dialogue between the state and charitable organisations with bottom-up pressure on institutions. However, the decision-making process based on political considerations may undermine aid effectiveness if resources are tied to the volatile and changing political dynamics of recipient contexts. Finally, this process of institutionalisation has gained legitimacy through increased engagement in multilateral channels, as demonstrated by the case of Syria.

While Qatar's identity is shaped by its autonomy in the region, the UAE's identity is characterised by its securitisation approach. This securitisation is defined by both internal and external dynamics, as well as perceptions of threats, including Islamist movements in the region (and domestically), and the subsequent promotion of a moderate form of Islam. This allows the UAE to portray itself as a natural ally of the West and as a reference point for the Arab counter-revolution following the Arab Spring (Boubtane, 2021). But what would happen if the revolution were to succeed? The situation in Syria following the fall of Bashar al-Assad presents several challenges for the UAE's approach in the region, requiring it to adapt its pragmatism to new political dynamics.

However, examining the UAE's foreign aid structure and approach, the securitisation that characterises its foreign policy is reflected in two main dynamics. The first aspect is that institutional centralisation leads to the prioritisation of bilateral interventions over multilateral contributions, as the UAE seeks to retain greater control over funding and its impact on the political objectives of the donor. This is the case in Syria, though it is not the only example, as seen in Sudan (Donelli & Pericoli, 2024).

The second aspect is the centralisation of policy formulation and the establishment of a single entity, the Ministry of Foreign Affairs and International

Cooperation, responsible for formulating policies and coordinating the operations of implementing agencies and foundations. The Abu Dhabi Fund for Development serves as a parallel entity, focusing on development interventions through soft loans and grants. Compared to Qatar, the absence of a meso-level in the aid structure (represented by entities such as the QFFD and RACA) reduces the negotiation space between the implementing agencies and institutional levels. Moreover, despite the presence of numerous charitable organisations and foundations – related to the UAE's federal structure – the predominance of bilateral interventions limits the 'space of existence' for small implementing agencies in each emirate, with the Emirates Red Crescent serving as the primary actor.

Aid for Donors or Aid for Recipients?

Considering that political implications and conditions are intrinsic to the aid system, this book has demonstrated that separating politics from humanitarian practices is not feasible, as aid is driven by political factors and can influence political dynamics on the ground.

> The aid system does not operate as an organic whole but involves asymmetrical power, contested sovereignties, and competing, often contradictory goals. Recognising these tensions challenges the optimistic assumptions used to legitimate the system but does not undermine the case for aid itself. Instead, it provides us with a more realistic approach to the complex and contested processes involved in donor–recipient attempts to negotiate mutually beneficial agreements, and to the adequacy of the regulatory framework that governs them. (Brett, 2016: 3)

Recognising the political nature of aid and the political involvement of donors does not necessarily undermine the aid system itself, or the legitimacy of donors. As Slim (2002) wrote, the philanthropy-only approach that persists in international humanitarianism, which bases humanitarian action primarily on the ethic of charity, is insufficient. He argues, instead, that respect for international humanitarian law (IHL) can provide 'an effective bridge between a potentially utopian theory and effective humanitarian protection' (Slim 2002: 1). If IHL regulates the negative political implications of aid on the ground and the asymmetrical relationships between donors and recipients, the political drivers of donors, and their different values, can be harmonised in the system and aligned with the real needs of affected populations, especially during conflicts and emergencies. However, IHL is derived from a series of moral norms that collectively reflect a humanitarian ideal. One of the law's roles is to reproduce and reinforce these norms (Gordon, 2021: 59). In analysing the relationship between IHL and the healthcare system during the Syrian war, Gordon raises important questions regarding the role of the law in either undermining or protecting healthcare, highlighting the tension between norms and law.

The case of Syria highlights the failure of the international community, IHL and the conflicting parties to protect civilians and ensure safe and sufficient access to aid throughout the years of conflict. Aid became a tool within the conflict in both opposition- and government-controlled areas. For the rebels, it was a means of survival, while for the regime, it was a way to ensure basic needs for the population, thereby reinforcing sovereignty through external resources. In both contexts, the inclusion or exclusion from aid access became a political decision; similarly, for donors, choosing to intervene in areas controlled by either the Assad regime or the rebels was also a political choice. Furthermore, some state actors involved in humanitarian aid, such as Qatar and the UAE, were indirectly engaged in the conflict while providing resources to assist the civilian population. I analysed the aid strategies from the perspective of donors while keeping in mind that aid should ultimately serve the needs of the recipients, or at least this is what it is supposed to do. Instead, it became part of the conflict ecosystem and the war economy, with a lack of responsibility at all levels, including the donors (McLean, 2021).

Following nearly fourteen years of conflict, over 16 million Syrians need humanitarian assistance, with 90 per cent of the population living in poverty. The country's economic situation has deteriorated over time.[2] The budget estimated by OCHA in the HRP has increased from 2016 to 2024, accompanied by a growing gap between the funding received by donors and the unmet requirements. In 2022, only 53 per cent of the required funding was received, and this figure is projected to drop to 35 per cent in 2024. The contraction of funds from USAID, which was one of the major donors in Syria and the largest donor in the HRP, is likely to have a significant impact on the humanitarian response.[3]

After al-Assad's removal, Ahmad al-Sharaa's HTS group emerged as the *de facto* governing party, facing a challenging future. The reconstruction efforts following the conflict and the restoration of the country's economy were hindered by sanctions, imposed by the United States, European Union and the United Kingdom on the former government of Bashar al-Assad. The sanctions were lifted by the US in May 2025 after a meeting between President Trump and Ahmad al-Sharaa in Saudi Arabia (Al Jazeera, 2025c). They included a total arms embargo, restrictions on all imports of Syrian oil, bans on all forms of public and private financial support to Syria, bans on telecommunications equipment exports to Syria, prohibitions of financial transactions with Syrian financial institutions, and the control of exports to Syria of any goods or material that might be used for internal repression (Abboud, 2017).

Moreover, al-Sharaa needs both new and old international and regional allies to implement the political transition and the post-war reconstruction. However, attracting funds for reconstruction from donors and actors with differing interests in the country could, once again, compromise the country's stability due to external interference.

Does Islam Really Matter?

Despite the predominance of political considerations over religious values and norms, the analysis of Islamic concepts of humanitarianism and charity provides a foundational framework for evaluating the aid phenomenon in and from Muslim-majority countries. This phenomenon should be understood as a multidimensional process that requires consideration of various levels of analysis, values and interactions.

The analysis of the top-down decision-making process in aid strategies by state entities overlooks the role of faith-based organisations, transnational Muslim NGOs and other grassroots groups, and their interactions with recipients, as well as their understanding of Islam and the intersection between aid and Islamic principles. In comparing different Muslim organisations, Petersen (2012) distinguishes between two approaches to the interpretation of religion within aid practices: the maximalist approach, in which Islam constitutes the central framework of the organisational community, shaping all discourses, practices and structures, and the minimalist approach, where Islam is relegated to a quasi-secular, almost invisible role, confined to the personal sphere. The process of institutionalisation of the aid sector in Qatar and the UAE has led to a secularisation of aid, where Islam, and its different understandings, are either associated with personal values or used to justify the moral duty of wealth redistribution and assisting those in need. As stated by Sheikh Zayed bin Sultan al-Nahyan: 'The rich must help the poor, and God Almighty granted us this fortune to develop our country and help develop other countries as well' (Gulf News, 2022).

The marginalisation of religion in favour of a more 'neutral' and institutionalised approach to aid is also evident in the case of Saudi Arabia, particularly with the transformation of its aid landscape following the establishment of the King Salman Humanitarian Aid and Relief Centre in 2015. Through its mandate, this institution, which is responsible for managing and channelling all humanitarian aid from the kingdom, is reorienting humanitarian practices towards a unified approach that aligns with the dominant paradigm of 'the global moral community', which emphasises universality (Derbal, 2022b: 122). However, this reorientation of the aid landscape comes at the expense of organisational freedom and the loss of a multiplicity of values (Derbal, 2022b: 127). The centralisation of humanitarian operations under state control has indeed diminished the operations of other organisations, such as the Saudi Red Crescent and the International Islamic Relief Organization.

With the aim of operating within the international humanitarian landscape, the idea of acting in the name of Islamic solidarity may be perceived as partial and misleading, potentially diminishing the credibility of these donors within the international community. This is even though the concentration of aid from all these three Gulf states remains primarily focused on Muslim-majority or Arab countries. Therefore, the process of institutionalisation and centralisation of aid has resulted in a model that maintains their identities in terms of structure and approaches but diminishes the religion-based focus in their discourses.

In the ongoing transformation of the Gulf States' aid landscape, and of the humanitarian space itself, various levels of analysis are required to understand the asymmetrical structure of the system. This book has explored the conceptual framework and the institutional transformations of Qatar and the UAE as donors, actors and agents in emergency and conflict zones, contributing to the debate on Gulf States' foreign aid in constantly changing crises and regional political dynamics.

Notes

1. UNHCR budget and expenditure per year. Retreived from https://reporting.unhcr.org/dashboards/budget-and-expenditure
2. IOM, Crisis in the Syrian Arab Republic. Retrieved from https://www.iom.int/crisis-syrian-arab-republic
3. OCHA FTS, Syria Humanitarian Response Plan 2016–24. Retrieved from https://fts.unocha.org/plans/1175/summary

APPENDICES

This section offers data on the aid resources provided by Qatar and the UAE in Syria in the period 2015–23. The two tables show the aid flow per year, donor agency, and geographical, sectoral and channel allocation of resources.

Appendix 1

Qatar Fund for Development Aid Allocation in Syria from 2015 to 2023

Appendix 1 Qatar Fund for Development aid allocation in Syria from 2015 to 2023.

Year	Donor agency	Implementing agency/ channel	Sector	Geographical location	Total amount in USD million
2015	Education Above All	HRP	Multisector	Syria	1.3
2016	QFFD, Education Above All	Through charities	QUEST Education	Syria & neighbours	150
2016	QFFD	(Pledged)	Relief/ Humanitarian	Aleppo	100
2016	QFFD	Joint Humanitarian Trust	Refugees	Türkiye	5.0

(Continued)

Year	Donor agency	Implementing agency/ channel	Sector	Geographical location	Total amount in USD million
2016	QFFD	HRP	Multisector	Syria	1.6
2017	QFFD	QRCS	Reconstruction	Homs (al-Waar)	0.5
2017	QFFD	QRCS–HRP	Multisector		12.0
2018	QFFD, Education Above All	Not specified	Education – IDPs	Idlib, Aleppo, Hama, Homs, *Dar'a*, Quneitra, rural Damascus, Damascus	21.4
2018	QFFD	QC, QRCS	Emergency	Deraa, eastern Ghouta	2.9
2018	QFFD	QRCS	Health	Northwest al-Bab	7.0
2018	QFFD	QRCS	Refugees	Jordan	2.0
2018	QFFD	HRP	Multisector	Syria	39.8
2019	QFFD, QC	HRP	Multisector	Syria	68.8
2020	QFFD	SPARK	Refugees, IDPs	Jordan, Türkiye, northern Syria	10.0
2020	QFFD	UNHCR	Syrian refugees	Lebanon	2.0
2020	QFFD	UNRWA	Palestinian Refugees	Syria	20.7
2020	QFFD	HRP	Multisector	Syria	41.0
2021	QFFD	HRP	Multisector	Syria	9.5
2021	QFFD	Shafak, IOM	IDPs (protection)	Northern Syria	1.3
2021	QFFD, FCDO		Education	Northern Syria	1.6
2021	QFFD	Lebanese Red Cross	Refugees (protection)	Lebanon	0.9
2021	QFFD	UNRWA	Palestinian refugees	Syria	4.0
2021	QFFD	Cross-border Humanitarian Fund, pooled funds	Refugees and IDPs	Northern Syria, Lebanon, Jordan	2.0

(Continued)

Year	Donor agency	Implementing agency/ channel	Sector	Geographical location	Total amount in USD million
2022	QFFD	UNHCR	Syrian refugees	Lebanon, Jordan	2.6
2022	QFFD	UNRWA	Palestinian refugees	Syria	5.5
2022	QFFD	IOM	IDPs	Northwest Syria	0.7
2022	QFFD	HRP	Multisector	Syria	54.3
2022	QFFD	WHO (pledge)	Health	Not specified	10.0
2023	QFFD	HRP	Multisector	Syria	73.0
2023	QFFD	Türkiye Disaster and Emergency Management Authority	Infrastructure/ development	Northern Syria	98.0

Appendix 2

UAE Aid Allocation in Syria from 2015 to 2023

Appendix 2 UAE aid allocation in Syria from 2015 to 2023 (MOFAIC, ADFD, charitable organisations and foundations). The table includes multilateral funds to the Syrian Humanitarian Response Plan and SRTF.

Year	Donor agency	Implementing agency / channel	Sector	Geographical location	Total amount in USD million
2015	UAE	HRP	Multisector	Syria	1.1
2016	UAE government	Bilateral – Syrian Government	Emergency	Syria (government-controlled areas (GCA))	40.5
2016	UAE government	Emirates Red Crescent	Refugee response	Jordan, Lebanon, Türkiye, Greece, Iraq	89.5
2017	UAE government	Bilateral	Humanitarian response	Syria (GCA)	22.4
2017	UAE government	ERC	Refugee response	Jordan, Lebanon	41.9
2018	UAE government	Bilateral	Humanitarian response	Syria (GCA)	60.3
2018	UAE government	ERC	Refugee Response	Jordan, Lebanon, Iraq	49.7
2019	UAE government	Bilateral	Humanitarian response	Syria (GCA)	5.8
2019	UAE government	Bilateral / ERC	Refugee Response	Jordan, Lebanon, Iraq	53.9
2020	UAE government	HRP	Multisector	Syria	9.5
2020	UAE government	Bilateral	Humanitarian – health	Syria (GCA)	22.2
2020	UAE government	ACTED	Humanitarian	Kurdistan	2.0
2020	UAE government	ERC / bilateral	Refugee response	Jordan	38.4
2021	UAE government	Bilateral	Humanitarian	Syria (GCA)	30.5

(Continued)

Year	Donor agency	Implementing agency / channel	Sector	Geographical location	Total amount in USD million
2021	UAE government	Bilateral	Refugee response	Jordan	56.7
2022	UAE government	HRP	Multisector		7.0
2022	UAE government	Bilateral	Humanitarian – health	Syria	30.0
2022	UAE government	ERC / bilateral	Refugee response	Jordan	10.0
2023	UAE government ERC	Bilateral	Humanitarian (earthquake response)	Syria	281.3
2023	UAE government	HRP (earthquake flash appeal)	Humanitarian – shelter and food	Syria	15.0
2023	UAE government	Bilateral	Refugee response	Jordan	41.2
2014–2024	UAE government	SRTF	Multisector	Syria	19.4

BIBLIOGRAPHY

Abboud, S. (2017, 31 January). The economics of war and peace in Syria: stratification and factionalization in the business community. Century Foundation. Retrieved from https://tcf.org/content/report/economics-war-peace-Syria/

ACAPS. (2023, 4 August). *Northern Syria: Key crises to watch*. Retrieved from https://www.acaps.org/fileadmin/Data_Product/Main_media/20230804_ACAPS_Thematic_report_Northern_Syria_key_crises_to_watch.pdf

Adamczyk, S., & Doumit, J. (2023). Legal identity in limbo: Humanitarian challenges and responses to civil documentation issued by *de facto* authorities in Northwest Syria. *Citizenship Studies, 27*, 866–82. https://doi.org/10.1080/13621025.2024.2321719

Adleh, F., & Favier, A. (2017). 'Local reconciliation agreements' in Syria: A non-starter for peacebuilding. Middle East Directions (MED), 2017/01.

Ahmad, K. (1994). *Islamic approach to development: Some policy implications*. Islamabad: Institute of Policy Studies.

Ahmad, K. (2003). The challenge of global capitalism. In J. H. Dunning (Ed.), *Making globalization good: The moral challenges of global capitalism*. Oxford: Oxford University Press.

Ahmed, C. (2009). Networks of Islamic NGOs in sub-Saharan Africa: Bilal Muslim Mission, African Muslim Agency (Direct Aid) and *al-Haramayn*. *Journal of Eastern African Studies, 3*, 426–37. https://doi.org/10.1080/17531050903273727

Ahmed, H. (2004). *Role of zakah and awqaf in poverty alleviation*. Jeddah: Islamic Development Bank, Islamic Research and Training Institute.

Ahmed, H. (2020). The Islamic social sector (zakat and waqf) and development: Principles, status and prospects. In A. A. Khan & A. Cheema (Eds), *Islam and international development: Insights for working with Muslim communities*. Rugby: Practical Action.

Ahmed, Z. S., & Akbarzadeh, S. (2021). Sectarianism and the Organisation of Islamic Cooperation (OIC). *Territory, Politics, Governance, 9*, 76–93. https://doi.org/10.1080/21622671.2019.1643779.

Akbarzadeh, S., & Ahmed, Z. S. (2018). Impacts of Saudi hegemony on the Organization of Islamic Cooperation (OIC). *International Journal of Politics, Culture, and Society, 31*, 297–311. https://doi.org/10.1007/s10767-017-9270-x

Akgündüz, A. (2011). The Ottoman waqf administration in the 19th and early-20th centuries: Continuities and discontinuities. *Acta Orientalia Academiae Scientiarum Hungaricae, 64*, 71–87. https://doi.org/10.1556/aorient.64.2011.1.5

Al-Ansari, M. M. H., Aras, B., & Yorulmazlar, E. (2021). The new Gulf order: Crisis, mediation, and reconciliation. *Middle East Policy, 28*(1), 23–35. https://doi.org/10.1111/mepo.12544

Al-Daghistani, S. (2021). *The making of Islamic economic thought: Islamization, law, and moral discourses*. Cambridge: Cambridge University Press.

Aldassouky, A., and Hatahet, S. (2020, 11 June). *The role of philanthropy in the Syrian war: Regime-sponsored NGOs and armed group charities*. Research Project Report 2020/09, European University Institute. Retrieved from https://cadmus.eui.eu/server/api/core/bitstreams/0e8d2bef-90be-5c3b-be41-d2f4322e5646/content

Al Fahad, A. H. (2015). Rootless trees: Genealogical politics in Saudi Arabia. In B. Haykel, T. Hegghammer & S. Lacroix (Eds), *Saudi Arabia in transition: Insights on social, political, economic and religious change*. New York: Cambridge University Press, pp. 263–91.

al-Ghithami, A. (2009). *Tribe and tribalism or postmodern identities*. Casablanca, Morocco: Arab Cultural Centre.

Ali, S. S. (Ed.). (2019). *Towards a maqāṣid al-sharīʿah index of socio-economic development: Theory and application*. Cham: Palgrave Macmillan.

Al-Jabassini, A. (2024). From rebel leaders to post-war intermediaries: Evidence from Southern Syria. *Small Wars & Insurgencies, 35*(4), 656–77. https://doi.org/10.1080/09592318.2024.2312626

Al Jazeera. (2024a, 8 December). Celebrations in Damascus as Syrian opposition declares end of al-Assad rule. Retrieved from https://www.aljazeera.com/gallery/2024/12/8/celebrations-in-damascus-as-syrian-opposition-declares-end-of-al-assad-rule

Al Jazeera. (2024b, 8 December). What happened in Syria? How did al-Assad fall? Retrieved from https://www.aljazeera.com/news/2024/12/8/what-happened-in-syria-has-al-assad-really-fallen

Al Jazeera. (2025a, 29 January). Qatari emir to visit Syria on Thursday: Al Jazeera sources. Retrieved from https://www.aljazeera.com/news/2025/1/29/qatari-emir-to-visit-syria-on-thursday-al-jazeera-sources

Al Jazeera. (2025b, 2 January). Syria FM in Saudi Arabia on maiden trip as new rulers reset regional ties. Retrieved from https://www.aljazeera.com/news/2025/1/2/syria-fm-in-saudi-arabia-on-maiden-trip-as-new-rulers-reset-regional-ties

Al Jazeera. (2025c, 23 May). US lifts first sanctions on Syria following Trump's surprise announcement. Retrieved from https://www.aljazeera.com/news/2025/5/23/us-lifts-first-sanctions-on-syria-following-trumps-surprise-announcement

Al Kaabi, M., Yaaqeib, S., & Bin Touq, A. (2023). The landscape of the third sector in the United Arab Emirates. *Journal of Muslim Philanthropy & Civil Society*, *7*(1). https://scholarworks.iu.edu/iupjournals/index.php/muslimphilanthropy/index

Alkahlout, O. M. (2023). *Zakat* restrictions: Religious, social, institutional, and political. Case study: Qatar. *Asian Social Science*, *19*(3), 32–44. https://doi.org/10.5539/ass.v19n3p32

Al Khalifa, H. H. (2019). Aljazeera's coverage of the Qatar crisis on June 5th, 2017: A frame analysis. *Global Media Journal*, *17*(32). https://www.globalmediajournal.com/

Alkubaisi, H. J. (2020, January). *Sponsorship and donations in Qatar Foundation: An empirical investigation to the foundation's fundraising efforts.* MBA project, Qatar University. Retrieved from https://qspace.qu.edu.qa/handle/10576/12648

Al-Kuwari, M. (2019). Tribe and tribalism: The Trojan horse of GCC states? In A. Krieg (Ed.), *Divided Gulf: The anatomy of a crisis.* Singapore: Palgrave Macmillan.

Almezaini, K. S. (2012). *The UAE and foreign policy: Foreign aid, identities and interest.* Abingdon: Routledge.

Almezaini, K. (2017). From identities to politics: UAE foreign aid. In I. Bergamaschi, P. Moore & A. B. Tickner (Eds), *South–south cooperation beyond the myths: Rising donors, new aid practices?* London: Palgrave Macmillan.

Almezaini, K. (2021). The changing dynamics in the UAE–Syria relationship. In B. Balci & N. Monceau (Eds), *Turkey, Russia and Iran in the Middle East: Establishing a new regional order.* Cham: Palgrave Macmillan.

Almezaini, K. (2024). The politics of Gulf foreign aid: From survival and solidarity to political and military influence. *Third World Quarterly*, *45*, 2190–2207. https://doi.org/10.1080/01436597.2024.2394618

Aloudat, T., & Khan, T. (2022). Decolonising humanitarianism or humanitarian aid? *PLOS Global Public Health, 2*(4), e0000179. https://doi.org/10.1371/journal.pgph.0000179

Al-Qaradawi, Y. (2002). Zakah role in curing social and economic malaises. In M. Kahf (Ed.), *Economics of* zakah: *A book of readings* (2nd ed.). Jeddah: Islamic Research and Training Institute.

Al-Qaradawi, Y. (2011). *Fiqh al-zakāh: A comprehensive study of zakah regulations and philosophy in the light of the Qur'an and Sunnah*. Kuala Lumpur: Islamic Book Trust.

Al-Saif, T. (2014). Political Islam in Saudi Arabia: Recent trends and prospects. *Contemporary Arab Affairs, 7*, 398–420. https://doi.org/10.1080/17550912.2014.936122

Alsharif, A. (2012, 16 August). Organization of Islamic Cooperation suspends Syria. Reuters. Retrieved from https://www.reuters.com/article/us-syria-crisis-islamic-summit-idUSBRE87E19F/

AlShehabi, O. H. (2019). Policing labour in empire: The modern origins of the Kafala sponsorship system in the Gulf Arab States. *British Journal of Middle Eastern Studies, 48*, 291–310. https://doi.org/10.1080/13530194.2019.1580183

Alterman, B., & von Hippel, K. (2007). *Understanding Islamic charities*. Washington, DC: Center for Strategic and International Studies.

AP. (2015, 10 September). UAE home to 242,000 Syrians. *Khaleej Times*. Retrieved from https://www.khaleejtimes.com/

Arar, R. (2017a, March). Leveraging sovereignty: The case of Jordan and the international refugee regime. In *Refugees and migration movements in the Middle East*. POMEPS Studies 25, Project on Middle East Political Science. Retrieved from https://pomeps.org/wp-content/uploads/2017/03/POMEPS_Studies_25_Refugees_Web.pdf

Arar, R. (2017b). The new grand compromise: How Syrian refugees changed the stakes in the global refugee assistance regime. *Middle East Law and Governance, 9*, 298–312. https://doi.org/10.1163/18763375-00903007

Arif, M. (1989). Towards establishing the microfoundations of Islamic economics: The basis of the basics. In A. Ghazali and S. Omar (Eds.), *Readings in the concept and methodology of Islamic economics*. Petaling Jaya, Malaysia: Pelanduk.

Asseburg, M. (2020, July). *Reconstruction in Syria: Challenges and policy options for the EU and its member states*. SWP Research Paper 11, Stiftung Wissenschaft und Politik. Retrieved from https://www.swp-berlin.org/publications/products/research_papers/2020RP11_ReconstructionSyria.pdf

Asseburg, M., & Henkel, S. C. (2021, July). *Normalisation and realignment in the Middle East: A new, conflict-prone regional order takes shape*. SWP Comment No. 45, Stiftung Wissenschaft und Politik. Retrieved from https://nbn-resolving.org/urn:nbn:de:0168-ssoar-76039-4

Asutay, M. (2007). A political economy approach to Islamic economics: Systemic understanding for an alternative economic system. *Kyoto Bulletin of Islamic Area Studies, 1*(2), 3–18. https://ssrn.com/abstract=1735619

Asutay, M. (2012). Conceptualising and locating the social failure of Islamic finance: Aspirations of Islamic moral economy vs the realities of Islamic finance. *Asian and African Area Studies, 11*, 93–113.

Asutay, M. (2025). Islamic moral economy: Bringing back substantive morality to humanise Islamic finance. *Global Policy, 16*(S1), 7–11. https://doi.org/10.1111/1758-5899.13487

Asutay, M., & Yilmaz, I. (2018). Re-embedding Maqāṣid al-Sharīʿah in the essential methodology of Islamic economics. In M. E. El-Mesawi (Ed.), *Maqāṣid Al-Sharīʿah: Explorations and implications*. Kuala Lumpur: Islamic Book Trust

Atia, M. (2013). *Building a house in Heaven: Pious neoliberalism and Islamic charity in Egypt*. Minneapolis: University of Minnesota Press.

Aydin, N. (2019). Paradigmatic and conceptual framework for Islamic HDI. In S. S. Ali (Ed.), *Towards a maqāṣid al-sharīʿah index of socio-economic development*. Cham: Palgrave Macmillan.

Baabood, A. (2019). The future of the GCC amid the Gulf divide. In A. Krieg (Ed.), *Divided Gulf: The anatomy of a crisis*. Singapore: Palgrave Macmillan.

Babar, Z. (2014, March). *Working for the neighbors: Arab migrants in Qatar*. Paper presented at the Arab Migrant Communities in the GCC Working Group Conference, Centre for International and Regional Studies, School of Foreign Service in Qatar, Georgetown University, Doha, Qatar.

Bacik, G. (2011). The genesis, history, and functioning of the Organization of Islamic Cooperation (OIC): A formal-institutional analysis. *Journal of Muslim Minority Affairs, 31*, 594–614. https://doi.org/10.1080/13602004.2011.630864

Bakeer, A. (2019, 8 January). Why did the UAE and Bahrain re-open their embassies in Syria? Al Jazeera. Retrieved from https://www.aljazeera.com/opinions/2019/1/8/why-did-the-uae-and-bahrain-re-open-their-embassies-in-syria

Baldwin, D. A. (1966). *Foreign aid and American foreign policy: A documentary analysis*. New York: Praeger.

Banna, H. (1993). *The message of the Teachings*. London: Ta-Ha.

Barakat, S. (2012, July). *The Qatari Spring: Qatar's emerging role in peacemaking*. Kuwait Programme on Development, Governance and Globalisation in the Gulf States No. 24, London School of Economics and Politics Science. Retrieved from https://eprints.lse.ac.uk/59266/1/The-Qatari-Spring%20-%20 Qatars-Emerging-Role-in-Peacemaking.pdf

Barakat, S. (2014, November). *Qatari mediation: Between ambition and achievement.* Brookings Doha Center Analysis Paper No 12. Retrieved from https://www.brookings.edu/wp-content/uploads/2016/06/Final-PDF-English.pdf

Barakat, S. (2019, July). *Priorities and challenges of Qatar's humanitarian diplomacy.* CMI Brief No. 07, Chr. Michelsen Institute. Retrieved from https://www.cmi.no/publications/6906-priorities-and-challenges-of-qatars-humanitarian-diplomacy

Barakat, S. (2024). Niche small states in humanitarian diplomacy: Qatar's positionality in the protection ecosystem. *International Review of the Red Cross, 106,* 585–609. https://doi.org/10.1017/S1816383124000602

Barakat, S., & Milton, S. (2019). Qatar as an emerging power in post-conflict reconstruction and conflict mediation. In A. Paczyńska (Ed.), *Emerging powers and post-conflict reconstruction.* Boulder, CO: Lynne Rienner.

Barakat, S., & Zyck, S. A. (2010). *Gulf state assistance to conflict-affected environments.* London: London School of Economics and Political Science.

Barakat, S., Milton, S., and Elkahlout, G. (2020). The impact of the Gulf crisis on Qatar's humanitarian sector. *Disasters, 44,* 63–84. https://doi.org/10.1111/disa.12407

Barnett, M. N. (1996). Identity and alliances in the Middle East. In P. J. Katzenstein (Ed.), *The culture of national security: Norms and identity in world politics.* New York: Columbia University Press.

Barnett, M., & Weiss, T. G. (2013). *Humanitarianism contested: Where angels fear to tread.* Abingdon: Routledge.

Bartlotti, L. N. (2002). Development in Islamic contexts: Christian NGOS and best practice under the Taliban. *Transformation, 19,* 107–17. https://doi.org/10.1177/026537880201900204

Bashir, F. A., & Abdelsalam, F. (2021). Qatar's foreign aid policy: Evolution, motives and values. *Al-Hikmah: International Journal of Islamic Studies and Human Sciences, 4*(1), 1–26. https://doi.org/10.46722/hikmah.v4i1.83

Başkan, B. (2021). *The politics of Islam: The Muslim Brothers and the state in the Arab Gulf.* Edinburgh: Edinburgh University Press.

Bennett, J. (2013). Afghanistan: cross-border NGO coordination, 1985–93. In *Meeting needs: NGO coordination in practice.* Abingdon: Earthscan.

Bedoui, H. E., & Mansour, W. (2015). Performance and *maqasid al-shari'ah*'s pentagon-shaped ethical measurement. *Science and Engineering Ethics, 21,* 555–76. https://doi.org/10.1007/s11948-014-9561-9

Benthall, J. (2007). Islamic charities, faith-based organizations, and the international aid system. In J. B. Alterman & K. von Hippel (Eds), *Understanding Islamic charities.* Washington, DC: Center for Strategic and International Studies.

Benthall J. C. M. (2018a). Charitable activities of the Muslim Brotherhood, *Journal of Muslim Philanthropy & Civil Society, 2*(2). Retrieved from https://scholarworks.iu.edu

Benthall, J. (2018b). *The rise and decline of Saudi overseas humanitarian charities.* CIRS Occasional Papers 20, Center for International and Regional Studies. Retrieved from https://cirs.qatar.georgetown.edu/publications/rise-and-decline-saudi-overseas-humanitarian-charities-0/

Benthall, J., & Bellion-Jourdan, J. (2003). *The charitable crescent: Politics of aid in the Muslim world,* New York: I. B. Tauris.

Berg, H. (2025). Five-star humanitarianism? Navigating Gulf aid in the aftermath of the Syrian refugee crisis in Jordan. *Middle East Critique, 34*, 263–86. https://doi.org/10.1080/19436149.2025.2453316

Bianco, C. (2024). *The Gulf monarchies after the Arab Spring: Threats and security.* Manchester: Manchester University Press.

Bianco, C., & Stansfield, G. (2018). The intra-GCC crises: Mapping GCC fragmentation after 2011. *International Affairs, 94*, 613–35. https://doi.org/10.1093/ia/iiy025

Bonner, M. (2003). Poverty and charity in the rise of Islam. In M. Bonner, M. Ener & A. Singer (Eds), *Poverty and charity in Middle Eastern contexts.* Albany: State University of New York Press.

Borck, T. (2024). *Seeking stability amidst disorder: The foreign policies of Saudi Arabia, the UAE and Qatar, 2010–20.* London: Hurst.

Boubtane, D. (2021). *From soft power to sharp power? The United Arab Emirates religious policy and the promotion of a moderate Islam.* Sciences Po Kuwait Program. Retrieved from https://www.sciencespo.fr/kuwait-program/wp-content/uploads/2021/11/sciencespo-kuwait-program-2021-boutane-dhiya.pdf

Bradley, M. (2023). *The politics and everyday practice of international humanitarianism.* Oxford: Oxford University Press.

Brehony, N. (2020). The UAE's role in the Yemen crisis. In S. W. Day and N. Brehony (Eds), *Global, regional, and local dynamics in the Yemen Crisis.* Cham: Palgrave Macmillan.

Brett, E. A. (2016, April). *Explaining aid (in)effectiveness: The political economy of aid relationships.* LSE International Development Working Paper 176.

Bseiso, J., Hofman, M., & Whittall, J. (Eds). (2021). *Everybody's war: The politics of aid in the Syria crisis*. New York: Oxford University Press.

Bulut, M., & Korkut, C. (2022). The Ottoman cash waqf as altruistic finance model. In A. G. Ismail, R. Abdullah & M. H. Zaenal (Eds), *Islamic philanthropy: Exploring zakat, waqf, and sadaqah in Islamic finance and economics*. Cham: Palgrave Macmillan.

Bunzel, C. M. (2025). Refounding the Kingdom: Saudi Arabia from Islamism and Wahhabism to 'moderate' Islam. *Middle Eastern Studies*. Advance online publication. https://doi.org/10.1080/00263206.2025.2482632

Bürcky, U. (2011, June). *Trends in in-country aid fragmentation and donor proliferation: An analysis of changes in aid allocation patterns between 2005 and 2009.* Report on behalf of the OECD Task Team on Division of Labour and Complementarity.

Carnegie, A., Howe, K., Lichtenheld, A. G., & Mukhopadhyay, D. (2022). Winning hearts and minds for rebel rulers: Foreign aid and military contestation in Syria. *British Journal of Political Science, 52*, 1333–54. doi:10.1017/S0007123421000156

Carpi, E. (2015, February). *The UAE-funded Mrajeeb al-Fhood Syrian refugee camp in Jordan: Can humanitarianism ever upgrade?* Trends Research & Advisory – Abu Dhabi.

Carpi, E. (2020). Different shades of 'neutrality': Arab Gulf NGO responses to Syrian refugees in northern Lebanon. In E. Fiddian-Qasmiyeh (Ed.), *Refuge in a moving world: Tracing refugee and migrant journeys across disciplines*. London: UCL Press.

Carpi, E. (2023). *The politics of crisis-making: Forced displacement and cultures of assistance in Lebanon*. Bloomington: Indiana University Press.

Center for Conflict and Humanitarian Studies. (2024, 7 December). The Center for Conflict and Humanitarian Studies signs agreement with Qatar Charity. Retrieved from https://chs-doha.org/en/News/Pages/The-Center-for-Conflict-and-Humanitarian-Studies-signs-agreement-with-Qatar-Charity-.aspx

Chapra, M. U. (2001). *What is Islamic economics?* Islamic Research and Training Institute, IsDB Prize Winners' Lecture Series No. 9.

Chapra, M. U. (2008a). Ibn Khaldun's theory of development: Does it help explain the low performance of the present-day Muslim world? *Journal of Socioeconomics, 37*, 836–63. https://doi.org/10.1016/j.socec.2006.12.051

Chapra, M. U. (2008b). *The Islamic vision of development in the light of* maqāṣid al-sharīʿah. London: International Institute of Islamic Thought.

Charles, L. (2021). Refugees but not refugees: The UAE's response to the Syrian refugee crisis viewed through the lived experience of Syrians in Abu Dhabi. *Journal of Refugee Studies, 34*, 1423–40. https://doi.org/10.1093/jrs/feab014.

Chenery, H. B., & Strout, A. M. (1966). Foreign assistance and economic development. *American Economic Review, 56*, 679–733. https://www.jstor.org/stable/1813524

Çizakça, M. (2000). *History of Awqaf in the Ottoman Empire and the Turkish Republic.* Paper, Fifth Draft.

Clark, J. A. (2004). *Islam, charity, and activism: Middle-class networks and social welfare in Egypt, Jordan, and Yemen*. Bloomington: Indiana University Press.

Clark, M. (2012a). Haunted by history: The power politics of the Sunni–Shi'a divide. *Popular Social Science*, Fall.

Clark, J. A. (2012b). Patronage, prestige, and power: the Islamic Center Charity Society's political role within the Muslim Brotherhood. In S. S. Shehata (Ed.), *Islamist politics in the Middle East: Movements and change*. Abingdon: Routledge.

Clarke, G. (2007). Agents of transformation? Donors, faith-based organisations and international development. *Third World Quarterly, 28*, 77–96. https://doi.org/10.1080/01436590601081880

Coates Ulrichsen, K. (2024a). *Centers of power in the Arab Gulf states*. London: Hurst.

Coates Ulrichsen, K. (2024b). The changing role of Gulf-based non-state actors in foreign aid. *Third World Quarterly, 45*, 2175–89. https://doi.org/10.1080/01436597.2024.2307552

Cochrane, L. (2021). The United Arab Emirates as a global donor: What a decade of foreign aid data transparency reveals. *Development Studies Research, 8*, 49–62. https://doi,org/10.1080/21665095.2021.1883453.

Colombo, S. (2017). Foreign policy activism in Saudi Arabia and Oman: Diverging narratives and stances towards the Syrian and Yemeni conflicts. *International Spectator, 52*(2), 54–70. https://doi.org/10.1080/03932729.2017.1303965

Costa, A., & Macmillan, M. (2018, July). *From rebel to regime: Barriers of return to Aleppo for internally displaced people (IDPs).* Shattuck Center, Central European University School of Public Policy. Retrieved from https://www.thealeppoproject.com/papers/from-rebel-to-regime-barriers-of-return-to-aleppo-for-internally-displaced-people-idps/

Cuéller, M. (2006). Refugee security and the organizational logic of legal mandates. *Georgetown Journal of International Law, 37*, 583–723.

Daher, J. (2018, December). *The political-economic context of Syria's reconstruction: A prospective in light of a legacy of unequal development.* European University Institute. Retrieved from https://cadmus.eui.eu/server/api/core/bitstreams/2ae39891-e03d-5ff5-b737-2230f54448a7/content

Daher, J. (2019, 25 October). *The dynamics and evolution of UAE–Syria relations: Between expectations and obstacles.* Research Project Report 2019/14, Robert Schuman Centre for Advanced Studies, European University Institute. Retrieved from https://cadmus.eui.eu/entities/publication/9131db63-1d38-5e9a-a14c-06e390e2812f

Daher, J. (2020, 25 April). Syria, the Gulf, and reconstruction – what possible future? *Journal of Middle Eastern Politics & Policy*. Retrieved from https://studentreview.hks.harvard.edu/syria-the-gulf-and-reconstruction-what-possible-future/

DanishSyrian. (2016, 15 October). Interview with Syrian president Bashar al Assad on Danish TV. [Video file]. Retrieved from https://youtu.be/KSWu1n7I2_A?si=s52vESqQgo5cijA9

Dany, C. (2015). Politicization of humanitarian aid in the European Union. *European Foreign Affairs Review, 20*, 419–38. https://doi.org/10.54648/eerr2015035

Dawisha, A. (1988). Arab regimes: Legitimacy and foreign policy. In A. Dawisha and I. W. Zartman (Eds), *Beyond coercion: The durability of the Arab state*. London: Croom Helm.

De Bel-Air, F. (2015). *A note on Syrian refugees in the Gulf: Attempting to assess data and policies.* Explanatory Note No. 11/2015, Gulf Labour Markets and Migration. Retrieved from https://gulfmigration.grc.net/media/pubs/exno/GLMM_EN_2015_11.pdf

De Cordier, B. (2009). Faith-based aid, globalisation and the humanitarian frontline: An analysis of Western-based Muslim aid organisations. *Disasters, 33*, 608–28. https://doi.org/10.1111/j.1467-7717.2008.01090.x

Degg, M. (1993). The 1992 'Cairo earthquake': cause, effect and response. *Disasters*, 17, 226–38. https://doi.org/10.1111/j.1467-7717.1993.tb00496.x

De Lauri, A. (2018, June). *Humanitarian diplomacy: A new research agenda.* CMI Brief No. 2018:4, Chr. Michelsen Institute. Retrieved from https://www.cmi.no/publications/6536-humanitarian-diplomacy-a-new-research-agenda

Derbal, N. (2022a). *Charity in Saudi Arabia: Civil society under authoritarianism.* Cambridge: Cambridge University Press.

Derbal, N. (2022b). Humanitarian and relief organizations in global Saudi *da'wa?* In P. Mandaville (Ed.), *Wahhabism and the world: Understanding Saudi Arabia's global influence on Islam.* New York: Oxford University Press.

Desportes, I., Corbet, A., & Siddiqi, A. (Eds.). (2024). *Depoliticising humanitarian action: Paradigms, dilemmas, resistance.* Abingdon and New York: Routledge.

Dewachi, O., Marei, F. G., & Whittall, J. (2021). Contested statehood: the politics of health care in Syria. In J. Bseiso, M. Hofman & J. Whittall (Eds), *Everybody's war: The politics of aid in the Syria crisis.* New York: Oxford University Press.

De Zayas, F. G. (2003). *The law and institution of zakat.* Kuala Lumpur: Other Press.

Diwan, K. (2021). Clerical associations in Qatar and the United Arab Emirates: Soft power competition in Islamic politics. *International Affairs, 97*, 945–63. https://doi.org/10.1093/ia/iiab083

Donelli, F., and Pericoli, A. (2024). Foreign aid, identities and interests: Qatar and the UAE in Sudan. *International Spectator.* Advance online publication. https://doi.org/10.1080/03932729.2024.2416892

Drevon, J. (2021). Ahrar al-Sham's politicisation during the Syrian conflict. In M. Bano (Ed.), *Salafi social and political movements: National and transnational contexts.* Edinburgh: Edinburgh University Press.

Drevon, J. (2024). *From jihad to politics: How Syrian jihadis embraced politics.* New York: Oxford University Press.

Drevon, J., & Haenni, P. (2021, January). *How global jihad relocalises and where it leads: The case of HTS, the former AQ franchise in Syria.* EUI Working Papers RSC 2021/08, European University Institute. Retrieved from https://cadmus.eui.eu/entities/publication/749ae446-0ee0-5505-93e9-2a9d75f6e33d

Drevon, J., & Haenni, P. (2025). The end of Jihadi Salafism? The religious governance of HTS, the Post-Jihadi rebel ruler in Northern Syria. *Mediterranean Politics.* Advance online publication. https://doi.org/10.1080/13629395.2024.2410119

Dukhan, H. (2014). Tribes and tribalism in the Syrian uprising. *Syria Studies, 6*(2), 1–28. Retrieved from https://ojs.st-andrews.ac.uk/index.php/syria/index

Dunn, E. C. (2012). The chaos of humanitarian aid: adhocracy in the Republic of Georgia. *Humanity: An International Journal of Human Rights, Humanitarianism, and Development, 3*, 1–23. https://doi.org/10.1353/hum.2012.0005

Economist Intelligence Unit. (2023). *Democracy index 2023.* Retrieved from https://www.eiu.com/n/campaigns/democracy-index-2023/

Eickelman. D. F. (2016). Tribes and tribal identity in the Arab Gulf states. In J. E. Peterson (Ed.), *The emergence of the Gulf states: Studies in modern history.* London: Bloomsbury Academic.

Elayah, M., & al-Awami, H. (2024). Exploring the preference for bilateral aid: Gulf oil states' aid to Yemen. *Third World Quarterly, 45*, 2266–86. https://doi.org/10.1080/01436597.2024.2327451

Elkahlout, G. (2020). Post-conflict housing reconstruction in the Gaza Strip: A case study of agency-driven housing in Sheikh Hamad city. International Journal of Housing Markets and Analysis, 13(2), 317–30.

Elkahlout, G., & Hedaya, M. (2024). Examining Qatari humanitarian diplomacy: Key features, challenges and prospects. *Third World Quarterly, 45*, 1813–31. https://doi.org/10.1080/01436597.2024.2379345

Elkahlout, G., Milton, S., Yaseen, T., & Raweh, E. (2022). Localisation of humanitarian action in war-torn countries: The experience of local NGOs in Yemen. *International Journal of Disaster Risk Reduction, 75*, 102921. https://doi.org/10.1016/j.ijdrr.2022.102921

El Kurd, D. (2023). The paradox of peace: The impact of normalization with Israel on the Arab world. *Global Studies Quarterly, 3*(3), ksad042. https://doi.org/10.1093/isagsq/ksad042

Emirates News Agency – WAM (2023, 18 February). UAE's rapid response to support victims of earthquake in Türkiye, Syria made a difference. Retrieved from https://www.wam.ae/en/article/hszrghcs-uae%E2%80%99s-rapid-response-support-victims-earthquake

ESCWA (2017). *Arab multidimensional poverty report.* ESCWA. Retrieved from https://ophi.org.uk/sites/default/files/2023-08/multidimensional-arab-poverty-report-english.pdf

Evans-Pritchard, E. (1969). *The Nuer: A description of the modes of livelihood and political institutions of a Nilotic people.* Oxford: Clarendon Press.

Facon, C. (2023). Depoliticization and (re)politicization tactics in refugee governance in Lebanon: Comparing Western and Gulf donors' interventions. *Territory, Politics, Governance, 11*, 712–29. https://doi.org/10.1080/21622671.2021.2011776

Facon, C. (2024). Gulf responses to Syrian refugee arrivals in Lebanon: Narratives of legitimisation. *Third World Quarterly, 45*, 2287–2304. https://doi.org/10.1080/01436597.2023.2188187

Facon-Salelles, C. (2025). Adhocracy in action: Gulf humanitarian interventions in Lebanon. *International Spectator*. Advance online publication. https://doi.org/10.1080/03932729.2024.2441668

Fakhoury, T. (2019). Multi-level governance and migration politics in the Arab world: The case of Syria's displacement. *Journal of Ethnic and Migration Studies, 45*, 1310–26. https://doi.org/10.1080/1369183X.2018.1441609

Fawcett, L. (2017). States and sovereignty in the Middle East: Myths and realities. *International Affairs, 93*, 789–807. https://doi.org/10.1093/ia/iix122

Fawcett, L. (Ed.). (2023a). *International relations of the Middle East* (6th ed.). Oxford: Oxford University Press.

Fawcett, L. (2023b). Regionalism and shifting alliance in the Middle East. In L. Fawcett (Ed.), *International relations of the Middle East* (6th ed.). Oxford: Oxford University Press.

Fraihat, I. (2020). Superpower and small-state mediation in the Qatar Gulf crisis. *International Spectator, 55*(2), 79–91. https://doi.org/10.1080/03932729.2020.1741268

Freer, C. J. (2018). *Rentier Islamism: The influence of the Muslim Brotherhood in Gulf monarchies*. New York: Oxford University Press.

Gellner, E. (1995). *Anthropology and politics: Revolutions in the sacred grove*. Oxford: Blackwell.

Glaberson, W. (2001, 9 December). A nation challenged: the law; US asks to use secret evidence in many cases of deportation. *New York Times*. Retrieved from https://www.nytimes.com

GLMM (Gulf Labor Markets, Migration, and Population Programme). (n.d.). 'GCC: Total population and percentage of nationals and non-nationals in GCC countries (national statistics, 2017–2018) (with numbers)'. Retrieved from https://gulfmigration.grc.net/gcc-total-population-and-percentage-of-nationals-and-non-nationals-in-gcc-countries-national-statistics-2017-2018-with-numbers/

Global Centre for the Responsibility to Protect. (2014, 14 July). Resolution 2165 (Syria) S/RES/2165. Retrieved from https://www.globalr2p.org/resources/resolution-2165-syria-s-res-2165/

Gökalp, D. (2020, February). *The UAE's humanitarian diplomacy: Claiming state sovereignty, regional leverage and international recognition*. CMI Working Paper No. 1, Chr. Michelsen Institute.

Gordon, N. (2021). The moral norm, the law, and the limits of protection for wartime medical units. In J Bseiso, M. Hofman & J. Whittall (Eds), *Everybody's war: The politics of aid in the Syria crisis*. New York: Oxford University Press.

Gordon, S., & Donini, A. (2015). Romancing principles and human rights: Are humanitarian principles salvageable? *International Review of the Red Cross, 97*, 77–109. https://doi.org/10.1017/S1816383115000727

Government Communications Office. (2024). 'Qatar National Vision 2030'. Retrieved from https://www.gco.gov.qa/en/about-qatar/national-vision2030/

GRAIN (2024, 3 July). 'From land to logistics: UAE's growing power in the global food system'. Retrieved from https://grain.org/en/article/7170-from-land-to-logistics-uae-s-growing-power-in-the-global-food-system

Gray, M. (2011). *A theory of 'late rentierism' in the Arab states of the Gulf*. CIRS Occasional Papers 7, Center for International and Regional Studies.

Guéraiche, W. (2022). Between foreign policy and development assistance: The UAE international cooperation in Africa. *Forum for Development Studies, 49*, 211–32. https://doi.org/10.1080/08039410.2022.2080763

Gulf News. (2018, 16 September). UAE publishes list of terrorist organisations. Retrieved from https://gulfnews.com/uae/government/uae-publishes-list-of-terrorist-organisations-1.1412895

Gulf News. (2022, 6 August). UAE's Zayed bin Sultan Al Nahyan Foundation marks 30 years of helping the needy. Retrieved from https://gulfnews.com/uae/uaes-zayed-bin-sultan-al-nahyan-foundation-marks-30-years-of-helping-the-needy-1.89760464

Hall, N. (2022, February). *Rescuing Aid in Syria*. Center for Strategic & International Studies. Retrieved from https://www.csis.org/analysis/rescuing-aid-syria

Harmer, A., & Cotterrell L. (2005, September). *Diversity in donorship: The changing landscape of official humanitarian aid.* HPG Research Briefing No. 20, Overseas Development Institute. Retrieved from https://media.odi.org/documents/333.pdf

Hasan, S. (Ed.). (2015). *Human security and philanthropy: Islamic perspectives and Muslim majority country practices*. New York: Springer.

Hasan, Z. (1988). *Distributional equity in Islam*. MPRA Paper 2785.

Hassan, M. K., & Ashraf, A. (2010). An integrated poverty alleviation model combining zakat, awqaf and micro-finance. In A. G. Ismail, M. E. M. Hassan, N. Ismail & S. Shahimi (Eds), *Proceedings of Seventh International Conference: The Tawhidic epistemology – zakat and waqf economy*. Bangi, Malaysia: Institut Islam Hadhari.

Hatahet, S. (2023, 25 May). *Local governance structures and humanitarian responses to the earthquake in north-west Syria*. Syrian Trajectories Project, European University Institute. Retrieved from https://cadmus.eui.eu/entities/publication/f2d878c9-fb4a-5f08-a107-c8b38a62027a

Hatina, M. (2006). Restoring a lost identity: Models of education in modern Islamic thought. *British Journal of Middle Eastern Studies, 33*, 179–97. https://doi.org/10.1080/13530190600953328

Hattori, T. (2001). Reconceptualizing foreign aid. *Review of International Political Economy, 8*, 633–60. https://doi.org/10.1080/09692290110077610

Hegghammer, T. (2010). The rise of Muslim foreign fighters: Islam and the globalization of Jihad. *International Security, 35*(3), 53–94. https://doi.org/10.1162/ISEC_a_00023

Herb, M. F. (1997). *All in the family: Ruling dynasties, regime resilience, and democratic prospects in the middle eastern monarchies*. Doctoral thesis, University of California, Los Angeles.

Hernandez, D., & Vadlamannati, K. C. (2017). Politics of religiously motivated lending: An empirical analysis of aid allocation by the Islamic Development

Bank. *Journal of Comparative Economics, 45*, 910–29. https://doi.org/10.1016/j.jce.2016.09.008

Hertog, S. (2010). *Princes, brokers, and bureaucrats: Oil and the state in Saudi Arabia.* Ithaca, NY: Cornell University Press.

High Level Panel on Humanitarian Financing. (2016, January). *Too important to fail – addressing the humanitarian financing gap.* Report to the secretary-general. Retrieved from https://interagencystandingcommittee.org/sites/default/files/migrated/2017-02/hlp_report_too_important_to_failgcoaddressing_the_humanitarian_financing_gap.pdf

Hinnebusch, R., & Ehteshami, A. (2014). *The foreign policies of Middle East states.* Boulder, CO: Lynne Rienner.

Hitman, G. (2019). Gulf States' policy towards Syrian refugees: Charity before hospitality. *Asian Affairs, 50*, 80–101. https://doi.org/10.1080/03068374.2019.1567103

Hoffmann, M. (2017). Norms and social constructivism in international relations. In *Oxford research encyclopedia of international studies.* Retrieved from https://oxfordre.com/internationalstudies/view/10.1093/acrefore/9780190846626.001.0001/acrefore-9780190846626-e-60

Hook, S. W. (1995). *National interest and foreign aid.* Boulder, CO: Lynne Rienner.

Howell, J., & Lind, J. (2009). *Counter-terrorism, aid and civil society: Before and after the War on Terror.* Basingstoke: Palgrave Macmillan.

Human Rights Watch. (2018, 30 October). Qatar: Gulf's first refugee asylum law. Retrieved from https://www.hrw.org/news/2018/10/30/qatar-gulfs-first-refugee-asylum-law

Human Rights Watch. (2025, 18 February). US, EU, UK: lift Syria sanctions hindering recovery. Retrieved from https://www.hrw.org/news/2025/02/18/us-eu-uk-lift-syria-sanctions-hindering-recovery

Ibish, H. (2016). *What's at stake for the Gulf Arab states in Syria?* Arab Gulf States Institute in Washington.

International Rescue Committee. (2023, 13 December). The top ten crises the world can't ignore in 2024. Retrieved from https://www.rescue.org/article/top-10-crises-world-cant-ignore-2024

Iqbal, M. (2002). Introduction. In M. Iqbal (Ed.), *Islamic economic institutions and the elimination of poverty* (pp. 1–24). Leicester: Islamic Foundation.

IRTI & Thomson Reuters. (2015). *Islamic social finance report 2014.* Islamic Research and Training Institute & Thomson Reuters.

Isaac, S. K. (2014). Explaining the patterns of the Gulf monarchies' assistance after the Arab uprisings. *Mediterranean Politics, 19*(3), 413–30. https://doi.org/10.1080/13629395.2014.959759

IsDB & OPHI. (2016, July). *Multidimensional poverty assessment in IDB Sub-Saharan African member countries.* Islamic Development Bank and Oxford Poverty and Human Development Initiative. Retrieved from at https://www.mppn.org/wp-content/uploads/2017/03/IDB-Subsaharan-Africa-MPI-2016-1.pdf

Islamic Relief Worldwide. (2019). *Annual report and financial statements 2018.* Retrieved from https://islamic-relief.org/wp-content/uploads/2022/05/IslamicReliefWorld-AnnualReportandFinancialStatements-2018-1.pdf

Ismail, A. G., & Possumah, B. T. (2013). Theoretical model for *zakat*-based Islamic microfinance institutions in reducing poverty. *International Research Journal of Finance and Economics, 103*, 136–50.

Jabbour, S., Abbara, A., Ekzayez, A., Fouad, F. M., Katoub, M., & Nasser, R. (2023). The catastrophic response to the earthquake in Syria: The need for corrective actions and accountability. *The Lancet, 401*, 802–5. https://doi.org/10.1016/S0140-6736(23)00440-3

James, E. C. (Ed.). (2019). *Governing gifts: Faith, charity, and the security state.* Albuquerque: University of New Mexico Press.

James, R. (2009, February). *What is distinctive about FBOs? How European FBOs define and operationalise their faith.* Praxis Paper 22, INTRAC. Retrieved from https://www.intrac.org/resources/praxis-paper-22-distinctive-fbos-european-fbos-define-operationalise-faith/

Kagan, M. (2011, February). *'We live in a country of UNHCR': The UN surrogate state and refugee policy in the Middle East.* Research Paper 201, UNHCR. Retrieved from https://www.unhcr.org/media/we-live-country-unhcr-un-surrogate-state-and-refugee-policy-middle-east-michael-kagan

Kahf, M. (1989). Zakat: Unresolved issues in the contemporary Fiqh. *Journal of Islamic Economics, 2*(1): 1–22.

Kahf, M. (1999, August). *Zakah: performance in theory and practice.* Paper presented at the International Conference on Islamic Economics Towards the Twenty-First Century, Kuala Lumpur.

Kahf, M. (2003). Islamic economics: Notes on definition and methodology. *Review of Islamic Economics, 13*, 23–47.

Kahf, M. (2004). *Shariʿah and historical aspects of zakat and awqaf.* Background paper prepared for Islamic Research and Training Institute, Islamic Development Bank.

Kamrava, M. (2013). *The modern Middle East: A political history since the First World War.* Berkeley: University of California Press.

Kamrava, M. (2015). *Qatar: Small state, big politics.* Ithaca, NY: Cornell University Press.

Karagedikli, G., & Tunçer, A. C. (2018). Microcredit in the Ottoman Empire: A review of cash waqfs in transition to modern banking. In M. Lorenzini, C. Lorandini & D. Coffman (Eds), *Financing in Europe: Evolution, coexistence and complementarity of lending practices from the Middle Ages to modern times.* Cham: Palgrave Macmillan.

Katzman, K. (2014). *The United Arab Emirates (UAE): Issues for US policy.* CRS Report RS21852, Congressional Research Service.

Keser, A., & Fakhoury, F. (2025). Hay'at Tahrir Al-Sham (HTS) from an insurgent group to a local authority: emergence, development and social support base. *Studies in Conflict & Terrorism, 48*, 46–66. https://doi.org/10.1080/1057610X.2022.2082833

Khadhraoui, H. (2019). Fragmentation of armed non-state actors in protracted armed conflicts: some practical experiences on how to ensure compliance with humanitarian norms. *International Review of the Red Cross, 101*, 993–1000. https://doi.org/10.1017/S1816383119000572

Khan, M. A. (1984). Islamic economics: Nature and need. *Journal of Research in Islamic Economics, 1*(2), 51–8.

Kharas, M. (2015, June). *Trends and issues in Qatari Foreign Aid*, Global Economy and Development Working Paper 87, Brookings. Retrieved from https://web.archive.org/web/20150626142842/http://www.brookings.edu/~/media/Research/Files/Papers/2015/06/trends-issues-qatari-foreign-aid-kharas/Kharas-Trends-and-Issues-in-Qatar-Aid-v2.pdf?la=en

Khatib, D. K. (Ed.). (2021). *The Syrian crisis: Effects on the regional and international relations.* Singapore: Springer.

Khatib, L. (2019). Syria, Saudi Arabia, the UAE and Qatar: The 'sectarianization' of the Syrian conflict and undermining of democratization in the region. *British Journal of Middle Eastern Studies, 46*, 385–403. https://doi.org/10.1080/13530194.2017.1408456.

Kuran, T. (2004). Why the Middle East is economically underdeveloped: Historical mechanisms of institutional stagnation. *Journal of Economic Perspectives, 18*(3), 71–90. https://doi.org/10.1257/0895330042162421

Kuran, T. (2023). *Freedoms delayed: Political legacies of Islamic law in the Middle East.* Cambridge: Cambridge University Press.

Kusuma, D. B. W. (2010). *Economic development in an Islamic perspective.* Retrieved from http://repo.unand.ac.id/5033/1/Dimas%20Bagus%20Wiranata%20Kusuma.pdf

Lacroix, S. (2011). *Awakening Islam: The politics of religious dissent in contemporary Saudi Arabia.* Cambridge, MA: Harvard University Press.

Lacroix, S. (2015). Understanding stability and dissent in the kingdom: The role of the *jama'at* in Saudi politics. In B. Haykel, T. Hegghammer & S. Lacroix (Eds), *Saudi Arabia in transition: Insights on social, political, economic and religious change*. New York: Cambridge University Press.

Leenders, R., & Mansour, K. (2018). Humanitarianism, state sovereignty, and authoritarian regime maintenance in the Syrian war. *Political Science Quarterly, 133*, 225–57. https://doi.org/10.1002/polq.12773.

Lessy, Z. (2013). *Philanthropic zakat for empowering Indonesia's poor: A qualitative study of recipient experiences at Rumah Zakat*. PhD thesis, Indiana University.

Lestra, M. (2017). The more it's centralized, the more it's divided: A historical-institutionalist reading of Qatar's foreign aid landscape. *Oxford Middle East Review, 1*, 67–89.

Li, Y. 2019. Saudi Arabia's economic diplomacy through foreign aid: Dynamics, objectives and mode. *Asian Journal of Middle Eastern and Islamic Studies*, 13:110–22. https://doi.org/10.1080/25765949.2019.1586367

Lindstaedt, N. (2025, 4 February). USAid shutdown isn't just a humanitarian issue – it's a threat to American interests. *The Conversation*. Retrieved from https://theconversation.com

Liska, G. (1960). *The new statecraft: Foreign aid in American foreign policy*. Chicago: University of Chicago Press.

Loewenthal, A., Miaari, S. H., & Hoeffler, A. (2023). Aid and radicalization: The case of Hamas in the West Bank and Gaza. *Journal of Development Studies, 59*, 1187–1212. https://doi.org/10.1080/00220388.2023.2197546

Lowi, M. R. (2024). *Refining the common good: Oil, Islam and politics in Gulf monarchies*. New York: Cambridge University Press.

Lysa, C. (2023). Are there really no refugees in the GCC states? Establishing a basis for further research. *Journal of Arabian Studies, 13*, 258–75. https://doi.org/10.1080/21534764.2024.2387238

Madani, L. (2024). Reassessing peace: The implications of the Abraham Accords for conflict resolution in the Gulf region. *Asian Journal of Middle Eastern and Islamic Studies, 18*, 260–81. https://doi.org/10.1080/25765949.2024.2416845

Maestri, E. (2021). Migration and the Muslim world: Perspectives and challenges. In A. Profanter & E. Maestri (Eds), *Migration and integration challenges of Muslim immigrants in Europe: Debating policies and cultural approaches*. Cham: Palgrave Macmillan.

Makdisi, K. (2019, February). *Contested multilateralism: The United Nations and the Middle East.* MENARA Working Paper No. 31, MENARA Project. Retrieved from https://www.iai.it/sites/default/files/menara_wp_31.pdf

Mandaville, J. E. (1979). Usurious piety: the cash waqf controversy in the Ottoman Empire. *International Journal of Middle East Studies, 10*, 289–308. https://doi.org/10.1017/S0020743800000118

Mandaville, P. (2007). *Global political Islam.* Abingdon: Routledge.

Mandaville, P. (2023). *Islam and international relations in the Middle East: From* umma *to nation state.* In L. Fawcett (Ed.), *International relations of the Middle East* (6th ed.). Oxford: Oxford University Press.

Mason, R. (2023). *Saudi Arabia and the United Arab Emirates: Foreign policy and strategic alliances in an uncertain world.* Manchester: Manchester University Press.

Mason, R. (2024). Power and competition in the transitions toward postrentierism: The cases of Saudi Arabia and the United Arab Emirates. *Digest of Middle East Studies, 33*, 225–44. https://doi.org/10.1111/dome.12331

McLean, D. (2021). The business of the conflict: Humanitarian assistance and the war economy in Syria. In J. Bseiso, M. Hofman & J. Whittall (Eds), *Everybody's war: The politics of aid in the Syria crisis.* New York: Oxford University Press.

MDX. (n.d.). 'Syrian Arab Republic: humanitarian access'. Retrieved from https://data.humdata.org/dataset/syria-humanitarian-access-severity

Meininghaus, E. (2016). Humanitarianism in intra-state conflict: Aid inequality and local governance in government- and opposition-controlled areas in the Syrian war. *Third World Quarterly, 37*, 1454–82. https://doi.org/10.1080/01436597.2016.1159509

Menshawy, M. (2019). Constructing state, territory, and sovereignty in the Syrian conflict. *Politics, 39*, 332–46. https://doi.org/10.1177/0263395718770348

Milton, S., & Elkahlout, G. (2025). Qatar's multifaceted humanitarian role in Afghanistan since August 2021. *Development Policy Review, 43*(1), e12793. https://doi.org/10.1111/dpr.12793

Milton, S., Elkahlout, G., & Tariq, S. (2025). Qatar's evolving role in conflict mediation. *Mediterranean Politics, 30*, 53–77. https://doi.org/10.1080/13629395.2023.2266665

Minear, L. (2002). *The humanitarian enterprise: Dilemmas and discoveries.* Bloomfield, CT: Kumarian Press.

Ministry of Foreign Affairs (Iraq). (2024, 14 December). Final Statement of the Meeting of Arab Ministerial Contact Committee on Syria. Retrieved from https://mofa.gov.iq/2024/52505/

Ministry of Foreign Affairs (Qatar). (2025, 3 June). Qatar, Syria issue joint statement. Retrieved from https://mofa.gov.qa/en/latest-articles/statements/qatar--syria-issue-joint-statement

Mitchell, R. P. (1969). *The Society of the Muslim Brothers*. London: Oxford University Press.

Momani, B., & Ennis, C. A. (2012). Between caution and controversy: Lessons from the Gulf Arab states as (re-)emerging donors. *Cambridge Review of International Affairs, 25*, 605–27. https://doi.org/10.1080/09557571.2012.734786

Morgenthau, H. (1962). A political theory of foreign aid. *American Political Science Review, 56*, 301–9. https://doi.org/10.2307/1952366

Moumtaz, N. (2021). *God's property: Islam, charity and the modern state*. Oakland: University of California Press.

Muhammad, I. (2019). Analysis of Zakat system in high-income Islamic countries. *Journal of Muamalat and Islamic Finance Research, 16*(2), 1–11. https://doi.org/10.33102/jmifr.v16i2.219

Munson, Z. (2001). Islamic mobilization: Social movement theory and the Egyptian Muslim Brotherhood. *Sociological Quarterly, 42*, 487–510. https://doi.org/10.1111/j.1533-8525.2001.tb01777.x

Musallam, A. A. (1993). Sayyid Qutb and social justice, 1945–1948. *Journal of Islamic Studies, 4*, 52–70. https://doi.org/10.1093/jis/4.1.52

Mustafa, D., and Razak, N. A. A. (2012). Islamic Development Bank, foreign aid and economic growth in Africa: A simultaneous equations model approach. *International Journal of Economics and Finance, 4*(6), 94–107. https://doi.org/10.5539/ijef.v4n6p94

Naqvi, S. N. H. (1994). *Islam, economics and society*. London: Kegan Paul International.

Narang, N. (2015). Assisting uncertainty: How humanitarian aid can inadvertently prolong civil war. *International Studies Quarterly, 59*, 184–95. https://doi.org/10.1111/isqu.12151

Natter, K. (2023). Ad-hocratic immigration governance: How states secure their power over immigration through intentional ambiguity. *Territory, Politics, Governance, 11*, 677–94. https://doi.org/10.1080/21622671.2021.1877189

Neumayer, E. (2004). Arab-related bilateral and multilateral sources of development finance: Issues, trends, and the way forward. *World Economy, 27*, 281–300. https://doi.org/10.1111/j.1467-9701.2004.00600.x

Nurlaelawati, E. (2010). Zakat and the concept of ownership in Islam: Yusuf Qaradawi's perspective on Islamic economics. *Journal of Islamic Studies, 48*, 365–85. https://doi.org/10.14421/ajis.2010.482.365-385.

OCHA. (2024, March). Syrian Arab Republic: humanitarian access severity overview. Retrieved from https://www.unocha.org/publications/report/syrian-arab-republic/syrian-arab-republic-humanitarian-access-severity-overview-march-2024

OECD. (2020). *Development co-operation profile: UAE.*

OECD. (2024). *Development co-operation profile: Qatar.*

OIC. (2013). *Resolutions on humanitarian affairs adopted by the fortieth session of the Council of Foreign Ministers, Conakry, Republic of Guinea, 6–8 Safar 1435H (09–11 December 2013).* Retrieved from https://www.oic-oci.org/docdown/?docID=343&refID=25

OIC. (2016). *Final communique of the 13th Islamic summit of the heads of state/government (unity and solidarity for justice and peace), Istanbul, Republic of Turkey, 14–15 April 2016.* Retrieved from https://www.oic-oci.org/docdown/?docID=14&refID=5

Onuf, N. G. (2023). *International theory at the margins: Neglected essays, recurring themes.* Bristol: Bristol University Press.

Owoyemi, M. Y. (2020). Zakat management: The crisis of confidence in zakat agencies and the legality of giving zakat directly to the poor. *Journal of Islamic Accounting and Business Research, 11*, 498–510. https://doi.org/10.1108/JIABR-07-2017-0097.

Palmer, V. (2011). Analysing cultural proximity: Islamic Relief Worldwide and Rohingya refugees in Bangladesh. *Development in Practice, 21*, 96–108. https://doi.org/10.1080/09614524.2011.530226

Pericoli, A. (2020). Building the humanitarian–development–peace nexus: The relevance of cooperation between UN agencies and Islamic actors. *Global Affairs Review, 1*. https://doi.org/10.51330/gar.002011.

Pericoli, A. (2021, December). *Organization of Islamic Cooperation and the Islamic Development Bank: The regional dimension of humanitarian diplomacy.* Norwegian Centre for Humanitarian Studies. Retrieved from https://www.humanitarianstudies.no/resource/the-organization-of-islamic-cooperation-and-the-islamic-development-bank/

Pericoli, A. (2023a). Qatar and the UAE in the Syrian early recovery: Top-down strategies of foreign aid. *Third World Quarterly, 45*, 2305–22. https://doi.org/10.1080/01436597.2023.2216141

Pericoli, A. (2023b). The use of *zakat* in the pandemic response: The case of Islamic Relief and BAZNAS in Indonesia. *Third World Quarterly,* 44, 405–22. https://doi.org/10.1080/01436597.2022.2150161

Pericoli, A. (2024). Overcoming obstacles in regional crises: The role of the OIC and IsDB in the MENA region. In M. Elaya & B. Alzandani (Eds), *Conflicts in the*

Middle East and Africa: State, non-state actors and unheard voices (pp. 121–37). Abingdon & New York: Routledge.

Pericoli, A. (2025a). Islamic Instruments for Refugee Financing: the IsDB and UNHCR Collaborative Approach. *Global Policy, 16*(S1), 46–56. https://doi.org/10.1111/1758-5899.13476

Pericoli, A. (2025b). Understanding Gulf States' foreign aid: a conceptual framework. *International Spectator.* Advance online publication. https://doi.org/10.1080/03932729.2025.2510985f

Pericoli, A. (2025c). UNHCR Refugee Zakat Fund in Bangladesh: Sustainable religious funds for stateless refugees. In A. Thomas (Ed.), *Islamic finance and sustainable development: The water, food, energy, and climate nexus* (pp. 14–28). Abingdon: Routledge.

Pericoli, A., & Donelli, F. (2024). Qatar's foreign aid and political strategies in the Horn of Africa: The case of Somalia. *Global Policy*, *15*(1), 53–65. https://doi.org/10.1111/1758-5899.13294

Petersen, M. J. (2012). Islamizing aid: Transnational Muslim NGOs after 9.11. *Voluntas: International Journal of Voluntary and Nonprofit Organizations*, *23*, 126–55. https://doi.org/10.1007/s11266-011-9185-5

Petersen, M. J. (2015). *For humanity or for the umma? Aid and Islam in transnational Muslim NGOs*. London: Hurst.

Peterson, J. E. (2012, December). *The GCC states: Participation, opposition, and the fraying of the social contract*. Kuwait Programme on Development, Governance and Globalisation in the Gulf States 26, London School of Economics and Political Science. Retrieved from https://eprints.lse.ac.uk/55258/1/Peterson_2012.pdf

Philpott, D. (2020). Sovereignty. In E. N. Zalta (Ed.), *The Stanford Encyclopedia of Philosophy* (Fall 2020 ed.). Retrieved from https://plato.stanford.edu/archives/fall2020/entries/sovereignty/

Porter, R. S. (1986). Arab economic aid. *Development Policy Review, 4*, 44–68. https://doi.org/10.1111/j.1467-7679.1986.tb00496.x

Powell, R. (2010). Zakat: Drawing insights for legal theory and economic policy from Islamic jurisprudence. *Pittsburgh Tax Review 7*, 43ff. Retrieved from https://home.heinonline.org/

Qadir, M. I., & Rehman, M. S. (2015). Organization of Islamic Co-operation (OIC) and prospects of Yemeni conflict resolution: Delusion or plausible reality. *Journal of Political Studies, 22*, 367–81. Retrieved from https://home.heinonline.org/

Qatar Charity. (2020–2). Annual impact reports. Retrieved from https://www.qcharity.org/en/qa/media/electronicbooks?type=85&view=Reports

QFFD (Qatar Fund for Development). (2016–23). Annual reports. Retrieved from https://www.qatarfund.org.qa/media-center/reports-publications/

Quamar, M. M. (2020). Changing regional geopolitics and the foundations of a rapprochement between Arab Gulf and Israel. *Global Affairs*, *6*, 593–608. https://doi.org/10.1080/23340460.2020.1865110

Rasmi, A. (2013, 23 September). A tale of two refugee cities. Al Jazeera. Retrieved from https://www.aljazeera.com/features/2013/9/23/a-tale-of-two-refugee-cities

Razavy, M. (2005). Hawala: An underground haven for terrorists or social phenomenon? *Crime, Law and Social Change, 44*, 277–99. https://doi.org/10.1007/s10611-006-9019-3

Refugee Zakat Fund. (2020, April). *Islamic philanthropy: 2020 annual report*. Retrieved from https://zakat.unhcr.org/wp-content/uploads/2020/04/IP-English-Impact-Full-Final.pdf

Reliefweb. (n.d.). Türkiye/Syria: earthquakes – Feb 2023. Retrieved from https://reliefweb.int/disaster/eq-2023-000015-tur

Reuters. (2022, 13 December). Sudan to develop Red Sea port in $6-bln initial pact with Emirati group. Retrieved from https://www.reuters.com/markets/sudan-signs-6-bln-agreement-with-emirati-consortium-develop-red-sea-port-2022-12-13/

Riddell, R. C. (1996). The moral case for post-Cold War development aid. *International Journal, 51*, 191–210. https://doi.org/10.1177/002070209605100201

Riddell, R. C. (2007). *Does foreign aid really work?* Oxford: Oxford University Press.

Roberts, D. (2012). Understanding Qatar's foreign policy objectives. *Mediterranean Politics, 17*, 233–9. https://doi.org/10.1080/13629395.2012.695123

Roberts, D. (2014). Qatar and the Muslim Brotherhood: pragmatism or preference? *Middle East Policy, 21*(3), 84–94. https://doi.org/10.1111/mepo.12084

Roberts, D. B. (2017). Qatar and the UAE: Explaining divergent responses to the Arab Spring. *Middle East Journal 71*, 544–62. https://doi.org/10.3751/71.4.12

Rouis, M., & Shomakhmadova, O. (2018, February). *Arab aid on the rise 2011–2016*. MENA Knowledge and Learning Quick Notes, No. 163. Retrieved from https://openknowledge.worldbank.org/server/api/core/bitstreams/8c909d61-3c25-5c2f-8f45-2c427fa05a63/content

Ruiz de Elvira, L. (2024). *Charities and politics in Bashar al-Asad's Syria: The unravelling of the old social contract*. Edinburgh: Edinburgh University Press.

Sadeq, A. M. (1997). Poverty alleviation: An Islamic perspective. *Humanomics, 13*(3), 110–34. https://doi.org/10.1108/eb018797

Said, S., & Yazigi, J. (2018, December). *The reconstruction of Syria: Socially just re-integration and peace building or regime re-consolidation?* Friedrich Ebert Stiftung. Retrieved from http://library.fes.de/pdf-files/iez/14939.pdf

Salih, M. A. R. M. (2002, March). *Islamic NGOs in Africa: The promise and peril of Islamic voluntarism.* Occasional paper, Centre of African Studies, University of Copenhagen. Retrieved from https://teol.ku.dk/cas/publications/publications/occ._papers/salih2001.pdf

Salleh, M. S. (2017). Contemporary vision of poverty and Islamic strategy for poverty alleviation. *SAGE Open, 7*(2). https://doi.org/10.1177/2158244017697153

Salloukh, B. F. (2013). The Arab uprisings and the geopolitics of the Middle East. *International Spectator, 48*(2), 32–46. https://doi.org/10.1080/03932729.2013.787830

Shirazi, N. S. (2006). Providing for the resource shortfall for poverty elimination through the institution of Zakat in low-income Muslim countries. *International Journal of Economics, Management and Accounting, 14*(1). https://doi.org/10.31436/ijema.v14i1.116

Silbey, S. S. (1992). Making a place for cultural analyses of law. *Law and Social Inquiry, 17*, 39–48. https://doi.org/10.1111/j.1747-4469.1992.tb00928.x

Singer, A. (2008). *Charity in Islamic societies.* Cambridge: Cambridge University Press.

SIPRI. (n.d.). SIPRI military expenditure database. Stockholm International Peace Research Institute. Retrieved from https://www.sipri.org/databases/milex.

Slim, H. (2002). Not philanthropy but rights: The proper politicisation of humanitarian philosophy. *International Journal of Human Rights, 6*(2), 1–22. https://doi.org/10.1080/714003759

Soage, A. B. (2008). Shaykh Yusuf al-Qaradawi: Portrait of a leading Islamist cleric. *Middle East Review of International Affairs, 12*(1), 51–68.

Solberg, A. (2007). The role of Turkish Islamic networks in the western Balkans. *Südosteuropa: Zeitschrift für Politik und Gesellschaft,4*, 429–62. Retrieved from https://www.ceeol.com/

Solomon, C. (2022, 13 July). HTS: Evolution of a jihadi group. Wilson Center. Retrieved from https://www.wilsoncenter.org/article/hts-evolution-jihadist-group

SPA. (2025a, 27 April). Joint press statement by the Kingdom of Saudi Arabia, the State of Qatar on settlement of Syria's outstanding arrears to the World Bank Group. Retrieved from https://www.spa.gov.sa/N2307023

SPA. (2025b, 9 March). OIC secretary-general welcomes Syria's resumption of OIC membership. Retrieved from https://www.spa.gov.sa/en/N2278017

Sparre, S. L., & Petersen, M. J. (2007). *Islam and civil society: Case studies from Jordan and Egypt.* Copenhagen: Danish Institute for International Studies.

Svoboda, E., Zyck, S. A., Osman, D., & Hashi, A. (2015, February). *Islamic humanitarianism? The evolving role of the Organisation for Islamic Cooperation in Somalia and beyond.* Humanitarian Policy Group Working Paper, Overseas Development Institute. Retrieved from https://media.odi.org/documents/9457.pdf

Swiss, L. (2021). The globalisation of foreign aid: Global influences and the diffusion of aid priorities. In S. Chaturvedi, H. Janus, S. Klingebiel, X. Li, A. de Mello e Souza, E. Sidiropoulos & D. Wehrmann (Eds), *The Palgrave handbook of development cooperation for achieving the 2030 agenda: Contested collaboration.* Cham: Palgrave Macmillan.

Tharoor, I. (2023, 15 February). Syria's Assad regime sees opportunity in earthquake aftermath. *The Washington Post.* Retrieved from https://www.washingtonpost.com

Thomson, J. E. (1995). State sovereignty in international relations: Bridging the gap between theory and empirical research. *International Studies Quarterly, 39,* 213–33. https://doi.org/10.2307/2600847

Tok, M. E., & D'Alessandro, C. (2019). Global governance and the informal nature of Islamic development assistance: The peculiar case of Gulf states. In L. A. Pal & M. E. Tok (Eds), *Global governance and Muslim organizations.* Cham: Palgrave Macmillan.

Tokmajyan, A. (2020, July). *How southern Syria has been transformed into a regional powder keg.* Working paper, Carnegie Middle East Center. Retrieved from https://carnegie-production-assets.s3.amazonaws.com/static/files/files__Tokmajyan_DFID_Syria-updated.pdf

UAE MOFA. (2022). The United Arab Emirates policy for foreign assistance: 2022 update. Retrieved from https://www.mofa.gov.ae/en/the-ministry/uae-international-development-cooperation/uae-foreign-aid-policy

UAE MOFAIC (2016-2023). UAE foreign aid reports. Retrieved from https://www.mofaic.gov.ae/en/the-ministry/uae-international-development-cooperation/annual-foreign-aid-report

UNHCR (2019, 28 August). 100% zakat distribution policy. Retrieved from https://zakat.unhcr.org/blog/en/refugee-zakat-fund/100-zakat-policy

UNHCR (2020, 3 September). Tabah Foundation / UAE. Retrieved from https://zakat.unhcr.org/blog/en/fatwa/tabah-foundation

UNHCR (2021, 6 May). Zakat al fitr / Egypt. Retrieved from https://zakat.unhcr.org/blog/en/fatwa/you-can-give-your-zakat-el-fitr-to-unhcr-in-cash

UNHCR (2022, 17 February). Fiqh Majlis of Canada / Canada. Retrieved from https://zakat.unhcr.org/blog/en/fatwa/fiqh-majlis-of-canada-canada

United Nations (2023, 19 July). In meeting following Russian Federation's veto of cross-border aid text, General Assembly speakers highlight humanitarian consequences for millions. Meeting coverage. Retrieved from https://press.un.org/en/2023/ga12517.doc.htm

Valbjørn, M., & Gunning, J. (2025). 'The more, the merrier': three ways of case universe extension – reflections on bringing Shia into Islamism studies. *International Studies Review*, 27(1), viaf001. https://doi.org/10.1093/isr/viaf001

Vignal, L. (2017). The changing borders and borderlands of Syria in a time of conflict. *International Affairs, 93*, 809–27. https://doi.org/10.1093/ia/iix113

Warde, I. (2000). *Islamic finance in the global economy*. Edinburgh: Edinburgh University Press.

Wendt, A. E., & Duvall, R. (1989). Institutions and international order. In E.O. Czempiel & J. N. Rosenau (Eds), *Global changes and theoretical challenges: Approaches to world politics for the 1990s*. Lexington, MA: Lexington.

Wintour, P. (2017, 23 June). Qatar given 10 days to meet 13 sweeping demands by Saudi Arabia. *The Guardian*. Retrieved from https://www.theguardian.com

Wood, R. E. (1986). *From Marshall Plan to debt crisis: Foreign aid and development choices in the world economy*. Berkeley: University of California Press.

Wood, R. M., & Sullivan, C. (2015). Doing harm by doing good? The negative externalities of humanitarian aid provision during civil conflict. *Journal of Politics, 77*, 736–48. https://doi.org/10.1086/681239

World Bank & Islamic Development Bank Group (2016), *Islamic finance: A catalyst for shared prosperity?* Washington, DC: World Bank.

Yasin, H. M., & Tahir, S. (2002). Poverty elimination in an Islamic perspective: An applied general equilibrium approach. In M. Iqbal (Ed.), *Islamic economic institutions and the elimination of poverty*. Leicester: Islamic Foundation.

Yaylaci, I. (2007, 3–5 June). *Communitarian humanitarianism: The politics of IHOs*. Paper presented at the Workshop on Religion and Humanitarianism, American University of Cairo.

Yazigi, J. (2016, September). *No going back: Why decentralisation is the future for Syria*. Policy Brief ECFR/185, European Council on Foreign Relations. Retrieved from https://ecfr.eu/publication/no_going_back_why_decentralisation_is_the_future_for_syria7107/

Younis, H., & Sundarakani, B. (2010, November). *How UAE is positioned on the Humanitarian Logistics map*. Conference paper. Retrieved from https://www.researchgate.

net/profile/Balan-Sundarakani-2/publication/329034685_How_UAE_is_positioned_on_the_Humanitarian_Logistics_map/links/5bf28476a6fdcc3a8de10cec/How-UAE-is-positioned-on-the-Humanitarian-Logistics-map.pdf.

Zaman, M. (2004). The 'ulama of contemporary Islam and their conceptions of the common good. In A. Salvatore & D. F. Eickelman (Eds), *Public Islam and the common good*. Leiden: Brill.

Ziadah, R. (2019). Circulating power: Humanitarian logistics, militarism, and the United Arab Emirates. *Antipode, 51*, 1684–1702. https://doi.org/10.1111/anti.12547

Zweiri, M., Rahman, M. M. & Kamal, A. (2021). The 2017 Gulf crisis: An introduction. In M. Zweiri, M. M. Rahman & A. Kamal (Eds), *The 2017 Gulf crisis: An interdisciplinary approach* (pp. 1–18). Singapore: Springer.

INDEX

Note: **bold** indicates figure; *italic* indicates table; n indicates note

EU Authorised Representative:
Easy Access System Europe Mustamäe tee 50, 10621 Tallinn, Estonia
gpsr.requests@easproject.com

Printed and bound by CPI Group (UK) Ltd, Croydon, CR0 4YY
12/02/2026
02052822-0007